Oliver Wendell Holmes

Over the teacups by Oliver Wendell Holmes

Oliver Wendell Holmes

Over the teacups by Oliver Wendell Holmes

ISBN/EAN: 9783743303485

Manufactured in Europe, USA, Canada, Australia, Japa

Cover: Foto ©Andreas Hilbeck / pixelio.de

Manufactured and distributed by brebook publishing software
(www.brebook.com)

Oliver Wendell Holmes

Over the teacups by Oliver Wendell Holmes

OVER THE TEACUPS

BY

OLIVER WENDELL HOLMES
AUTHOR OF "THE AUTOCRAT OF THE BREAKFAST-TABLE"

BOSTON AND NEW YORK
HOUGHTON, MIFFLIN AND COMPANY
The Riverside Press, Cambridge
1891

SEVENTEENTH THOUSAND.

The Riverside Press, Cambridge, Mass., U. S. A.
Electrotyped and Printed by H. O. Houghton & Company.

THE Teapot represented on the title-page seems entitled to special mention. Its inscription shows it to be the gift of pupils to their Instructor, in the year 1738. The pupils were students of Harvard College; the Instructor was Henry Flynt, Fellow and Tutor from 1699 to 1754. The three nodules of *flint* on the escutcheon belong to what are called in heraldry "canting arms."

Henry Flynt was a bachelor. The Teapot passed by descent to his niece Dorothy (Quincy) Jackson, from her to her daughter Mary (Jackson) Wendell, then to *her* daughter Sarah (Wendell) Holmes, and from her to her son, the present owner,

O. W. H.

OVER THE TEACUPS.

I.

INTRODUCTION.

THIS series of papers was begun in March, 1888.
A single number was printed, when it was interrupted
by the course of events, and not resumed until nearly
two years later, in January, 1890. The plan of the
series was not formed in my mind when I wrote the
first number. In returning to my task I found that
my original plan had shaped itself in the underground
laboratory of my thought so that some changes had
to be made in what I had written. As I proceeded,
the slight story which formed a part of my programme
developed itself without any need of much contrivance
on my part. Given certain characters in a writer's
conception, if they are real to him, as they ought to
be, they will act in such or such a way, according to
the law of their nature. It was pretty safe to assume
that intimate relations would spring up between some
members of our mixed company ; and it was not rash
to conjecture that some of these intimacies might end
in such attachment as would furnish us hints, at least,
of a love-story.

As to the course of the conversations which would
take place, very little could be guessed beforehand.

Various subjects of interest would be likely to present themselves, without definite order, oftentimes abruptly and, as it would seem, capriciously. Conversation in such a mixed company as that of "The Teacups" is likely to be suggestive rather than exhaustive. Continuous discourse is better adapted to the lecture-room than to the tea-table. There is quite enough of it, — I fear too much, — in these pages. But the reader must take the reports of our talks as they were jotted down. A patchwork quilt is not like a piece of Gobelin tapestry; but it has its place and its use.

Some will feel a temptation to compare these conversations with those earlier ones, and remark unamiably upon their difference. This is hardly fair, and is certainly not wise. They are produced under very different conditions, and betray that fact in every line. It is better to take them by themselves; and, if my reader finds anything to please or profit from, I shall be contented, and he, I feel sure, will not be ungrateful.

The readers who take up this volume may recollect a series of conversations held many years ago over the breakfast-table, and reported for their more or less profitable entertainment. Those were not very early breakfasts at which the talks took place, but at any rate the sun was rising, and the guests had not as yet tired themselves with the labors of the day. The morning cup of coffee has an exhilaration about it which the cheering influence of the afternoon or evening cup of tea cannot be expected to reproduce. The toils of the forenoon, the heats of midday, in the warm season, the slanting light of the descending sun, or the sobered translucency of twilight have subdued the

vivacity of the early day. Yet under the influence of
the benign stimulant many trains of thought which
will bear recalling, may suggest themselves to some of
our quiet circle and prove not uninteresting to a certain number of readers.

How early many of my old breakfast companions
went off to bed! I am thinking not merely of those
who sat round our table, but of that larger company
of friends who listened to our conversations as reported. Dear girl with the silken ringlets, dear boy
with the down-shadowed cheek, your grandfather,
your grandmother, turned over the freshly printed
leaves that told the story of those earlier meetings
around the plain board where so many things were
said and sung, not all of which have quite faded from
the memory of this overburdened and forgetful time.
Your father, your mother, found the scattered leaves
gathered in a volume, and smiled upon them as not
uncompanionable acquaintances. My tea-table makes
no promises. There is no programme of exercises to
be studied beforehand. What if I should content
myself with a single report of what was said and done
over our teacups? Perhaps my young reader would
be glad to let me off, for there are talkers enough
who have not yet left their breakfast-tables; and nobody can blame the young people for preferring the
thoughts and the language of their own generation,
with all its future before it, to those of their grand-
fathers' contemporaries.

My reader, young or old, will please to observe that
I have left myself entire freedom as to the sources of
what may be said over the teacups. I have not told
how many cups are commonly on the board, but by
using the plural I have implied that there is at least

one other talker or listener beside myself, and for all that appears there may be a dozen. There will be no regulation length to my reports, — no attempt to make out a certain number of pages. I have no contract to fill so many columns, no pledge to contribute so many numbers. I can stop on this first page if I do not care to say anything more, and let this article stand by itself if so minded. What a sense of freedom it gives not to write by the yard or the column!

When one writes for an English review or magazine at so many guineas a sheet, the temptation is very great to make one's contribution cover as many sheets as possible. We all know the metallic taste of articles written under this powerful stimulus. If Bacon's Essays had been furnished by a modern hand to the "Quarterly Review" at fifty guineas a sheet, what a great book it would have taken to hold them!

The first thing which suggests itself to me, as I contemplate my slight project, is the liability of repeating in the evening what I may have said in the morning in one form or another, and printed in these or other pages. When it suddenly flashes into the consciousness of a writer who has been long before the public, "Why, I have said all that once or oftener in my books or essays, and here it is again, the same old thought, the same old image, the same old story!" it irritates him, and is likely to stir up the monosyllables of his unsanctified vocabulary. He sees in imagination a thousand readers, smiling or yawning as they say to themselves, "We have had all that before," and turn to another writer's performance for something not quite so stale and superfluous. This is what the writer says to himself about the reader.

The idiot! Does the simpleton really think that

everybody has read all he has written? Does he really believe that everybody remembers all of his, the writer's, words he may happen to have read? At one of those famous dinners of the Phi Beta Kappa Society, where no reporter was ever admitted, and from which nothing ever leaks out about what is said and done, Mr. Edward Everett, in his after-dinner speech, quoted these lines from the Æneid, giving a very liberal English version of them, which he applied to the Oration just delivered by Mr. Emerson: —

Tres imbris torti radios, tres nubis aquosæ
Addiderant, rutili tres ignis, et alitis Austri.

His nephew, the ingenious, inventive, and inexhaustible Dr. Edward Everett Hale, tells the story of this quotation, and of the various uses to which it might be applied in after-dinner speeches. How often he ventured to repeat it at the Phi Beta Kappa dinners I am not sure; but as he reproduced it with his lively embellishments and fresh versions and artful circumlocutions, not one person in ten remembered that he had listened to those same words in those same accents only a twelvemonth ago. The poor deluded creatures who take it for granted that all the world remembers what they have said, and laugh at them when they say it over again, may profit by this recollection. But what if one does say the same things, — of course in a little different form each time, — over and over? If he has anything to say worth saying, that is just what he ought to do. Whether he ought to or not, it is very certain that this is what all who write much or speak much necessarily must and will do. Think of the clergyman who preaches fifty or a hundred or more sermons every year for fifty years! Think of the stump speaker who shouts before a hun-

dred audiences during the same political campaign,
always using the same arguments, illustrations, and
catchwords! Think of the editor, as Carlyle has pictured him, threshing the same straw every morning,
until we know what is coming when we see the first
line, as we do when we read the large capitals at the
head of a thrilling story, which ends in an advertise-
ment of an all-cleansing soap or an all-curing remedy!

The latch-key which opens into the inner chambers
of my consciousness fits, as I have sufficient reason to
believe, the private apartments of a good many other
people's thoughts. The longer we live, the more we
find we are like other persons. When I meet with
any facts in my own mental experience, I feel almost
sure that I shall find them repeated or anticipated in
the writings or the conversation of others. This feeling gives one a freedom in telling his own personal
history he could not have enjoyed without it. My
story belongs to you as much as to me. *De te fabula
narratur.* Change the personal pronoun, — that is
all. It gives many readers a singular pleasure to find
a writer telling them something they have long known
or felt, but which they have never before found any
one to put in words for them. An author does not
always know when he is doing the service of the angel
who stirred the waters of the pool of Bethesda. Many
a reader is delighted to find his solitary thought has a
companion, and is grateful to the benefactor who has
strengthened him. This is the advantage of the humble reader over the ambitious and self-worshipping
writer. It is not with him *pereant illi*, but *beati sunt
illi qui pro nobis nostra dixerunt*, — Blessed are those
who have said our good things for us.

What I have been saying of repetitions leads me

into a train of reflections like which I think many readers will find something in their own mental history. The area of consciousness is covered by layers of habitual thoughts, as a sea-beach is covered with wave-worn, rounded pebbles, shaped, smoothed, and polished by long attrition against each other. These thoughts remain very much the same from day to day, even from week to week; and as we grow older, from month to month, and from year to year. The tides of wakening consciousness roll in upon them daily as we unclose our eyelids, and keep up the gentle movement and murmur of ordinary mental respiration until we close them again in slumber. When we think we are thinking, we are for the most part only listening to the sound of attrition between these inert elements of our intelligence. They shift their places a little, they change their relations to each other, they roll over and turn up new surfaces. Now and then a new fragment is cast in among them, to be worn and rounded and take its place with the others, but the pebbled floor of consciousness is almost as stationary as the pavement of a city thoroughfare.

It so happens that at this particular time I have something to tell which I am quite sure is not one of the rolled pebbles which my reader has seen before in any of my pages, or, as I feel confident, in those of any other writer.

If my reader asks why I do not send the statement I am going to make to some one of the special periodicals that deal with such subjects, my answer is, that I like to tell my own stories at my own time, in my own chosen columns, where they will be read by a class of readers with whom I like to talk.

All men of letters or of science, all writers well

known to the public, are constantly tampered with, in these days, by a class of predaceous and hungry fellow-laborers who may be collectively spoken of as the *brain-tappers*. They want an author's ideas on the subjects which interest them, the inquirers, from the gravest religious and moral questions to the most trivial matters of his habits and his whims and fancies. Some of their questions he cannot answer; some he does not choose to answer; some he is not yet ready to answer, and when he is ready he prefers to select his own organ of publication. I do not find fault with all the brain-tappers. Some of them are doing excellent service by accumulating facts which could not otherwise be attained. But one gets tired of the strings of questions sent him, to which he is expected to return an answer, plucked, ripe or unripe, from his private tree of knowledge. The brain-tappers are like the owner of the goose that laid the golden eggs. They would have the embryos and germs of one's thoughts out of the mental oviducts, and cannot wait for their spontaneous evolution and extrusion.

The story I have promised is, on the whole, the most remarkable of a series which I may have told in part at some previous date, but which, if I have not told, may be worth recalling at a future time.

Some few of my readers may remember that in a former paper I suggested the possibility of the existence of an *idiotic area* in the human mind, corresponding to the blind spot in the human retina. I trust that I shall not be thought to have let my wits go wandering in that region of my own intellectual domain, when I relate a singular coincidence which very lately occurred in my experience, and add a few

remarks made by one of our company on the delicate
and difficult but fascinating subject which it forces
upon our attention. I will first copy the memorandum
made at the time : —

"Remarkable coincidence. On Monday, April 18th,
being at table from 6.30 P. M. to 7.30, with —— and
—— [the two ladies of my household], I told them of
the case of 'trial by battel' offered by Abraham
Thornton in 1817. I mentioned his throwing down
his glove, which was not taken up by the brother of
his victim, and so he had to be let off, for the old law
was still in force. I mentioned that Abraham Thornton was said to have come to this country, 'and [I
added] he may be living near us, for aught that I
know.' I rose from the table, and found an English
letter waiting for me, left while I sat at dinner. I
copy the first portion of this letter : —

'20 ALFRED PLACE, West (near Museum),
South Kensington, LONDON, S. W.
April 7, 1887.

DR. O. W. HOLMES :

DEAR SIR, — In travelling, the other day, I met
with a reprint of the very interesting case of Thornton for murder, 1817. The prisoner pleaded success-
fully the old Wager of Battel. I thought you would
like to read the account, and send it with this. . . .
Yours faithfully,
FRED. RATHBONE.' "

Mr. Rathbone is a well-known dealer in old Wedg-
wood and eighteenth-century art. As a friend of my
hospitable entertainer, Mr. Willett, he had shown me
many attentions in England, but I was not expecting
any communication from him ; and when, fresh from

my conversation, I found this letter just arrived by
mail, and left while I was at table, and on breaking
the seal read what I had a few moments before been
telling, I was greatly surprised, and immediately made
a note of the occurrence, as given above.

I had long been familiar with all the details of this
celebrated case, but had not referred to it, so far as I
can remember, for months or years. I know of no
train of thought which led me to speak of it on that
particular day. I had never alluded to it before in
that company, nor had I ever spoken of it with Mr.
Rathbone.

I told this story over our teacups. Among the
company at the table is a young English girl. She
seemed to be amused by the story. "Fancy!" she
said, — "how very very odd!" "It was a striking
and curious coincidence," said the professor who was
with us at the table. "As remarkable as two teaspoons in one saucer," was the comment of a college
youth who happened to be one of the company. But
the member of our circle whom the reader will hereafter know as Number Seven, began stirring his tea in
a nervous sort of way, and I knew that he was getting
ready to say something about the case. An ingenious
man he is, with a brain like a tinder-box, its contents
catching at any spark that is flying about. I always
like to hear what he says when his tinder brain has a
spark fall into it. It does not follow that because he
is often wrong he may not sometimes be right, for he
is no fool. He treated my narrative very seriously.

The reader need not be startled at the new terms
he introduces. Indeed, I am not quite sure that some
thinking people will not adopt his view of the matter,
which seems to have a degree of plausibility as he
states and illustrates it.

" The impulse which led you to tell that story passed
directly from the letter, which came charged from the
cells of the cerebral battery of your correspondent.
The distance at which the action took place [the letter was left on a shelf twenty-four feet from the place
where I was sitting] shows this charge to have been
of notable intensity.

" Brain action through space without material symbolism, such as speech, expression, etc., is analogous
to electrical induction. Charge the prime conductor
of an electrical machine, and a gold-leaf electrometer,
far off from it, will at once be disturbed. Electricity,
as we all know, can be stored and transported as if it
were a measurable fluid.

" Your incident is a typical example of *cerebral induction* from a source containing stored *cerebricity*.
I use this word, not to be found in my dictionaries, as
expressing the brain-cell power corresponding to electricity. Think how long it was before we had attained any real conception of the laws that govern the
wonderful agent, which now works in harness with the
other trained and subdued forces! It is natural that
cerebricity should be the last of the unweighable
agencies to be understood. The human eye had seen
heaven and earth and all that in them is before it saw
itself as our instruments enable us to see it. This
fact of yours, which seems so strange to you, belongs
to a great series of similar facts familiarly known now
to many persons, and before long to be recognized as
generally as those relating to the electric telegraph
and the slaving 'dynamo.'

" What! you cannot conceive of a charge of cerebricity fastening itself on a letter-sheet and clinging
to it for weeks, while it was shuffling about in mail-

bags, rolling over the ocean, and shaken up in railroad cars? And yet the odor of a grain of musk will hang round a note or a dress for a lifetime. Do you not remember what Professor Silliman says, in that pleasant journal of his, about the little ebony cabinet which Mary, Queen of Scots, brought with her from France, — how ' its drawers still exhale the sweetest perfumes ' ? If they could hold their sweetness for more than two hundred years, why should not a written page retain for a week or a month the equally mysterious effluence poured over it from the thinking marrow, and diffuse its vibrations to another excitable nervous centre ? "

I have said that although our imaginative friend is given to wild speculations, he is not always necessarily wrong. We know too little about the laws of brain-force to be dogmatic with reference to it. I am, myself, therefore, fully in sympathy with the psychological investigators. When it comes to the various pretended sciences by which men and women make large profits, attempts at investigation are very apt to be used as lucrative advertisements for the charlatans. But a series of investigations of the significance of certain popular beliefs and superstitions, a careful study of the relations of certain facts to each other, — whether that of cause and effect, or merely of coincidence, — is a task not unworthy of sober-minded and well-trained students of nature. Such a series of investigations has been recently instituted, and was reported at a late meeting held in the rooms of the Boston Natural History Society. The results were mostly negative, and in one sense a disappointment. A single case, related by Professor Royce, attracted a good deal of attention. It was reported in the next morning's newspapers, and will be given at full length, doubtless, in the next number of the Psychological Journal. The leading facts were, briefly, these: A lady in Hamburg, Germany, wrote, on the 22d of June last, that she had what she supposed to be nightmare on the night of the 17th, five days before. "It seemed," she wrote, "to belong to you; to be a horrid pain in your head, as if it were being forcibly jammed into an iron casque, or some such pleasant instrument of torture." It proved that on that same 17th of June her sister was undergoing a painful operation at the hands of a dentist. "No single case," adds Professor Royce, "proves, or even makes probable, the existence of telepathic toothaches; but if there are any more cases of this sort, we want to hear of them, and that all the more because no folk-lore and no supernatural horrors have as yet mingled with the natural and well-known impressions that people associate with the dentist's chair."

The case I have given is, I am confident, absolutely free from every source of error. I do not remember that Mr. Rathbone had communicated with me since he sent me a plentiful supply of mistletoe a year ago last Christmas. The account I received from him was cut out of "The Sporting Times" of March 5, 1887. My own knowledge of the case came from "Kirby's Wonderful Museum," a work presented to me at least thirty years ago. I had not looked at the account, spoken of it, nor thought of it for a long time, when it came to me by a kind of spontaneous generation, as it seemed, having no connection with any previous train of thought that I was aware of. I consider the evidence of entire independence, apart from possible "telepathic" causation, completely water-proof, air-tight, incombustible, and unassailable.

I referred, when first reporting this curious case of coincidence, with suggestive circumstances, to two others, one of which I said was the most picturesque and the other the most unlikely, as it would seem, to happen. This is the first of those two cases : —

Grenville Tudor Phillips was a younger brother of George Phillips, my college classmate, and of Wendell Phillips, the great orator. He lived in Europe a large part of his life, but at last returned, and, in the year 1863, died at the house of his brother George. I read his death in the paper ; but, having seen and heard very little of him during his life, should not have been much impressed by the fact, but for the following occurrence : between the time of Grenville Phillips's death and his burial, I was looking in upon my brother, then living in the house in which we were both born. Some books which had been my father's were stored in shelves in the room I used to occupy when at Cambridge. Passing my eye over them, an old dark quarto attracted my attention. It must be a Bible, I said to myself, — perhaps a rare one, — the "Breeches" Bible or some other interesting specimen. I took it from the shelves, and, as I did so, an old slip of paper fell out and fluttered to the floor. On lifting it I read these words : —

The name is Grenville Tudor.

What was the meaning of this slip of paper coming to light at this time, after reposing undisturbed so long ? There was only one way of explaining its presence in my father's old Bible, — a copy of the Scriptures which I did not remember ever having

handled or looked into before. In christening a child
the minister is liable to forget the name, just at the
moment when he ought to remember it. My father
preached occasionally at the Brattle Street Church.
I take this for granted, for I remember going with
him on one occasion when he did so. Nothing was
more likely than that he should be asked to officiate
at the baptism of the younger son of his wife's first
cousin, Judge Phillips. This slip was handed him to
remind him of the name. He brought it home, put it
in that old Bible, and there it lay quietly for nearly
half a century, when, as if it had just heard of Mr.
Phillips's decease, it flew from its hiding-place and
startled the eyes of those who had just read his name
in the daily column of deaths. It would be hard to
find anything more than a mere coincidence here; but
it seems curious enough to be worth telling.

The second of these two last stories must be told in
prosaic detail to show its whole value as a coincidence.

One evening while I was living in Charles Street,
I received a call from Dr. S., a well-known and
highly respected Boston physician, a particular friend
of the late Alexander H. Stephens, vice-president of
the Southern Confederacy. It was with reference to
a work which Mr. Stephens was about to publish that
Dr. S. called upon me. After talking that matter
over we got conversing on other subjects, among the
rest a family relationship existing between us, — not
a very near one, but one which I think I had seen
mentioned in genealogical accounts. Mary S. (the
last name being the same as that of my visitant), it
appeared, was the great-great-grandmother of Mrs. H.
and myself. After cordially recognizing our forgotten
relationship, now for the first time called to mind, we

parted, my guest leaving me for his own home. We
had been sitting in my library on the lower floor. On
going up-stairs where Mrs. II. was sitting alone, just
as I entered the room she pushed a paper across the
table towards me, saying that perhaps it might interest me. It was one of a number of old family papers
which she had brought from the house of her mother,
recently deceased.

I opened the paper, which was an old-looking docu-
ment, and found that it was a copy, perhaps made in
this century, of the will of that same Mary S. about
whom we had been talking down-stairs.

If there is such a thing as a purely accidental coincidence this must be considered an instance of it.

All one can say about it is that it seems very unlikely that such a coincidence should occur, *but it did*.

I have not tried to keep my own personality out of
these stories. But after all, how little difference it
makes whether or not a writer appears with a mask
on which everybody can take off, — whether he bolts
his door or not, when everybody can look in at his
windows, and all his entrances are at the mercy of the
critic's skeleton key and the jimmy of any ill-disposed
assailant!

The company have been silent listeners for the most
part; but the reader will have a chance to become
better acquainted with some of them by and by.

II.

I KNOW that it is a hazardous experiment to address myself again to a public which in days long past has given me a generous welcome. But my readers have been, and are, a very faithful constituency. I think there are many among them who would rather listen to an old voice they are used to than to a new one of better quality, even if the "childish treble" should betray itself now and then in the tones of the over-tired organ. But there must be others, — I am afraid many others, — who will exclaim: "He has had his day, and why can't he be content? We don't want literary *revenants*, superfluous veterans, writers who have worn out their welcome and still insist on being attended to. Give us something fresh, something that belongs to our day and generation. Your morning draught was well enough, but we don't care for your evening slip-slop. You are not in relation with us, with our time, our ideas, our aims, our aspirations."

Alas, alas! my friend, — my young friend, for your hair is not yet whitened, — I am afraid you are too nearly right. No doubt, — no doubt. Tea-cups are not coffee-cups. They do not hold so much. Their pallid infusion is but a feeble stimulant compared with the black decoction served at the morning board. And so, perhaps, if wisdom like yours were compatible with years like mine, I should drop my pen and make no further attempts upon your patience.

But suppose that a writer who has reached and passed the natural limit of serviceable years feels that he has some things which he would like to say, and which may have an interest for a limited class of readers, — is he not right in trying his powers and calmly taking the risk of failure? Does it not seem rather lazy and cowardly, because he cannot " beat his record," or even come up to the level of what he has done in his prime, to shrink from exerting his talent, such as it is, now that he has outlived the period of his greatest vigor? A singer who is no longer equal to the trials of opera on the stage may yet please at a chamber concert or in the drawing-room. There is one gratification an old author can afford a certain class of critics: that, namely, of comparing him as he is with what he was. It is a pleasure to mediocrity to have its superiors brought within range, so to speak; and if the ablest of them will only live long enough, and keep on writing, there is no pop-gun that cannot reach him. But I fear that this is an unamiable reflection, and I am at this time in a very amiable mood.

I confess that there is something agreeable to me in renewing my relations with the reading public. Were it but a single appearance, it would give me a pleasant glimpse of the time when I was known as a frequent literary visitor. Many of my readers — if I can lure any from the pages of younger writers — will prove to be the children, or the grandchildren, of those whose acquaintance I made something more than a whole generation ago. I could depend on a kind welcome from my contemporaries, — my coevals. But where *are* those contemporaries? *Ay de mi!* as Carlyle used to exclaim, — Ah, dear me! as our old

women say, — I look round for them, and see only
their vacant places. The old vine cannot unwind its
tendrils. The branch falls with the decay of its support, and must cling to the new growths around it, if
it would not lie helpless in the dust. This paper is a
new tendril, feeling its way, as it best may, to whatever it can wind around. The thought of finding here
and there an old friend, and making, it may be, once
in a while a new one, is very grateful to me. The
chief drawback to the pleasure is the feeling that I
am submitting to that inevitable exposure which is the
penalty of authorship in every form. A writer must
make up his mind to the possible rough treatment of
the critics, who swarm like bacteria whenever there is
any literary material on which they can feed. I have
had as little to complain of as most writers, yet I
think it is always with reluctance that one encounters
the promiscuous handling which the products of the
mind have to put up with, as much as the fruit and
provisions in the market-stalls. I had rather be criti-
cised, however, than criticise; that is, express my
opinions in the public prints of other writers' work, if
they are living, and can suffer, as I should often have
to make them. There are enough, thank Heaven,
without me. We are literary cannibals, and our writers live on each other and each other's productions to
a fearful extent. What the mulberry leaf is to the
silk-worm, the author's book, treatise, essay, poem, is
to the critical larvæ that feed upon it. It furnishes
them with food and clothing. The process may not
be agreeable to the mulberry leaf or to the printed
page; but without it the leaf would not have become
the silk that covers the empress's shoulders, and but
for the critic the author's book might never have

reached the scholar's table. Scribblers will feed on
each other, and if we insist on being scribblers we
must consent to be fed on. We must try to endure
philosophically what we cannot help, and ought not, I
suppose, to wish to help.

It is the custom at our table to vary the usual talks
by the reading of short papers, in prose or verse, by
one or more of The Teacups, as we are in the habit
of calling those who make up our company. Thirty
years ago, one of our present circle — "Teacup Number Two," The Professor, — read a paper on Old Age,
at a certain Breakfast-table, where he was in the habit
of appearing. That paper was published at the time,
and has since seen the light in other forms. He did
not know so much about old age then as he does now,
and would doubtless write somewhat differently if he
took the subject up again. But I found that it was
the general wish that another of our company should
let us hear what he had to say about it. I received a
polite note, requesting me to discourse about old age,
inasmuch as I was particularly well qualified by my
experience to write in an authoritative way concerning
it. The fact is that I, — for it is myself who am speaking, — have recently arrived at the age of threescore
years and twenty, — fourscore years we may otherwise
call it. In the arrangement of our table, I am Teacup Number One, and I may as well say that I am
often spoken of as The Dictator. There is nothing
invidious in this, as I am the oldest of the company,
and no claim is less likely to excite jealousy than that
of priority of birth.

I received congratulations on reaching my eightieth
birthday, not only from our circle of Teacups, but

from friends, near and distant, in large numbers. I tried to acknowledge these kindly missives with the aid of a most intelligent secretary; but I fear that there were gifts not thanked for, and tokens of good-will not recognized. Let any neglected correspondent be assured that it was not intentionally that he or she was slighted. I was grateful for every such mark of esteem; even for the telegram from an unknown friend in a distant land, for which I cheerfully paid the considerable charge which the sender doubtless knew it would give me pleasure to disburse for such an expression of friendly feeling.

I will not detain the reader any longer from the essay I have promised.

This is the paper read to The Teacups.

It is in A Song of Moses that we find the words, made very familiar to us by the Episcopal Burial Service, which place the natural limit of life at three-score years and ten, with an extra ten years for some of a stronger constitution than the average. Yet we are told that Moses himself lived to be a hundred and twenty years old, and that his eye was not dim nor his natural strength abated. This is hard to accept literally, but we need not doubt that he was very old, and in remarkably good condition *for a man of his age.* Among his followers was a stout old captain, Caleb, the son of Jephunneh. This ancient warrior speaks of himself in these brave terms: " Lo, I am this day fourscore and five years old. As yet, I am as strong this day as I was in the day that Moses sent me; as my strength was then, even so is my strength now, for war, both to go out and to come in." It is not likely that anybody believed his brag about his being as good a man for active service at eighty-five as he was at forty, when Moses sent him out to spy the land of Canaan. But he was, no doubt, lusty and vigorous *for his years*, and ready to smite the Canaanites hip and thigh, and drive them out, and take possession of their land, as he did forthwith, when Moses gave him leave.

Grand old men there were, three thousand years ago! But not all octogenarians were like Caleb, the son of Jephunneh. Listen to poor old Barzillai, and hear him piping: "I am this day-fourscore years old; and can I discern between good and evil? Can thy servant taste what I eat or what I drink? Can I hear any more the voice of singing men and singing women? Wherefore, then, should thy servant be yet a burden unto my lord the king?" And poor King David was worse off than this, as you all remember, at the early age of seventy.

Thirty centuries do not seem to have made any very great difference in the extreme limits of life. Without pretending to rival the alleged cases of life prolonged beyond the middle of its second century, such as those of Henry Jenkins and Thomas Parr, we can make a good showing of centenarians and nonagenarians. I myself remember Dr. Holyoke, of Salem, son of a president of Harvard College, who answered a toast proposed in his honor at a dinner given to him on his hundredth birthday.

"Father Cleveland," our venerated city missionary, was born June 21, 1772, and died June 5, 1872, within a little more than a fortnight of his hundredth birthday. Colonel Perkins, of Connecticut, died recently after celebrating his centennial anniversary.

Among nonagenarians, three whose names are well

known to Bostonians, Lord Lyndhurst, Josiah Quincy, and Sidney Bartlett, were remarkable for retaining their faculties in their extreme age. That patriarch of our American literature, the illustrious historian of his country, is still with us, his birth dating in 1800.

Ranke, the great German historian, died at the age of ninety-one, and Chevreul, the eminent chemist, at that of a hundred and two.

Some English sporting characters have furnished striking examples of robust longevity. In Gilpin's "Forest Scenery" there is the story of one of these horseback heroes. Henry Hastings was the name of this old gentleman, who lived in the time of Charles the First. It would be hard to find a better portrait of a hunting squire than that which the Earl of Shaftesbury has the credit of having drawn of this very peculiar personage. His description ends by saying, "He lived to be an hundred, and never lost his eyesight nor used spectacles. He got on horseback without help, and rode to the death of the stag till he was past fourscore."

Everything depends on habit. Old people can do, of course, more or less well, what they have been doing all their lives; but try to teach them any new tricks, and the truth of the old adage will very soon show itself. Mr. Henry Hastings had done nothing but hunt all his days, and his record would seem to have been a good deal like that of Philippus Zachdarm in that untranslatable epitaph which may be found in "Sartor Resartus." Judged by its products, it was a very short life of a hundred useless twelvemonths.

It is something to have climbed the white summit, the Mont Blanc of fourscore. A small number only of mankind ever see their eightieth anniversary. I

might go to the statistical tables of the annuity and
life insurance offices for extended and exact information, but I prefer to take the facts which have impressed themselves upon me in my own career.

The class of 1829 at Harvard College, of which I
am a member, graduated, according to the triennial,
fifty-nine in number. It is sixty years, then, since that
time ; and as they were, on an average, about twenty
years old, those who survive must have reached fourscore years. Of the fifty-nine graduates ten only are
living, or were at the last accounts ; one in six, very
nearly. In the first ten years after graduation, our
third decade, when we were between twenty and thirty
years old, we lost three members, — about one in
twenty ; between the ages of thirty and forty, eight
died, — one in seven of those the decade began with ;
from forty to fifty, only two, — or one in twenty-four ;
from fifty to sixty, eight, — or one in six ; from sixty
to seventy, fifteen, — or two out of every five ; from
seventy to eighty, twelve, — or one in two. The
greatly increased mortality which began with our
seventh decade went on steadily increasing. At sixty
we come " within range of the rifle-pits," to borrow
an expression from my friend Weir Mitchell.

Our eminent classmate, the late Professor Benjamin
Peirce, showed by numerical comparison that the men
of superior ability outlasted the average of their fel-
low-graduates. He himself lived a little beyond his
threescore and ten years. James Freeman Clarke
almost reached the age of eighty. The eighth decade
brought the fatal year for Benjamin Robbins Curtis,
the great lawyer, who was one of the judges of the
Supreme Court of the United States ; for the very
able chief justice of Massachusetts, George Tyler

Bigelow; and for that famous wit and electric centre
of social life, George T. Davis. At the last annual
dinner every effort was made to bring all the survivors
of the class together. Six of the ten living members
were there, — six old men in the place of the thirty or
forty classmates who surrounded the long, oval table
in 1859, when I asked, " Has there any old fellow got
mixed with the boys ? " — " boys " whose tongues were
as the vibrating leaves of the forest; whose talk was
like the voice of many waters ; whose laugh was as
the breaking of mighty waves upon the seashore.
Among the six at our late dinner was our first scholar,
the thorough-bred and accomplished engineer who held
the city of Lawrence in his brain before it spread
itself out along the banks of the Merrimac. There,
too, was the poet whose National Hymn, " My Country, 't is of thee," is known to more millions, and
dearer to many of them, than all the other songs written since the Psalms of David. Four of our six were
clergymen; the engineer and the present writer completed the list. Were we melancholy? Did we talk
of graveyards and epitaphs? No, — we remembered
our dead tenderly, serenely, feeling deeply what we
had lost in those who but a little while ago were with
us. How could we forget James Freeman Clarke,
that man of noble thought and vigorous action, who
pervaded this community with his spirit, and was felt
through all its channels as are the light and the
strength that radiate through the wires which stretch
above us? It was a pride and a happiness to have
such classmates as he was to remember. We were
not the moping, complaining graybeards that many
might suppose we must have been. We had been
favored with the blessing of long life. We had seen

the drama well into its fifth act. The sun still warmed
us, the air was still grateful and life-giving. But there
was another underlying source of our cheerful equanimity, which we could not conceal from ourselves if
we had wished to do it. Nature's kindly anodyne is
telling upon us more and more with every year. Our
old doctors used to give an opiate which they called
" the black drop." It was stronger than laudanum,
and, in fact, a dangerously powerful narcotic. Something like this is that potent drug in Nature's pharma-
copœia which she reserves for the time of need, — the
later stages of life. She commonly begins adminis-
tering it at about the time of the " grand climacteric,"
the ninth septennial period, the sixty-third year.
More and more freely she gives it, as the years go on,
to her grey-haired children, until, if they last long
enough, every faculty is benumbed, and they drop off
quietly into sleep under its benign influence.

Do you say that old age is unfeeling? It has not
vital energy enough to supply the waste of the more
exhausting emotions. Old Men's Tears, which furnished the mournful title to Joshua Scottow's Lamen-
tations, do not suggest the deepest grief conceivable.
A little breath of wind brings down the raindrops
which have gathered on the leaves of the tremulous
poplars. A very slight suggestion brings the tears
from Marlborough's eyes, but they are soon over, and
he is smiling again as an allusion carries him back to
the days of Blenheim and Malplaquet. Envy not the
old man the tranquillity of his existence, nor yet blame
him if it sometimes looks like apathy. Time, the inexorable, does not threaten him with the scythe so
often as with the sand-bag. He does not cut, but he
stuns and stupefies. One's fellow-mortals can afford

to be as considerate and tender with him as Time and Nature.

There was not much boasting among us of our present or our past, as we sat together in the little room at the great hotel. A certain amount of self-deception is quite possible at threescore years and ten, but at threescore years and twenty Nature has shown most of those who live to that age that she is earnest, and means to dismantle and have done with them in a very little while. As for boasting of our past, the *laudator temporis acti* makes but a poor figure in our time. Old people used to talk of their youth as if there were giants in those days. We knew some tall men when we were young, but we can see a man taller than any one among them at the nearest dime museum. We had handsome women among us, of high local reputation, but nowadays we have professional beauties who challenge the world to criticise them as boldly as Phryne ever challenged her Athenian admirers. We had fast horses, — did not " Old Blue " trot a mile in three minutes ? True, but there is a three-year-old colt just put on the track who has done it in a little more than two thirds of that time. It seems as if the material world had been made over again since we were boys. It is but a short time since we were counting up the miracles we had lived to witness. The list is familiar enough: the railroad, the ocean steamer, photography, the spectroscope, the telegraph, telephone, phonograph, anæsthetics, electric illumination, — with such lesser wonders as the friction match, the sewing machine, and the bicycle. And now, we said, we must have come to the end of these unparalleled developments of the forces of nature. We must rest on our achievements. The nineteenth century is not

likely to add to them; we must wait for the twentieth
century. Many of us, perhaps most of us, felt in that
way. We had seen our planet furnished by the art of
man with a complete nervous system: a spinal cord
beneath the ocean, secondary centres, — ganglions, —
in all the chief places where men are gathered together, and ramifications extending throughout civilization. All at once, by the side of this talking and
light-giving apparatus, we see another wire stretched
over our heads, carrying force to a vast metallic muscular system, — a slender cord conveying the strength
of a hundred men, of a score of horses, of a team of
elephants. The lightning is tamed and harnessed,
the thunderbolt has become a common carrier. No
more surprises in this century! A voice whispers,
What next?

It will not do for us to boast about our young days
and what they had to show. It is a great deal better
to boast of what they could *not* show, and, strange as
it may seem, there is a certain satisfaction in it. In
these days of electric lighting, when you have only to
touch a button and your parlor or bedroom is instantly
flooded with light, it is a pleasure to revert to the era
of the tinder-box, the flint and steel, and the brimstone match. It gives me an almost proud satisfaction
to tell how we used, when those implements were not
at hand or not employed, to light our whale-oil lamp
by blowing a live coal held against the wick, often
swelling our cheeks and reddening our faces until we
were on the verge of apoplexy. I love to tell of our
stage-coach experiences, of our sailing-packet voyages,
of the semi-barbarous destitution of all modern comforts and conveniences through which we bravely lived
and came out the estimable personages you find us.

Think of it! All my boyish shooting was done with a flint-lock gun; the percussion lock came to me as one of those new-fangled notions people had just got hold of. We ancients can make a grand display of minus quantities in our reminiscences, and the figures look almost as well as if they had the plus sign before them.

I am afraid that old people found life rather a dull business in the time of King David and his rich old subject and friend, Barzillai, who, poor man, could not have read a wicked novel, nor enjoyed a symphony concert, if they had had those luxuries in his day. There were no pleasant firesides, for there were no chimneys. There were no daily newspapers for the old man to read, and he could not read them if there were, with his dimmed eyes, nor hear them read, very probably, with his dulled ears. There was no tobacco, a soothing drug, which in its various forms is a great solace to many old men and to some old women, — Carlyle and his mother used to smoke their pipes together, you remember.

Old age is infinitely more cheerful, for intelligent people at least, than it was two or three thousand years ago. It is our duty, so far as we can, to keep it so. There will always be enough about it that is solemn, and more than enough, alas! that is saddening. But how much there is in our times to lighten its burdens! If they that look out at the windows be darkened, the optician is happy to supply them with eye-glasses for use before the public, and spectacles for their hours of privacy. If the grinders cease because they are few, they can be made many again by a third dentition, which brings no toothache in its train. By temperance and good habits of life, proper

clothing, well-warmed, well-drained, and well-venti-
lated dwellings, and sufficient, not too much exercise,
the old man of our time may keep his muscular
strength in very good condition.   I doubt if Mr.
Gladstone, who is fast nearing his eightieth birthday,
would boast, in the style of Caleb, that he was as good
a man with his axe as he was when he was forty, but
I would back him, — if the match were possible, —
for a hundred shekels, against that over-confident old
Israelite, to cut down and chop up a cedar of Leba-
non.   I know a most excellent clergyman, not far
from my own time of life, whom I would pit against
any old Hebrew rabbi or Greek philosopher of his
years and weight, if they could return to the flesh, to
run a quarter of a mile on a good, level track.

We must not make too much of such exceptional
cases of prolonged activity.   I often reproached my
dear friend and classmate, James Freeman Clarke,
that his ceaseless labors made it impossible for his coevals to enjoy the luxury of that repose which their
years demanded.   A wise old man, the late Dr. James
Walker, president of Harvard University, said that
the great privilege of old age was the *getting rid of
responsibilities*.   These hard-working veterans will
not let one get rid of them until he drops in his harness, and so gets rid of them and his life together.
How often has many a tired old man envied the super-
annuated family cat, stretched upon the rug before
the fire, letting the genial warmth tranquilly diffuse
itself through all her internal arrangements!   No
more watching for mice in dark, damp cellars, no
more awaiting the savage gray rat at the mouth of
his den, no more scurrying up trees and lamp-posts
to avoid the neighbor's cur who wishes to make her

acquaintance! It is very grand to "die in harness," but it is very pleasant to have the tight straps unbuckled and the heavy collar lifted from the neck and shoulders.

It is natural enough to cling to life. We are used to atmospheric existence, and can hardly conceive of ourselves except as breathing creatures. We have never tried any other mode of being, or, if we have, we have forgotten all about it, whatever Wordsworth's grand ode may tell us we remember. Heaven itself must be an experiment to every human soul which shall find itself there. It may take time for an earthborn saint to become acclimated to the celestial ether, — that is, if time can be said to exist for a disembodied spirit. We are all sentenced to capital punishment for the crime of living, and though the condemned cell of our earthly existence is but a narrow and bare dwelling-place, we have adjusted ourselves to it, and made it tolerably comfortable for the little while we are to be confined in it. The prisoner of Chillon

regained [his] freedom with a sigh,

and a tender-hearted mortal might be pardoned for looking back, like the poor lady who was driven from her dwelling-place by fire and brimstone, at the home he was leaving for the "undiscovered country."

On the other hand, a good many persons, not suicidal in their tendencies, get more of life than they want. One of our wealthy citizens said, on hearing that a friend had dropped off from apoplexy, that it made his mouth water to hear of such a case. It was an odd expression, but I have no doubt that the fine old gentleman to whom it was attributed made use of it. He had had enough of his gout and other infirmi-

ties.   Swift's account of the Struldbrugs is not very
amusing reading for old people, but some may find it
a consolation to reflect on the probable miseries they
escape in not being doomed to an undying earthly existence.

There are strange diversities in the way in which
different old persons look upon their prospects. A
millionaire whom I well remember confessed that he
should like to live long enough to learn how much a
certain fellow-citizen, a multimillionaire, was worth.
One of the three nonagenarians before referred to expressed himself as having a great *curiosity* about the
new sphere of existence to which he was looking forward.

The feeling must of necessity come to many aged
persons that they have outlived their usefulness ; that
they are no longer wanted, but rather in the way,
drags on the wheels rather than helping them forward.
But let them remember the often-quoted line of Milton, —

"They also serve who only stand and wait."

This is peculiarly true of them.   They are helping
others without always being aware of it.   They are
the shields, the breakwaters, of those who come after
them.   Every decade is a defence of the one next behind it.   At thirty the youth has sobered into manhood, but the strong men of forty rise in almost unbroken rank between him and the approaches of old
age as they show in the men of fifty.   At forty he
looks with a sense of security at the strong men of
fifty, and sees behind them the row of sturdy sexage-
narians.   When fifty is reached, somehow sixty does
not look so old as it once used to, and seventy is still
afar off.   After sixty the stern sentence of the burial

service seems to have a meaning that one did not notice in former years. There begins to be something personal about it. But if one lives to seventy he soon gets used to the text with the threescore years and ten in it, and begins to count himself among those who by reason of strength are destined to reach fourscore, of whom he can see a number still in reasonably good condition. The octogenarian loves to read about people of ninety and over. He peers among the asterisks of the triennial catalogue of the University for the names of graduates who have been seventy years out of college and remain still unstarred. He is curious about the biographies of centenarians. Such escapades as those of that terrible old sinner and ancestor of great men, the Reverend Stephen Bachelder, interest him as they never did before. But he cannot deceive himself much longer. See him walking on a level surface, and he steps off almost as well as ever; but watch him coming down a flight of stairs, and the family record could not tell his years more faithfully. He cut you dead, you say? Did it occur to you that he could not see you clearly enough to know you from any other son or daughter of Adam? He said he was very glad to hear it, did he, when you told him that your beloved grandmother had just deceased? Did you happen to remember that though he does not allow that he is deaf, he will not deny that he does not hear quite so well as he used to? No matter about his failings; the longer he holds on to life, the longer he makes life seem to all the living who follow him, and thus he is their constant benefactor.

Every stage of existence has its special trials and its special consolations. *Habits* are the crutches of old age; by the aid of these we manage to hobble along after the mental joints are stiff and the muscles rheumatic, to speak metaphorically, — that is to say, when every act of self-determination costs an effort and a pang. We become more and more automatic as we grow older, and if we lived long enough we should come to be pieces of creaking machinery like Maelzel's chess player, — or what that seemed to be.

Emerson was sixty-three years old, the year I have referred to as that of the grand climacteric, when he read to his son the poem he called "Terminus," beginning :

> "It is time to be old,
> To take in sail.
> The God of bounds,
> Who sets to seas a shore,
> Came to me in his fatal rounds
> And said, ' No more ! ' "

It was early in life to feel that the productive stage was over, but he had received warning from within, and did not wish to wait for outside advices. There is all the difference in the world in the mental as in the bodily constitution of different individuals. Some must "take in sail" sooner, some later. We can get a useful lesson from the American and the English elms on our Common. The American elms are quite bare, and have been so for weeks. They know very well that they are going to have storms to wrestle with ; they have not forgotten the gales of September and the tempests of the late autumn and early winter. It is a hard fight they are going to have, and they strip their coats off and roll up their shirt-sleeves, and show themselves bare-armed and ready for the contest. The English elms are of a more robust build, and stand defiant, with all their summer clothing about their sturdy frames. They may yet have to

learn a lesson of their American cousins, for notwithstanding their compact and solid structure they go to
pieces in the great winds just as ours do. We must
drop much of our foliage before winter is upon us.
We must take in sail and throw over cargo, if that is
necessary, to keep us afloat. We have to decide between our duties and our instinctive demand of rest.
I can believe that some have welcomed the decay of
their active powers because it furnished them with
peremptory reasons for sparing themselves during the
few years that were left them.

Age brings other obvious changes besides the loss
of active power. The sensibilities are less keen, the
intelligence is less lively, as we might expect under
the influence of that narcotic which Nature adminis-
ters. But there is another effect of her " black drop "
which is not so commonly recognized. Old age is like
an opium-dream. Nothing seems real except what is
unreal. I am sure that the pictures painted by the
imagination, — the faded frescos on the walls of memory, — come out in clearer and brighter colors than
belonged to them many years earlier. Nature has her
special favors for her children of every age, and this
is one which she reserves for our second childhood.

No man can reach an advanced age without thinking of that great change to which, in the course of
nature, he must be so near. It has been remarked
that the sterner beliefs of rigid theologians are apt to
soften in their later years. All reflecting persons,
even those whose minds have been half palsied by the
deadly dogmas which have done all they could to dis-
organize their thinking powers, — all reflecting persons, I say, must recognize, in looking back over a
long life, how largely their creeds, their course of life,

their wisdom and unwisdom, their whole characters, were shaped by the conditions which surrounded them. Little children they came from the hands of the Father of all ; little children in their helplessness, their ignorance, they are going back to Him. They cannot help feeling that they are to be transferred from the rude embrace of the boisterous elements to arms that will receive them tenderly. Poor planetary foundlings, they have known hard treatment at the hands of the brute forces of nature, from the control of which they are soon to be set free. There are some old pessimists, it is true, who believe that they and a few others are on a raft, and that the ship which they have quitted, holding the rest of mankind, is going down with all on board. It is no wonder that there should be such when we remember what have been the teachings of the priesthood through long series of ignorant centuries. Every age has to shape the Divine image it worships over again, — the present age and our own country are busily engaged in the task at this time. We unmake Presidents and make new ones. This is an apprenticeship for a higher task. Our doctrinal teachers are unmaking the Deity of the Westminster Catechism and trying to model a new one, with more of modern humanity and less of ancient barbarism in his composition. If Jonathan Edwards had lived long enough, I have no doubt his creed would have softened into a kindly, humanized belief.

Some twenty or thirty years ago, I said to Longfellow that certain statistical tables I had seen went to show that poets were not a long-lived race. He doubted whether there was anything to prove they were particularly short-lived. Soon after this, he handed me a list he had drawn up. I cannot lay my hand upon it at this moment, but I remember that Metastasio was the oldest of them all. He died at the age of eighty-four. I have had some tables made out, which I have every reason to believe are correct so far as they go. From these, it appears that twenty English poets lived to the average age of fifty-six years and a little over. · The eight American poets on the list averaged seventy-three and a half, nearly, and they are not all dead yet. The list including Greek, Latin, Italian, and German poets, with American and English, gave an average of a little over sixty-two years. Our young poets need not be alarmed. They can remember that Bryant lived to be eighty-three years old, that Longfellow reached seventy-five and Halleck seventy-seven, while Whittier is living at the age of nearly eighty-two. Tennyson is still writing at eighty, and Browning reached the age of seventy-seven.

Shall a man who in his younger days has written poetry, or what passed for it, continue to attempt it in his later years? Certainly, if it amuses or interests him, no one would object to his writing in verse as much as he likes. Whether he should continue to write for the public is another question. Poetry is a good deal a matter of heart-beats, and the circulation is more languid in the later period of life. The joints are less supple ; the arteries are more or less " ossified." Something like these changes has taken place in the mind. It has lost the flexibility, the plastic docility, which it had in youth and early manhood, when the gristle had but just become hardened into bone. It is the nature of poetry to writhe itself along through the tangled growths of the vocabulary, as a snake winds through the grass, in sinuous, complex,

and unexpected curves, which crack every joint that is
not supple as india-rubber.

I had a poem that I wanted to print just here. But
after what I have this moment said, I hesitated,
thinking that I might provoke the obvious remark
that I exemplified the unfitness of which I had been
speaking. I remembered the advice I had given to a
poetical aspirant not long since, which I think deserves
a paragraph to itself.

My friend, I said, I hope you will not write in verse.
When you write in prose you say what you *mean*.
When you write in rhyme you say what you *must*.

Should I send this poem to the publishers, or not?

"Some said, 'John, print it ;' others said, 'Not so.'"

I did not ask "some" or "others." Perhaps I
should have thought it best to keep my poem to myself and the few friends for whom it was written. All
at once, my *daimōn* — that other Me over whom I
button my waistcoat when I button it over my own
person — put it into my head to look up the story of
Madame Saqui. She was a famous *danseuse*, who
danced Napoleon in and out, and several other dynas-
ties besides. Her last appearance was at the age of
seventy-six, which is rather late in life for the tight
rope, one of her specialties. Jules Janin mummified
her when she died in 1866, at the age of eighty. He
spiced her up in his eulogy as if she had been the
queen of a modern Pharaoh. His foamy and flowery
rhetoric put me into such a state of good-nature that
I said, I will print my poem, and let the critical Gil
Blas handle it as he did the archbishop's sermon, —
or would have done, if he had been a writer for the
"Salamanca Weekly."

It must be premised that a very beautiful loving cup was presented to me on my recent birthday, by eleven ladies of my acquaintance. This was the most costly and notable of all the many tributes I received, and for which in different forms I expressed my gratitude.

TO THE ELEVEN LADIES

WHO PRESENTED ME WITH A SILVER LOVING CUP ON THE TWENTY-NINTH OF AUGUST, M DCCC LXXXIX.

"Who gave this cup?" The secret thou wouldst steal
Its brimming flood forbids it to reveal :
No mortal's eye shall read it till he first
    Cool the red throat of thirst.

If on the golden floor one draught remain,
Trust me, thy careful search will be in vain ;
Not till the bowl is emptied shalt thou know
    The names enrolled below.

Deeper than Truth lies buried in her well
Those modest names the graven letters spell
Hide from the sight ; but wait, and thou shalt see
    Who the good angels be

Whose bounty glistens in the beauteous gift
That friendly hands to loving lips shall lift :
Turn the fair goblet when its floor is dry, —
    Their names shall meet thine eye.

Count thou their number on the beads of Heaven, —
Alas ! the clustered Pleiads are but seven ;
Nay, the nine sister Muses are too few, —
    The Graces must add two.

"For whom this gift?" For one who all too long
Clings to his bough among the groves of song ;
Autumn's last leaf, that spreads its faded wing
    To greet a second spring.

Dear friends, kind friends, whate'er the cup may hold,
Bathing its burnished depths, will change to gold :
Its last bright drop let thirsty Mænads drain,
     Its fragrance will remain.

Better love's perfume in the empty bowl
Than wine's nepenthe for the aching soul ;
Sweeter than song that ever poet sung,
     It makes an old heart young !

III.

AFTER the reading of the paper which was reported in the preceding number of this record, the company fell into talk upon the subject with which it dealt.

The Mistress. "I could have wished you had said more about the religious attitude of old age as such. Surely the thoughts of aged persons must be very much taken up with the question of what is to become of them. I should like to have The Dictator explain himself a little more fully on this point."

My dear madam, I said, it is a delicate matter to talk about. You remember Mr. Calhoun's response to the advances of an over-zealous young clergyman who wished to examine him as to his outfit for the long journey. I think the relations between man and his Maker grow more intimate, more confidential, if I may say so, with advancing years. The old man is less disposed to argue about special matters of belief, and more ready to sympathize with spiritually minded persons without anxious questioning as to the fold to which they belong. That kindly judgment which he exercises with regard to others he will, naturally enough, apply to himself. The *caressing* tone in which the Emperor Hadrian addresses his soul is very much like that of an old person talking with a grandchild or some other pet: —

> "*Animula, vagula, blandula,*
> *Hospes comesque corporis.*"

> " Dear little, flitting, pleasing sprite,
> The body's comrade and its guest."

How like the language of Catullus to Lesbia's sparrow!

More and more the old man finds his pleasures in memory, as the present becomes unreal and dreamlike, and the vista of his earthly future narrows and closes in upon him. At last, if he live long enough, life comes to be little more than a gentle and peaceful delirium of pleasing recollections. To say, as Dante says, that there is no greater grief than to remember past happiness in the hour of misery is not giving the whole truth. In the midst of the *misery*, as many would call it, of extreme old age, there is often a divine consolation in recalling the happy moments and days and years of times long past. So beautiful are the visions of bygone delight that one could hardly wish them to become real, lest they should lose their ineffable charm. I can almost conceive of a dozing and dreamy centenarian saying to one he loves, " Go, darling, go! Spread your wings and leave me. So shall you enter that world of memory where all is lovely. I shall not hear the sound of your footsteps any more, but you will float before me, an aërial presence. I shall not hear any word from your lips, but I shall have a deeper sense of your nearness to me than speech can give. I shall feel, in my still solitude, as the Ancient Mariner felt when the seraph band gathered before him : —

> "' No voice did they impart —
> No voice ; but oh ! the silence sank
> Like music on my heart.' "

I said that the lenient way in which the old look at the failings of others naturally leads them to judge themselves more charitably. They find an apology for their short-comings and wrong-doings in another

consideration. They know very well that they are not
the same persons as the middle-aged individuals, the
young men, the boys, the children, that bore their
names, and whose lives were continuous with theirs.
Here is an old man who can remember the first time
he was allowed to go shooting. What a remorseless
young destroyer he was, to be sure! Wherever he
saw a feather, wherever a poor little squirrel showed
his bushy tail, bang! went the old " king's arm," and
the feathers or the fur were set flying like so much
chaff. *Now* that same old man, — the mortal that was
called by his name and has passed for the same person for some scores of years, — is considered absurdly
sentimental by kind-hearted women, because he opens
the fly-trap and sets all its captives free, — out-of-
doors, of course, but the dear souls all insisting, mean-
while, that the flies will, every one of them, be back
again in the house before the day is over. Do you
suppose that venerable sinner expects to be rigorously
called to account for the want of feeling he showed in
those early years, when the instinct of destruction, de-
rived from his forest-roaming ancestors, led him to
acts which he now looks upon with pain and aversion?

" Senex " has seen three generations grow up, the
son repeating the virtues and the failings of the father,
the grandson showing the same characteristics as the
father and grandfather. He knows that if such or
such a young fellow had lived to the next stage of
life he would very probably have caught up with his
mother's virtues, which, like a graft of a late fruit on
an early apple or pear tree, do not ripen in her children until late in the season. He has seen the successive ripening of one quality after another on the
boughs of his own life, and he finds it hard to condemn

himself for faults which only needed time to fall off
and be succeeded by better fruitage. I cannot help
thinking that the recording angel not only drops a
tear upon many a human failing, which blots it out
forever, but that he hands many an old record-book
to the imp that does his bidding, and orders him to
throw that into the fire instead of the sinner for whom
the little wretch had kindled it.

"And pitched him in after it, I hope," said Number
Seven, who is in some points as much of an optimist
as any one among us, in spite of the squint in his
brain, — or in virtue of it, if you choose to have it so.

"I like Wordsworth's 'Matthew,'" said Number
Five, "as well as any picture of old age I remember."

"Can you repeat it to us?" asked one of The
Teacups.

"I can recall two verses of it," said Number Five,
and she recited the two following ones. Number Five
has a very sweet voice. The moment she speaks all
the faces turn toward her. I don't know what its secret is, but it is a voice that makes friends of everybody.

> "'The sighs which Matthew heaved were sighs
> Of one tired out with fun and madness;
> The tears which came to Matthew's eyes
> Were tears of light, the dew of gladness.
>
> "'Yet, sometimes, when the secret cup
> Of still and serious thought went round,
> It seemed as if he drank it up,
> He felt with spirit so profound.'

"This was the way in which Wordsworth paid his
tribute to a

> "'Soul of God's best earthly mould.'"

The sweet voice left a trance-like silence after it,
which may have lasted twenty heart-beats. Then I

said, We all thank you for your charming quotation.
How much more wholesome a picture of humanity than
such stuff as the author of the "Night Thoughts"
has left us : —

> "Heaven's Sovereign saves all beings but Himself
> That hideous sight, a naked human heart."

Or the author of "Don Juan," telling us to look into ,

> "Man's heart, and view the hell that 's there!"

I hope I am quoting correctly, but I am more of a
scholar in Wordsworth than in Byron. Was Parson
Young's own heart such a hideous spectacle to himself?
If it was, he had better have stripped off his surplice.
No, — it was nothing but the cant of his calling. In
Byron it was a *mood*, and he might have said just the
opposite thing the next day, as he did in his two descriptions of the Venus de' Medici. That picture of
old Matthew abides in the memory, and makes one
think better of his kind. What nobler tasks has the
poet than to exalt the idea of manhood, and to make
the world we live in more beautiful?

We have two or three young people with us who
stand a fair chance of furnishing us the element without which life and tea-tables alike are wanting in
interest. We are all, of course, watching them, and
curious to know whether we are to have a romance or
not. Here is one of them ; others will show themselves presently.

I cannot say just how old the Tutor is, but I do not
detect a gray hair in his head. My sight is not so
good as it was, however, and he may have turned the
sharp corner of thirty, and even have left it a year
or two behind him. More probably he is still in the

twenties, — say twenty-eight or twenty-nine. He seems young, at any rate, excitable, enthusiastic, imaginative, but at the same time reserved. I am afraid that he is a poet. When I say "I am afraid," you wonder what I mean by the expression. I may take another opportunity to explain and justify it; I will only say now that I consider the Muse the most dangerous of sirens to a young man who has his way to make in the world. Now this young man, the Tutor, has, I believe, a future before him. He was born for a philosopher, — so I read his horoscope, — but he has a great liking for poetry and can write well in verse. We have had a number of poems offered for our entertainment, which I have commonly been requested to read. There has been some little mystery about their authorship, but it is evident that they are not all from the same hand. Poetry is as contagious as measles, and if a single case of it break out in any social circle, or in a school, there are certain to be a number of similar cases, some slight, some serious, and now and then one so malignant that the subject of it should be put on a spare diet of stationery, say from two to three penfuls of ink and a half sheet of notepaper *per diem*. If any of our poetical contributions are presentable, the reader shall have a chance to see them.

It must be understood that our company is not invariably made up of the same persons. The Mistress, as we call her, is expected to be always in her place. I make it a rule to be present. The Professor is almost as sure to be at the table as I am. We should hardly know what to do without Number Five. It takes a good deal of tact to handle such a little assembly as ours, which is a republic on a small scale, for

all that they give me the title of Dictator, and Number Five is a great help in every social emergency.
She sees when a discussion tends to become personal,
and heads off the threatening antagonists. She knows
when a subject has been knocking about long enough,
and dexterously shifts the talk to another track. It
is true that I am the one most frequently appealed to
as the highest tribunal in doubtful cases, but I often
care more for Number Five's opinion than I do for
my own. Who is this Number Five, so fascinating,
so wise, so full of knowledge, and so ready to learn?
She is suspected of being the anonymous author of a
book which produced a sensation when published, not
very long ago, and which those who read are very apt
to read a second time, and to leave on their tables for
frequent reference. But we have never asked her. I
do not think she wants to be famous. How she comes
to be unmarried is a mystery to me; it must be that
she has found nobody worth caring enough for. I wish
she would furnish us with the romance which, as I said,
our tea-table needs to make it interesting. Perhaps
the new-comer will make love to her, — I should think
it possible she might fancy him.

And who is the new-comer? He is a Counsellor
and a Politician. Has a good war record. Is about
forty-five years old, I conjecture. Is engaged in a
great law case just now. Said to be very eloquent.
Has an intellectual head, and the bearing of one who
has commanded a regiment or perhaps a brigade.
Altogether an attractive person, scholarly, refined;
has some accomplishments not so common as they
might be in the class we call *gentlemen*, with an accent
on the word.

There is also a young Doctor, waiting for his bald
spot to come, so that he may get into practice.

We have two young ladies at the table, — the English girl referred to in a former number, and an American girl of about her own age. Both of them are students in one of those institutions — I am not sure whether they call it an "annex" or not, but at any rate one of those schools where they teach the incomprehensible sort of mathematics and other bewildering branches of knowledge above the common level of high-school education. They seem to be good friends, and form a very pleasing pair when they walk in arm in arm; nearly enough alike to seem to belong together, different enough to form an agreeable contrast.

Of course we were bound to have a Musician at our table, and we have one who sings admirably, and accompanies himself, or one or more of our ladies, very frequently.

Such is our company when the table is full. But sometimes only half a dozen, or it may be only three or four, are present. At other times we have a visitor or two, either in the place of one of our habitual number, or in addition to it. We have the elements, we think, of a pleasant social gathering, — different sexes, ages, pursuits, and tastes, — all that is required for a "symphony concert" of conversation. One of the curious questions which might well be asked by those who had been with us on different occasions would be, "How many poets are there among you?" Nobody can answer this question. It is a point of etiquette with us not to press our inquiries about these anonymous poems too sharply, especially if any of them betray sentiments which would not bear rough handling.

I don't doubt that the different personalities at our table will get mixed up in the reader's mind if he is not particularly clear-headed. That happens very often, much oftener than all would be willing to confess, in reading novels and plays. I am afraid we should get a good deal confused even in reading our Shakespeare if we did not look back now and then at the *dramatis personæ.* I am sure that I am very apt to confound the characters in a moderately interesting novel; indeed, I suspect that the writer is often no better off than the reader in the dreary middle of the story, when his characters have all made their appearance, and before they have reached near enough to the *dénoûment* to have fixed their individuality by the position they have arrived at in the chain of the narrative.

My reader might be a little puzzled when he read that Number Five did or said such or such a thing, and ask, " Whom do you mean by that title? I am not quite sure that I remember." Just associate her with that line of Emerson, —

" Why nature loves the number five," —

and that will remind you that she is the favorite of our table.

You cannot forget who Number Seven is if I inform you that he specially prides himself on being a seventh son of a seventh son. The fact of such a descent is supposed to carry wonderful endowments with it. Number Seven passes for a natural healer. He is looked upon as a kind of wizard, and is lucky in living in the nineteenth century instead of the sixteenth or earlier. How much confidence he feels in himself as the possessor of half-supernatural gifts I cannot say. I think his peculiar birthright gives him a certain confidence in his whims and fancies which but for that he would hardly feel. After this explanation, when I speak of Number Five or Number Seven, you will know to whom I refer.

The company are very frank in their criticisms of each other. " I did not like that expression of yours, *planetary foundlings*," said the Mistress. " It seems to me that it is too like atheism for a good Christian like you to use."

Ah, my dear madam, I answered, I was thinking of the elements and the natural forces to which man was born an almost helpless subject in the rudimentary stages of his existence, and from which he has only partially got free after ages upon ages of warfare with their tyranny. Think what hunger forced the cave-man to do! Think of the surly indifference of the storms that swept the forest and the waters, the earth-quake chasms that engulfed him, the inundations that drowned him out of his miserable hiding-places, the pestilences that lay in wait for him, the unequal strife with ferocious animals! I need not sum up all the wretchedness that goes to constitute the " martyrdom of man." When our forefathers came to this wilderness as it then was, and found everywhere the bones of the poor natives who had perished in the great plague (which our Doctor there thinks was probably the small-pox), they considered this destructive malady as a special mark of providential favor for them. How about the miserable Indians? Were they anything but planetary foundlings? No! Civilization is a great foundling hospital, and fortunate are all those who get safely into the *crèche* before the frost or the malaria has killed them, the wild beasts or the venomous reptiles worked out their deadly appetites and instincts upon them. The very idea of humanity seems to be that it shall take care of itself and develop its powers in the "struggle for life." Whether we approve it or not, if we can judge by the material record, man was born a foundling, and fought his way as he best might to that kind of existence which we call civilized, — one which a considerable part of the inhabitants of our planet have reached.

If you do not like the expression planetary foundlings, I have no objection to your considering the race as put out to nurse. And what a nurse Nature is! She gives her charge a hole in the rocks to live in, ice for his pillow and snow for his blanket, in one part of the world; the jungle for his bedroom in another, with the tiger for his watch-dog and the cobra as his playfellow.

Well, I said, there may be other parts of the universe where there are no tigers and no cobras. It is not quite certain that such realms of creation are better off, on the whole, than this earthly residence of ours, which has fought its way up to the development of such centres of civilization as Athens and Rome, to such personalities as Socrates, as Washington.

"One of our company has been on an excursion among the celestial bodies of our system, I understand," said the Professor.

Number Five colored. "Nothing but a dream," she said. "The truth is, I had taken ether in the evening for a touch of neuralgia, and it set my imagination at work in a way quite unusual with me. I had been reading a number of books about an ideal condition of society, — Sir Thomas More's 'Utopia,' Lord Bacon's 'New Atlantis,' and another of more

recent date. I went to bed with my brain a good
deal excited, and fell into a deep slumber, in which I
passed through some experiences so singular that, on
awaking, I put them down on paper. I don't know
that there is anything very original about the experiences I have recorded, but I thought them worth pre-
serving. Perhaps you would not agree with me in
that belief."

"If Number Five will give us a chance to form our
own judgment about her dream or vision, I think we
shall enjoy it," said the Mistress. "She knows what
will please The Teacups in the way of reading as well
as I do how many lumps of sugar the Professor wants
in his tea and how many I want in mine."

The company was so urgent that Number Five sent
up-stairs for her paper.

Number Five reads the story of her dream.

It cost me a great effort to set down the words of
the manuscript from which I am reading. My dreams
for the most part fade away so soon after their occurrence that I cannot recall them at all. But in this
case my ideas held together with remarkable tenacity.
By keeping my mind steadily upon the work, I gradually unfolded the narrative which follows, as the famous Italian antiquary opened one of those fragile
carbonized manuscripts found in the ruins of Hercu-
laneum or Pompeii.

The first thing I remember about it is that I was
floating upward, without any sense of effort on my
part. The feeling was that of flying, which I have
often had in dreams, as have many other persons. It
was the most natural thing in the world, — a semi-
materialized volition, if I may use such an expression.

At the first moment of my new consciousness, — for I seemed to have just emerged from a deep slumber, — I was aware that there was a companion at my side. Nothing could be more gracious than the way in which this being accosted me. I will speak of it as *she*, because there was a delicacy, a sweetness, a divine purity, about its aspect that recalled my ideal of the loveliest womanhood.

" I am your companion and your guide," this being made me understand, as she looked at me. Some faculty of which I had never before been conscious had awakened in me, and I needed no interpreter to explain the unspoken language of my celestial attendant.

" You are not yet outside of space and time," she said, " and I am going with you through some parts of the phenomenal or apparent universe, — what you call the material world. We have plenty of what you call time before us, and we will take our voyage leisurely, looking at such objects of interest as may attract our attention as we pass. The first thing you will naturally wish to look at will be the earth you have just left. This is about the right distance," she said, and we paused in our flight.

The great globe we had left was rolling beneath us. No eye of one in the flesh could see it as I saw or seemed to see it. No ear of any mortal being could hear the sounds that came from it as I heard or seemed to hear them. The broad oceans unrolled themselves before me. I could recognize the calm Pacific and the stormy Atlantic, — the ships that dotted them, the white lines where the waves broke on the shore, — frills on the robes of the continents, — so they looked to my woman's perception; the vast

South American forests; the glittering icebergs about
the poles; the snowy mountain ranges, here and there
a summit sending up fire and smoke; mighty rivers,
dividing provinces within sight of each other, and
making neighbors of realms thousands of miles apart;
cities; light-houses to insure the safety of sea-going
vessels, and war-ships to knock them to pieces and
sink them.   All this, and infinitely more, showed itself to me during a single revolution of the sphere:
twenty-four hours it would have been, if reckoned by
earthly measurements of time.   I have not spoken of
the sounds I heard while the earth was revolving under us.   The howl of storms, the roar and clash of
waves, the crack and crash of the falling thunderbolt, — these of course made themselves heard as
they do to mortal ears.   But there were other sounds
which enchained my attention more than these voices
of nature.   As the skilled leader of an orchestra
hears every single sound from each member of the
mob of stringed and wind instruments, and above all
the screech of the straining soprano, so my sharpened
perceptions made what would have been for common
mortals a confused murmur audible to me as com-
pounded of innumerable easily distinguished sounds.
Above them all arose one continued, unbroken, ago-
nizing cry.   It was the voice of suffering womanhood,
— a sound that goes up day and night, one long cho-
rus of tortured victims.

"Let us get out of reach of this," I said; and we
left our planet, with its blank, desolate moon staring
at it, as if it had turned pale at the sights and sounds
it had to witness.

Presently the gilded dome of the State House,
which marked our starting-point, came into view for

the second time, and I knew that this side-show was over. I bade farewell to the Common with its Cogswell fountain, and the Garden with its last awe-inspiring monument.

"Oh, if I could sometimes revisit these beloved scenes!" I exclaimed.

"There is nothing to hinder that I know of," said my companion. "Memory and imagination as you know them in the flesh are two winged creatures with strings tied to their legs, and anchored to a bodily weight of a hundred and fifty pounds, more or less. When the string is cut you can *be* where you wish to be, — not merely a part of you, leaving the rest behind, but the whole of you. Why shouldn't you want to revisit your old home sometimes?"

I was astonished at the *human* way in which my guide conversed with me. It was always on the basis of my earthly habits, experiences, and limitations. "Your solar system," she said, "is a very small part of the universe, but you naturally feel a curiosity about the bodies which constitute it and about their inhabitants. There is your moon : a bare and desolate-looking place it is, and well it may be, for it has no respirable atmosphere, and no occasion for one. The Lunites do not breathe ; they live without waste and without supply. You look as if you do not understand this. Yet your people have, as you well know, what they call incandescent lights everywhere. You would have said there can be no lamp without oil or gas, or other combustible substance, to feed it ; and yet you see a filament which sheds a light like that of noon all around it, and does not waste at all. So the Lunites live by influx of divine energy, just as the incandescent lamp glows, — glows, and is not con-

sumed; receiving its life, if we may call it so, from
the central power, which wears the unpleasant name
of 'dynamo.'"

The Lunites appeared to me as pale phosphorescent
figures of ill-defined outline, lost in their own halos, as
it were. I could not help thinking of Shelley's

<blockquote>
" maiden
With white fire laden."
</blockquote>

But as the Lunites were after all but provincials, as
are the tenants of all the satellites, I did not care to
contemplate them for any great length of time.

I do not remember much about the two planets that
came next to our own, except the beautiful rosy atmosphere of one and the huge bulk of the other. Presently, we found ourselves within hailing distance of
another celestial body, which I recognized at once, by
the rings which girdled it, as the planet Saturn. A
dingy, dull-looking sphere it was in its appearance.
"We will tie up here for a while," said my attendant.
The easy, familiar way in which she spoke surprised
and pleased me.

Why, said I, — The Dictator, — what is there to
prevent beings of another order from being as cheerful, as social, as good companions, as the very liveliest
of God's creatures whom we have known in the flesh?
Is it impossible for an archangel to smile? Is such a
phenomenon as a laugh never heard except in our little
sinful corner of the universe? Do you suppose, that
when the disciples heard from the lips of their Master
the play of words on the name of Peter, there was no
smile of appreciation on the bearded faces of those
holy men? From any other lips we should have called
this pleasantry a —

Number Five shook her head very slightly, and gave me a look that seemed to say, " Don't frighten the other Teacups. We don't call things by the names that belong to them when we deal with celestial subjects."

We tied up, as my attendant playfully called our resting, so near the planet that I could know — I will not say see and hear, but apprehend — all that was going on in that remote sphere ; remote, as we who live in what we have been used to consider the centre of the rational universe regard it. What struck me at once was the deadness of everything I looked upon. Dead, uniform color of surface and surrounding atmosphere. Dead complexion of all the inhabitants. Dead-looking trees, dead-looking grass, no flowers to be seen anywhere.

" What is the meaning of all this? " I said to my guide.

She smiled good-naturedly, and replied, " It is a forlorn home for anything above a lichen or a toad-stool ; but that is no wonder, when you know what the air is which they breathe. It is pure nitrogen."

The Professor spoke up. "That can't be, madam," he said. " The spectroscope shows the atmosphere of Saturn to be — no matter, I have forgotten what; but it was not pure nitrogen, at any rate."

Number Five is never disconcerted. " Will you tell me, " she said, " where you have found any account of the bands and lines in the spectrum of dream-nitrogen? I should be so pleased to become acquainted with them."

The Professor winced a little, and asked Delilah,

the handmaiden, to pass a plate of muffins to him.
The dream had carried him away, and he thought
for the moment that he was listening to a scientific
paper.

Of course, my companion went on to say, the bodily
constitution of the Saturnians is wholly different from
that of air-breathing, that is oxygen-breathing, human
beings.   They are the dullest, slowest, most torpid of
mortal creatures.

All this is not to be wondered at when you remember the inert characteristics of nitrogen.   There are
in some localities natural springs which give out slender streams of oxygen.   You will learn by and by
what use the Saturnians make of this dangerous gas,
which, as you recollect, constitutes about one fifth of
your own atmosphere.   Saturn has large lead mines,
but no other metal is found on this planet.   The inhabitants have nothing else to make tools of, except
stones and shells.   The mechanical arts have therefore made no great progress among them.   Chopping
down a tree with a leaden axe is necessarily a slow
process.

So far as the Saturnians can be said to have any
pride in anything, it is in the absolute level which
characterizes their political and social order.   They
profess to be the only true republicans in the solar
system.   The fundamental articles of their Constitution are these : —

All Saturnians are born equal, live equal, and die
equal.

All Saturnians are born free, — free, that is, to
obey the rules laid down for the regulation of their

conduct, pursuits, and opinions, free to be married to the person selected for them by the physiological section of the government, and free to die at such proper period of life as may best suit the convenience and general welfare of the community.

The one great industrial product of Saturn is the bread-root. The Saturnians find this wholesome and palatable enough; and it is well they do, as they have no other vegetable. It is what I should call a most uninteresting kind of eatable, but it serves as food and drink, having juice enough, so that they get along without water. They have a tough, dry grass, which, matted together, furnishes them with clothes sufficiently warm for their cold-blooded constitutions, and more than sufficiently ugly.

A piece of ground large enough to furnish bread-root for ten persons is allotted to each head of a household, allowance being made for the possible increase of families. This, however, is not a very important consideration, as the Saturnians are not a prolific race. The great object of life being the product of the largest possible quantity of bread-roots, and women not being so capable in the fields as the stronger sex, females are considered an undesirable addition to society. The one thing the Saturnians dread and abhor is *inequality*. The whole object of their laws and customs is to maintain the strictest equality in everything, — social relations, property, so far as they can be said to have anything which can be so called, mode of living, dress, and all other matters. It is their boast that nobody ever starved under their government. Nobody goes in rags, for the coarse-fibred grass from which they fabricate their clothes is very durable. (I confess I wondered how a woman could live in Saturn. They have no looking-glasses. There is no such article as a ribbon known among them. All their clothes are of one pattern. I noticed that there were no pockets in any of their garments, and learned that a pocket would be considered *prima facie* evidence of theft, as no honest person would have use for such a secret receptacle.) Before the revolution which established the great law of absolute and lifelong equality, the inhabitants used to feed at their own private tables. Since the regeneration of society all meals are taken in common. The last relic of barbarism was the use of plates, — one or even more to each individual. This " odious relic of an effete civilization," as they called it, has long been superseded by oblong hollow receptacles, one of which is allotted to each twelve persons. A great riot took place when an attempt was made by some fastidious and exclusive egotists to introduce *partitions* which should partially divide one portion of these receptacles into individual compartments. The Saturnians boast that they have no paupers, no thieves, none of those fictitious values called money, — all which things, they hear, are known in that small Saturn nearer the sun than the great planet which is their dwelling-place.

" I suppose that now they have levelled everything they are quiet and contented. Have they any of those uneasy people called reformers ? "

" Indeed they have," said my attendant. " There are the Orthobrachians, who declaim against the shameful abuse of the left arm and hand, and insist on restoring their perfect equality with the right. Then there are Isopodic societies, which insist on bringing back the original equality of the upper and lower limbs. If you can believe it, they actually practise going on all fours, — generally in a private way, a few of them together, but hoping to bring the world round to them in the near future."

Here I had to stop and laugh.

"I should think life might be a little dull in Saturn," I said.

"It is liable to that accusation," she answered. "Do you notice how many people you meet with their mouths stretched wide open?"

"Yes," I said, "and I do not know what to make of it. I should think every fourth or fifth person had his mouth open in that way."

"They are suffering from the endemic disease of their planet, prolonged and inveterate gaping or yawning, which has ended in dislocation of the lower jaw. After a time this becomes fixed, and requires a difficult surgical operation to restore it to its place."

It struck me that, in spite of their boast that they have no paupers, no thieves, no money, they were a melancholy-looking set of beings.

"What are their amusements?" I asked.

"Intoxication and suicide are their chief recreations. They have a way of mixing the oxygen which issues in small jets from certain natural springs with their atmospheric nitrogen in the proportion of about twenty per cent, which makes very nearly the same thing as the air of your planet. But to the Saturnians the mixture is highly intoxicating, and is therefore a relief to the monotony of their every-day life. This mixture is greatly sought after, but hard to obtain, as the sources of oxygen are few and scanty. It shortens the lives of those who have recourse to it; but if it takes too long, they have other ways of escaping from a life which cuts and dries everything for its miserable subjects, defeats all the natural instincts, confounds all individual characteristics, and makes existence such a colossal *bore*, as your worldly people say, that self-destruction becomes a luxury."

Number Five stopped here.

Your imaginary wholesale Shakerdom is all very fine, said I. Your Utopia, your New Atlantis, and the rest are pretty to look at. But your philosophers are treating the world of living souls as if they were, each of them, playing a game of solitaire, — all the pegs and all the holes alike. Life is a very different sort of game. It is a game of chess, and not of solitaire, nor even of checkers. The men are not all pawns, but you have your knights, bishops, rooks, — yes, your king and queen, — to be provided for. Not with these names, of course, but all looking for their proper places, and having their own laws and modes of action. You can play solitaire with the members of your own family for pegs, if you like, and if none of them rebel. You can play checkers with a little community of meek, like-minded people. But when it comes to the handling of a great state, you will find that nature has emptied a box of chessmen before you, and you must play with them so as to give each its proper move, or sweep them off the board, and come back to the homely game such as I used to see played with beans and kernels of corn on squares marked upon the back of the kitchen bellows.

It was curious to see how differently Number Five's narrative was received by the different listeners in our circle. Number Five herself said she supposed she ought to be ashamed of its absurdities, but she did not know that it was much sillier than dreams often are, and she thought it might amuse the company. She was herself always interested by these ideal pictures of society. But it seemed to her that life must be dull in any of them, and with that idea in her head her dreaming fancy had drawn these pictures.

The Professor was interested in her conception of the existence of the Lunites without waste, and the death in life of the nitrogen-breathing Saturnians. Dream-chemistry was a new subject to him. Perhaps Number Five would give him some lessons in it.

At this she smiled, and said she was afraid she could not teach him anything, but if he would answer a few questions in matter-of-fact chemistry which had puzzled her she would be vastly obliged to him.

"You must come to my laboratory," said the Professor.

"I will come to-morrow," said Number Five.

Oh, yes! Much laboratory work they will do! Play of mutual affinities. Amalgamates. No freezing mixtures, I'll warrant!

Why shouldn't we get a romance out of all this, hey?

But Number Five looks as innocent as a lamb, and as brave as a lion. She does not care a copper for the looks that are going round The Teacups.

Our Doctor was curious about those cases of *anchylosis*, as he called it, of the lower jaw. He thought it a quite possible occurrence. Both the young girls thought the dream gave a very hard view of the optimists, who look forward to a reorganization of society which shall rid mankind of the terrible evils of over-crowding and competition.

Number Seven was quite excited about the matter. He had himself drawn up a plan for a new social arrangement. He had shown it to the legal gentleman who has lately joined us. This gentleman thought it well-intended, but that it would take one constable to every three inhabitants to enforce its provisions.

I said the dream could do no harm ; it was too outrageously improbable to come home to anybody's feelings. Dreams were like broken mosaics, — the separated stones might here and there make parts of pictures. If one found a caricature of himself made out of the pieces which had accidentally come together, he would smile at it, knowing that it was an accidental effect with no malice in it. If any of you really believe in a working Utopia, why not join the Shakers, and convert the world to this mode of life? Celibacy alone would cure a great many of the evils you complain of.

I thought this suggestion seemed to act rather unfavorably upon the ladies of our circle. The two Annexes looked inquiringly at each other. Number Five looked smilingly at them. She evidently thought it was time to change the subject of conversation, for she turned to me and said, " You promised to read us the poem you read before your old classmates the other evening."

I will fulfill my promise, I said. We felt that this might probably be our last meeting as a Class. The personal reference is to our greatly beloved and honored classmate, James Freeman Clarke.

AFTER THE CURFEW.

The Play is over. While the light
   Yet lingers in the darkening hall,
I come to say a last Good-night
   Before the final *Exeunt all.*

We gathered once, a joyous throng :
   The jovial toasts went gayly round ;
With jest, and laugh, and shout, and song,
   We made the floors and walls resound.

We come with feeble steps and slow,
   A little band of four or five,
Left from the wrecks of long ago,
   Still pleased to find ourselves alive.

Alive ! How living, too, are they
   Whose memories it is ours to share !
Spread the long table's full array, —
   There sits a ghost in every chair !

One breathing form no more, alas !
   Amid our slender group we see ;
With him we still remained "The Class," —
   Without his presence what are we ?

The hand we ever loved to clasp, —
   That tireless hand which knew no rest, —
Loosed from affection's clinging grasp,
   Lies nerveless on the peaceful breast.

The beaming eye, the cheering voice,
   That lent to life a generous glow,
Whose every meaning said " Rejoice,"
   We see, we hear, no more below.

The air seems darkened by his loss,
   Earth's shadowed features look less fair,
And heavier weighs the daily cross
   His willing shoulders helped us bear.

———————

Why mourn that we, the favored few
   Whom grasping Time so long has spared

Life's sweet illusions to pursue,
  The common lot of age have shared ?

In every pulse of Friendship's heart
  There breeds unfelt a throb of pain, —
One hour must rend its links apart,
  Though years on years have forged the chain.

So ends " The Boys," — a lifelong play.
  We too must hear the Prompter's call
To fairer scenes and brighter day :
  Farewell !   I let the curtain fall.

IV.

IF the reader thinks that all these talking Teacups came together by mere accident, as people meet at a boarding-house, I may as well tell him at once that he is mistaken. If he thinks I am going to explain how it is that he finds them thus brought together, — whether they form a secret association, whether they are the editors of this or that periodical, whether they are connected with some institution, and so on, — I must disappoint him. It is enough that he finds them in each other's company, a very mixed assembly, of different sexes, ages, and pursuits; and if there is a certain mystery surrounds their meetings, he must not be surprised. Does he suppose we want to be known and talked about in public as "Teacups"? No; so far as we give to the community some records of the talks at our table our thoughts become public property, but the sacred personality of every Teacup must be properly respected. If any wonder at the presence of one of our number, whose eccentricities might seem to render him an undesirable associate of the company, he should remember that some people may have relatives whom they feel bound to keep their eye on; besides, the cracked Teacup brings out the ring of the sound ones as nothing else does. Remember also that the soundest teacup does not always hold the best tea, nor the cracked teacup the worst.

This is a hint to the reader, who is not expected to

be too curious about the individual Teacups constituting our unorganized association.

The Dictator Discourses.

I have been reading Balzac's *Peau de Chagrin.* You have all read the story, I hope, for it is the first of his wonderful romances which fixed the eyes of the reading world upon him, and is a most fascinating if somewhat fantastic tale. A young man becomes the possessor of a certain magic skin, the peculiarity of which is that, while it gratifies every wish formed by its possessor, it shrinks in all its dimensions each time that a wish is gratified. The young man makes every effort to ascertain the cause of its shrinking; invokes the aid of the physicist, the chemist, the student of natural history, but all in vain. He draws a red line around it. That same day he indulges a longing for a certain object. The next morning there is a little interval between the red line and the skin, close to which it was traced. So always, so inevitably. As he lives on, satisfying one desire, one passion, after another, the process of shrinking continues. A mortal disease sets in, which keeps pace with the shrinking skin, and his life and his talisman come to an end together.

One would say that such a piece of integument was hardly a desirable possession. And yet, how many of us have at this very moment a *peau de chagrin* of our own, diminishing with every costly wish indulged, and incapable, like the magical one of the story, of being arrested in its progress!

Need I say that I refer to those *coupon bonds,* issued in the days of eight and ten per cent interest, and gradually narrowing as they drop their semiannual slips of paper, which represent wishes to be realized, as the roses let fall their leaves in July, as the icicles melt away in the thaw of January?

How beautiful was the coupon bond, arrayed in its golden raiment of promises to pay at certain stated intervals, for a goodly number of coming years! What annual the horticulturist can show will bear comparison with this product of auricultural industry, which has flowered in midsummer and midwinter for twenty successive seasons? And now the last of its blossoms is to be plucked, and the bare stem, stripped of its ever maturing and always welcome appendages, is reduced to the narrowest conditions of reproductive existence. Such is the fate of the financial *peau de chagrin*. Pity the poor fractional capitalist, who has just managed to live on the eight per cent of his coupon bonds. The shears of Atropos were not more fatal to human life than the long scissors which cut the last coupon to the lean proprietor, whose slice of dry toast it served to flatter with oleomargarine. Do you wonder that my thoughts took the poetical form, in the contemplation of these changes and their melancholy consequences? If the entire poem, of several hundred lines, was "declined with thanks" by an unfeeling editor, that is no reason why you should not hear a verse or two of it.

THE *PEAU DE CHAGRIN* OF STATE STREET.

> How beauteous is the bond
> In the manifold array
> Of its promises to pay,
> While the eight per cent it gives
> And the rate at which one lives
>   Correspond!

But at last the bough is bare
Where the coupons one by one
Through their ripening days have run,
And the bond, a beggar now,
Seeks investment anyhow,
          Anywhere !

The Mistress commonly contents herself with the
general supervision of the company, only now and
then taking an active part in the conversation.   She
started a question the other evening which set some of
us thinking.

"Why is it," she said, "that there is so common
and so intense a desire for poetical reputation?   It
seems to me that, if I were a man, I had rather have
done something worth telling of than make verses
about what other people had done."

"You agree with Alexander the Great," said the
Professor.   "You would prefer the fame of Achilles
to that of Homer, who told the story of his wrath and
its direful consequences.   I am afraid that I should
hardly agree with you.   Achilles was little better than
a Choctaw brave.   I won't quote Horace's line which
characterizes him so admirably, for I will take it for
granted that you all know it.   He was a gentleman,
— so is a first-class Indian, — a very noble gentleman
in point of courage, lofty bearing, courtesy, but an
unsoaped, ill-clad, turbulent, high-tempered young fellow, looked up to by his crowd very much as the
champion of the heavy weights is looked up to by his
gang of blackguards.   Alexander himself was not
much better, — a foolish, fiery young madcap.   How
often is he mentioned except as a warning?   His best
record is that he served to point a moral as ' Macedo-
nia's madman.'   He made a figure, it is true, in Dry-

den's great Ode, but what kind of a figure? He
got drunk, — in very bad company, too, — and then
turned fire-bug. He had one redeeming point, — he
did value his Homer, and slept with the Iliad under
his pillow. A poet like Homer seems to me worth a
dozen such fellows as Achilles and Alexander."

"Homer is all very well for those that can' read
him," said Number Seven, "but the fellows that tag
verses together nowadays are mostly fools. That's
my opinion. I wrote some verses once myself, but I
had been sick and was very weak; hadn't strength
enough to write in prose, I suppose."

This aggressive remark caused a little stir at our
tea-table. For you must know, if I have not told you
already, there are suspicions that we have more than
one. "poet" at our table. I have already confessed
that I do myself indulge in verse now and then, and
have given my readers a specimen of my work in that
line. · But there is so much difference of character in
the verses which are produced at our table, without
any signature, that I feel quite sure there are at least
two or three other contributors besides myself. There
is a tall, old-fashioned silver urn, a sugar-bowl of the
period of the Empire, in which the poems sent to be
read are placed by unseen hands. When the proper
moment arrives, I lift the cover of the urn and take
out any manuscript it may contain. If conversation
is going on and the company are in a talking mood, I
replace the manuscript or manuscripts, clap on the
cover, and wait until there is a moment's quiet before
taking it off again. I might guess the writers sometimes by the handwriting, but there is more trouble
taken to disguise the chirography than I choose to
take to identify it as that of any particular member
of our company.

The turn the conversation took, especially the slashing onslaught of Number Seven on the writers of verse, set me thinking and talking about the matter. Number Five turned on the stream of my discourse by a question.

"You receive a good many volumes of verse, do you not?" she said, with a look which implied that she knew I did.

I certainly do, I answered. My table aches with them. My shelves groan with them. Think of what a fuss Pope made about his trials, when he complained that

"All Bedlam or Parnassus is let out"!

What were the numbers of the

. "Mob of gentlemen who wrote with ease"

to that great multitude of contributors to our magazines, and authors of little volumes — sometimes, alas! big ones — of verse, which pour out of the press, not weekly, but daily, and at such a rate of increase that it seems as if before long every hour would bring a book, or at least an article which is to grow into a book by and by?

I thanked Heaven, the other day, that I was not a critic. These attenuated volumes of poetry in fancy bindings open their covers at one like so many little unfledged birds, and one does so long to drop a worm in, — a worm in the shape of a kind word for the poor fledgling! But what a desperate business it is to deal with this army of candidates for immortality! I have often had something to say about them, and I may be saying over the same things; but if I do not remember what I have said, it is not very likely that my reader will; if he does, he will find, I am very sure, that I say it a little differently.

What astonishes me is that this enormous mass of commonplace verse, which burdens the postman who brings it, which it is a serious task only to get out of its wrappers and open in two or three places, is on the whole of so good an average quality. The dead level of mediocrity is in these days a table-land, a good deal above the old sea-level of laboring incapacity. Sixty years ago verses made a local reputation, which verses, if offered to-day to any of our first-class magazines, would go straight into the waste-basket. To write " poetry " was an art and mystery in which only a few noted men and a woman or two were experts.

When " Potter the ventriloquist," the predecessor of the well-remembered Signor Blitz, went round giving his entertainments, there was something unexplained, uncanny, almost awful, and beyond dispute marvellous, in his performances. Those watches that disappeared and came back to their owners, those endless supplies of treasures from empty hats, and es. pecially those crawling eggs that travelled all over the magician's person, sent many a child home thinking that Mr. Potter must have ghostly assistants, and raised grave doubts in the minds of " professors," that is members of the church, whether they had not compromised their characters by being seen at such an unhallowed exhibition. Nowadays, a clever boy who has made a study of parlor magic can do many of those tricks almost as well as the great sorcerer himself. How simple it all seems when we have seen the mechanism of the deception!

It is just so with writing in verse. It was not understood that everybody can learn to *make poetry*, just as they can learn the more difficult tricks of juggling. M. Jourdain's discovery that he had been speaking and writing prose all his life is nothing to that of the man who finds out in middle life, or even later, that he might have been writing poetry all his days, if he had only known how perfectly easy and simple it is. Not everybody, it is true, has a sufficiently good ear, a sufficient knowledge of rhymes and capacity for handling them, to be what is called a poet. I doubt whether more than nine out of ten, in the average, have that combination of gifts required for the writing of readable verse.

This last expression of opinion created a sensation among The Teacups. They looked puzzled for a minute. One whispered to the next Teacup, " More than nine out of ten! I should think that was a pretty liberal allowance."

Yes, I continued ; perhaps ninety-nine in a hundred would come nearer to the mark. I have sometimes thought I might consider it worth while to set up a school for instruction in the art. "*Poetry taught in twelve lessons.*" Congenital idiocy is no disqualification. Anybody can write " poetry." It is a most unenviable distinction to have published a thin volume of verse, which nobody wanted, nobody buys, nobody reads, nobody cares for except the author, who cries over its pathos, poor fellow, and revels in its beauties, which he has all to himself. Come ! who will be my pupils in a Course, — Poetry taught in twelve lessons ?

That made a laugh, in which most of The Teacups, myself included, joined heartily. Through it all I heard the sweet tones of Number Five's caressing voice ; not because it was more penetrating or louder than the others, for it was low and soft, but it was so

different from the others, there was so much more
life, — the life of sweet womanhood, — dissolved
in it.

(Of course he will fall in love with her. "He?
Who?" Why, the new-comer, the Counsellor. Did
I not see his eyes turn toward her as the silvery notes
rippled from her throat? Did they not follow her in
her movements, as she turned her head this or that
way?

—What nonsense for me to be arranging matters
between two people strangers to each other before
to-day!)

"A fellow writes in verse when he has nothing to
say, and feels too dull and silly to say it in prose,"
said Number Seven.

This made us laugh again, good-naturedly. I was
pleased with a kind of truth which it seemed to me to
wrap up in its rather startling affirmation. I gave a
piece of advice the other day which I said I thought
deserved a paragraph to itself. It was from a letter
I wrote not long ago to an unknown young correspondent, who had a longing for seeing himself in
verse, but was not hopelessly infatuated with the idea
that he was born a "poet." "When you write in
prose," I said, "you say what you *mean*. When you
write in verse you say what you *must*." I was thinking more especially of *rhymed* verse. Rhythm alone
is a tether, and not a very long one. But rhymes are
iron fetters; it is dragging a chain and ball to march
under their incumbrance; it is a clog-dance you are
figuring in, when you execute your metrical *pas seul*.
Consider under what a disadvantage your thinking
powers are laboring when you are handicapped by the
inexorable demands of our scanty English rhyming

vocabulary! You want to say something about the
heavenly bodies, and you have a beautiful line ending
with the word *stars*. Were you writing in prose,
your imagination, your fancy, your rhetoric, your musical ear for the harmonies of language, would all
have full play. But there is your rhyme fastening
you by the leg, and you must either reject the line
which pleases you, or you must whip your hobbling
fancy and all your limping thoughts into the traces
which are hitched to one of three or four or half a
dozen serviceable words. You cannot make any use
of *cars*, I will suppose; you have no occasion to talk
about *scars*; "the red planet *Mars*" has been used
already; Dibdin has said enough about the gallant
tars; what is there left for you but *bars*? So you
give up your trains of thought, capitulate to necessity,
and manage to lug in some kind of allusion, in place
or out of place, which will allow you to make use of
bars. Can there be imagined a more certain process
for breaking up all continuity of thought, for taking
out all the vigor, all the virility, which belongs to natural prose as the vehicle of strong, graceful, spontaneous thought, than this miserable subjugation of in-
tellect to the clink of well or ill matched syllables?
I think you will smile if I tell you of an idea I have
had about teaching the art of writing "poems" to the
half-witted children at the Idiot Asylum. The trick
of rhyming cannot be more usefully employed than in
furnishing a pleasant amusement to the poor feeble-
minded children. I should feel that I was well employed in getting up a Primer for the pupils of the
Asylum, and other young persons who are incapable of
serious thought and connected expression. I would
start in the simplest way; thus: —

When darkness veils the evening . . . . .
I love to close my weary . . . .

The pupil begins by supplying the missing words, which most children who are able to keep out of fire and water can accomplish after a certain number of trials. When the poet that is to be has got so as to perform this task easily, a skeleton verse, in which two or three words of each line are omitted, is given the child to fill up. By and by the more difficult forms of metre are outlined, until at length a feeble-minded child can make out a sonnet, completely equipped with its four pairs of rhymes in the first section and its three pairs in the second part.

Number Seven interrupted my discourse somewhat abruptly, as is his wont; for we grant him a license, in virtue of his eccentricity, which we should hardly expect to be claimed by a perfectly sound Teacup.

"That's the way, — that's the way!" exclaimed he. "It's just the same thing as my plan for teaching drawing."

Some curiosity was shown among The Teacups to know what the queer creature had got into his head, and Number Five asked him, in her irresistible tones, if he would n't oblige us by telling us all about it.

He looked at her a moment without speaking. I suppose he has often been made fun of, — slighted in conversation, taken as a butt for people who thought themselves witty, made to feel as we may suppose a cracked piece of china-ware feels when it is clinked in the company of sound bits of porcelain. I never saw him when he was carelessly dealt with in conversation, — for it would sometimes happen, even at our table, — without recalling some lines of Emerson which always struck me as of wonderful force and almost terrible truthfulness : —

" Alas ! that one is born in blight,
  Victim of perpetual slight :
  When thou lookest in his face
  Thy heart saith, ' Brother, go thy ways !
  None shall ask thee what thou doest,
  Or care a rush for what thou knowest,
  Or listen when thou repliest,
  Or remember where thou liest,
  Or how thy supper is sodden ; '
  And another is born
  To make the sun forgotten."

Poor fellow !   Number Seven has to bear a good deal
in the way of neglect and ridicule, I do not doubt.
Happily, he is protected by an amount of belief in
himself which shields him from many assailants who
would torture a more sensitive nature.   But the sweet
voice of Number Five and her sincere way of addressing him seemed to touch his feelings.   That was the
meaning of his momentary silence, in which I saw
that his eyes glistened and a faint flush rose on his
cheeks.   In a moment, however, as soon as he was on
his hobby, he was all right, and explained his new and
ingenious system as follows : —

   " A man at a certain distance appears as a dark
spot, — nothing more.   Good.   Anybody, man, woman, or child, can make a dot, say a period, such as
we use in writing.   Lesson No. 1.   Make a dot ; that
is, draw your man, a mile off, if that is far enough.
Now make him come a little nearer, a few rods, say.
The dot is an oblong figure now.   Good.   Let your
scholar draw the oblong figure.   It is as easy as it
is to make a note of admiration.   Your man comes
nearer, and now some hint of a bulbous enlargement
at one end, and perhaps of lateral appendages and a
bifurcation, begins to show itself.   The pupil sets

down with his pencil just what he sees, — no more.
So by degrees the man who serves as model approaches.
A bright pupil will learn to get the outline of a human figure in ten lessons, the model coming five hundred feet nearer each time. A dull one may require
fifty, the model beginning a mile off, or more, and
coming a hundred feet nearer at each move."

The company were amused by all this, but could
not help seeing that there was a certain practical possibility about the scheme. Our two Annexes, as we
call them, appeared to be interested in the project, or
fancy, or whim, or whatever the older heads might
consider it. "I guess I'll try it," said the American
Annex. "Quite so," answered the English Annex.
Why the first girl "guessed" about her own intentions it is hard to say. What "Quite so" referred to
it would not be easy to determine. But these two
expressions would decide the nationality of our two
young ladies if we met them on the top of the great
Pyramid.

I was very glad that Number Seven had interrupted
me. In fact, it is a good thing once in a while to
break in upon the monotony of a steady talker at a
dinner-table, tea-table, or any other place of social
converse. The best talker is liable to become the
most formidable of bores. It is a peculiarity of the
bore that he is the last person to find himself out.
Many a terebrant I have known who, in that capacity,
to borrow a line from Coleridge,

"Was great, nor knew how great he was."

A line, by the way, which, as I have remarked, has in
it a germ like that famous "He builded better than
he knew" of Emerson.

There was a slight lull in the conversation. The

Mistress, who keeps an eye on the course of things, and feared that one of those *panic silences* was impending, in which everybody wants to say something and does not know just what to say, begged me to go on with my remarks about the " manufacture" of " poetry."

You use the right term, madam, I said. The manufacture of that article has become an extensive and therefore an important branch of industry. One must be an editor, which I am not, or a literary confidant of a wide circle of correspondents, which I am, to have any idea of the enormous output of verse which is characteristic of our time. There are many curious facts connected with this phenomenon. Educated people — yes, and many who are not educated — have discovered that rhymes are not the private property of a few noted writers who, having squatted on that part of the literary domain some twenty or forty or sixty years ago, have, as it were, fenced it in with their touchy, barbed-wire reputations, and have come to regard it and cause it to be regarded as their private property. The discovery having been made that rhyme is not a paddock for this or that race-horse, but a common, where every colt, pony, and donkey can range at will, a vast irruption into that once-privileged inclosure has taken place. The study of the great invasion is interesting.

Poetry is commonly thought to be the language of emotion. On the contrary, most of what is so called proves the absence of all passionate excitement. It is a cold-blooded, haggard, anxious, worrying hunt after rhymes which can be made serviceable, after images which will be effective, after phrases which are sonorous ; all this under limitations which restrict the natural movements of fancy and imagination. There is a secondary excitement in overcoming the difficulties of rhythm and rhyme, no doubt, but this is not the emotional heat excited by the subject of the "poet's" treatment. True poetry, the best of it, is but the ashes of a burnt-out passion. The flame was in the eye and in the cheek, the coals may be still burning in the heart, but when we come to the words it leaves behind it, a little warmth, a cinder or two just glimmering under the dead gray ashes, — that is all we can look for. When it comes to the manufactured article, one is surprised to find how well the metrical artisans have learned to imitate the real thing. They catch all the phrases of the true poet. They imitate his metrical forms as a mimic copies the gait of the person he is representing.

Now I am not going to abuse "these same metre ballad-mongers," for the obvious reason that, as all The Teacups know, I myself belong to the fraternity. I don't think that this reason should hinder my having my say about the ballad-mongering business. For the last thirty years I have been in the habit of receiving a volume of poems or a poem, printed or manuscript — I will not say daily, though I sometimes receive more than one in a day, but at very short intervals. I have been consulted by hundreds of writers of verse as to the merit of their performances, and have often advised the writers to the best of my ability. Of late I have found it impossible to attempt to read critically all the literary productions, in verse and in prose, which have heaped themselves on every exposed surface of my library, like snowdrifts along the railroad tracks, — blocking my literary pathway, so that I can hardly find my daily papers.

What is the meaning of this rush into rhyming of such a multitude of people, of all ages, from the infant phenomenon to the oldest inhabitant?

Many of my young correspondents have told me in so many words, "I want to be famous." Now it is true that of all the short cuts to fame, in time of peace, there is none shorter than the road paved with rhymes. Byron woke up one morning and found himself famous. Still more notably did Rouget de l'Isle fill the air of France, nay, the whole atmosphere of freedom all the world over, with his name wafted on the wings of the Marseillaise, the work of a single night. But if by fame the aspirant means having his name brought before and kept before the public, there is a much cheaper way of acquiring that kind of notoriety. Have your portrait taken as a "Wonderful Cure of a Desperate Disease given up by all the Doctors." You will get a fair likeness of yourself and a partial biographical notice, and have the satisfaction, if not of promoting the welfare of the community, at least that of advancing the financial interests of the benefactor whose enterprise has given you your coveted notoriety. If a man wants to be famous, he had much better try the advertising doctor than the terrible editor, whose waste-basket is a maw which is as insatiable as the temporary stomach of Jack the Giant-killer.

"You must not talk so," said Number Five. "I know you don't mean any wrong to the true poets, but you might be thought to hold them cheap, whereas you value the gift in others, — in yourself too, I rather think. There are a great many women, — and some men, — who write in verse from a natural instinct which leads them to that form of expression. If you could peep into the portfolio of all the cultivated women among your acquaintances, you would be surprised, I believe, to see how many of them trust their thoughts and feelings to verse which they never think of publishing, and much of which never meets any eyes but their own. Don't be cruel to the sensitive natures who find a music in the harmonies of rhythm and rhyme which soothes their own souls, if it reaches no farther."

I was glad that Number Five spoke up as she did. Her generous instinct came to the rescue of the poor poets just at the right moment. Not that I meant to deal roughly with them, but the " poets " I have been forced into relation with have impressed me with certain convictions which are not flattering to the fraternity, and if my judgments are not accompanied by my own qualifications, distinctions, and exceptions, they may seem harsh to many readers.

Let me draw a picture which many a young man and woman, and some no longer young, will recognize as the story of their own experiences.

— He is sitting alone with his own thoughts and memories. What is that book he is holding? Something precious, evidently, for it is bound in " tree calf," and there is gilding enough about it for a birthday present. The reader seems to be deeply absorbed in its contents, and at times greatly excited by what he reads; for his face is flushed, his eyes glitter, and — there rolls a large tear down his cheek. Listen to him ; he is reading aloud in impassioned tones : —

> And have I coined my soul in words for naught ?
> And must I, with the dim, forgotten throng
> Of silent ghosts that left no earthly trace

To show they once had breathed this vital air,
Die out of mortal memories ?

His voice is choked by his emotion. " How is it possible," he says to himself, " that any one can read my
' Gaspings for Immortality ' without being impressed
by their freshness, their passion, their beauty, their
originality ? " Tears come to his relief freely, — so
freely that he has to push the precious volume out of
the range of their blistering shower. Six years ago
" Gaspings for Immortality " was published, adver-
tised, praised by the professionals whose business it is
to *boost* their publishers' authors. A week and more
it was seen on the counters of the booksellers and at
the stalls in the railroad stations. Then it disappeared from public view. A few copies still kept
their place on the shelves of friends, — presentation
copies, of course, as there is no evidence that any
were disposed of by sale ; and now, one might as well
ask for the lost books of Livy as inquire at a bookstore for " Gaspings for Immortality."

The authors of these poems are all round us, men
and women, and no one with a fair amount of human
sympathy in his disposition would treat them otherwise than tenderly. Perhaps they do not need tender
treatment. How do you know that posterity may not
resuscitate these seemingly dead poems, and give their
author the immortality for which he longed and la-
bored ? It is not every poet who is at once appreci-
ated. Some will tell you that the best poets never
are. Who can say that you, dear unappreciated
brother or sister, are not one of those whom it is left
for after times to discover among the wrecks of the
past, and hold up to the admiration of the world ?

I have not thought it necessary to put in all the *interpellations*, as the French call them, which broke the course of this somewhat extended series of remarks; but the comments of some of The Teacups helped me to shape certain additional observations, and may seem to the reader as of more significance than what I had been saying.

Number Seven saw nothing but the folly and weakness of the "rhyming cranks," as he called them. He thought the fellow that I had described as blubbering over his still-born poems would have been better occupied in earning his living in some honest way or other. He knew one chap that published a volume of verses, and let his wife bring up the wood for the fire by which he was writing. A fellow says, "I am a poet!" and he thinks himself different from common folks. He ought to be excused from military service. He might be killed, and the world would lose the inestimable products of his genius. "I believe some of 'em think," said Number Seven, "that they ought not to be called upon to pay their taxes and their bills for household expenses, like the rest of us."

"If they would only study and take to heart Horace's 'Ars Poetica,'" said the Professor, "it would be a great benefit to them and to the world at large. I would not advise you to follow him too literally, of course, for, as you will see, the changes that have taken place since his time would make some of his precepts useless and some dangerous, but the spirit of them is always instructive. This is the way, somewhat modernized and accompanied by my running commentary, in which he counsels a young poet: —

"'Don't try to write poetry, my boy, when you are

not in the mood for doing it, — when it goes against the grain. You are a fellow of sense, — you understand all that.

" ' If you have written anything which you think well of, show it to Mr. ——, the well-known critic; to " the governor," as you call him, — your honored father; and to me, your friend.'

" To the critic is well enough, if you like to be over-hauled and put out of conceit with yourself, — it may do you good; but I would n't go to ' the governor' with my verses, if I were you. For either he will think what you have written is something wonderful, almost as good as he could have written himself, — in fact, he always *did* believe in hereditary genius, — or he will pooh-pooh the whole rhyming nonsense, and tell you that you had a great deal better stick to your business, and leave all the word-jingling to Mother Goose and her followers.

" ' Show *me* your verses,' says Horace. Very good it was in him, and mighty encouraging the first counsel he gives! ' Keep your poem to yourself for some eight or ten years; you will have time to look it over, to correct it and make it fit to present to the public.'

" ' Much obliged for your advice,' says the poor poet, thirsting for a draught of fame, and offered a handful of dust. And off he hurries to the printer, to be sure that his poem comes out in the next number of the magazine he writes for."

" Is not poetry the natural language of lovers? "

It was the Tutor who asked this question, and I thought he looked in the direction of Number Five, as if she might answer his question. But Number Five stirred her tea devotedly; there was a lump of sugar,

I suppose, that acted like a piece of marble. So there was a silence while the lump was slowly dissolving, and it was anybody's chance who saw fit to take up the conversation.

The voice that broke the silence was not the sweet, winsome one we were listening for, but it instantly arrested the attention of the company. It was the grave, manly voice of one used to speaking, and accustomed to be listened to with deference. This was the first time that the company as a whole had heard it, for the speaker was the new-comer who has been repeatedly alluded to, — the one of whom I spoke as " the Counsellor."

" I think I can tell you something about that, " said the Counsellor. " I suppose you will wonder how a man of my profession can know or interest himself about a question so remote from his arid pursuits. And yet there is hardly one man in a thousand who knows from actual experience a fraction of what I have learned of the lovers' vocabulary in my professional experience. I have, I am sorry to say, had to take an important part in a great number of divorce cases. These have brought before me scores and hundreds of letters, in which every shade of the great passion has been represented. What has most struck me in these amatory correspondences has been their remarkable sameness. It seems as if writing love-letters reduced all sorts of people to the same level. I don't remember whether Lord Bacon has left us anything in that line, — unless, indeed, he wrote ' Romeo and Juliet' and the ' Sonnets;' but if he has, I don't believe they differ so very much from those of his valet or his groom to their respective lady-loves. It is always, My darling! my darling! The words of endearment are the only ones the lover wants to employ, and he finds the vocabulary too limited for his vast desires. So his letters are apt to be rather tedious except to the personage to whom they are addressed. As to poetry, it is very common to find it in love-letters, especially in those that have no love in them. The letters of bigamists and polygamists are rich in poetical extracts. Occasionally, an original spurt in rhyme adds variety to an otherwise monotonous performance. I don't think there is much passion in men's poetry addressed to women. I agree with The Dictator that poetry is little more than the ashes of passion; still it may show that the flame has had its sweep where you find it, unless, indeed, it is shoveled in from another man's fireplace."

"What do you say to the love poetry of women?" asked the Professor. "Did ever passion heat words to incandescence as it did those of Sappho?"

The Counsellor turned, — not to Number Five, as he ought to have done, according to my programme, but to the Mistress.

"Madam," he said, "your sex is adorable in many ways, but in the *abandon* of a genuine love-letter it is incomparable. I have seen a string of women's love-letters, in which the creature enlaced herself about the object of her worship as that South American parasite which clasps the tree to which it has attached itself, begins with a slender succulent network, feeds on the trunk, spreads its fingers out to hold firmly to one branch after another, thickens, hardens, stretches in every direction, following the boughs, and at length gets strong enough to hold in its murderous arms, high up in air, the stump and shaft of the once sturdy growth that was its support and subsistence."

The Counsellor did not say all this quite so formally as I have set it down here, but in a much easier way. In fact, it is impossible to smooth out a conversation from memory without stiffening it; you can't have a dress shirt look quite right without starching the bosom.

Some of us would have liked to hear more about those letters in the divorce cases, but the Counsellor had to leave the table. He promised to show us some pictures he has of the South American parasite. I have seen them, and I can assure you they are very curious.

The following verses were found in the urn, or sugar-bowl.

CACOETHES SCRIBENDI.

If all the trees in all the woods were men,
And each and every blade of grass a pen;
If every leaf on every shrub and tree
Turned to a sheet of foolscap; every sea
Were changed to ink, and all earth's living tribes
Had nothing else to do but act as scribes,
And for ten thousand ages, day and night,
The human race should write, and write, and write,
Till all the pens and paper were used up,
And the huge inkstand was an empty cup,
Still would the scribblers clustered round its brink
Call for more pens, more paper, and more ink.

V.

"*Dolce, ma non troppo dolce,*" said the Professor to the Mistress, who was sweetening his tea. She always sweetens his and mine for us. He has been attending a series of concerts, and borrowed the form of the directions to the orchestra. "Sweet, but not too sweet," he said, translating the Italian for the benefit of any of the company who might not be linguists or musical experts.

"Do you go to those musical hullabaloos?" called out Number Seven. There was something very much like rudeness in this question and the tone in which it was asked. But we are used to the outbursts, and extravagances, and oddities of Number Seven, and do not take offence at his rough speeches as we should if any other of the company uttered them.

"If you mean the concerts that have been going on this season, yes, I do," said the Professor, in a bland, good-humored way.

"And do you take real pleasure in the din of all those screeching and banging and growling instruments?"

"Yes," he answered, modestly, "I enjoy the *brouhaha*, if you choose to consider it such, of all this quarrelsome menagerie of noise-making machines, brought into order and harmony by the presiding genius, the leader, who has made a happy family of these snarling stringed instruments and whining wind instruments, so that although

Linguæ centum sunt, oraque centum,

notwithstanding there are a hundred vibrating tongues and a hundred bellowing mouths, their one grand blended and harmonized uproar sets all my fibres tingling with a not unpleasing tremor."

"Do you understand it? Do you take any idea from it? Do you know what it all means?" said Number Seven.

The Professor was long-suffering under this series of somewhat peremptory questions. He replied very placidly, "I am afraid I have but a superficial outside acquaintance with the secrets, the unfathomable mysteries, of music. I can no more conceive of the working conditions of the great composer,

'Untwisting all the chains that tie
The hidden soul of harmony,'

than a child of three years can follow the reasonings of Newton's 'Principia.' I do not even pretend that I can appreciate the work of a great master as a born and trained musician does. Still, I do love a great crash of harmonies, and the oftener I listen to these musical tempests the higher my soul seems to ride upon them, as the wild fowl I see through my window soar more freely and fearlessly the fiercer the storm with which they battle."

"That's all very well," said Number Seven, "but I wish we could get the old-time music back again. You ought to have heard, — no, I won't mention her, — dead, poor girl, — dead and singing with the saints in heaven, — but the S—— girls. If you could have heard them as I did when I was a boy, you would have cried, as we all used to. Do you cry at those great musical smashes? How *can* you cry when you don't know what it is all about? We used to think

the words meant something, — we fancied that Burns
and Moore said some things very prettily. I suppose
you 've outgrown all that."

No one can handle Number Seven in one of his
tantrums half so well as Number Five can do it. She
can pick out what threads of sense may be wound off
from the tangle of his ideas when they are crowded
and confused, as they are apt to be at times. She
can soften the occasional expression of half-concealed
ridicule with which the poor old fellow's sallies are
liable to be welcomed — or unwelcomed. She knows
that the edge of a broken teacup may be sharper,
very possibly, than that of a philosopher's jackknife.
A mind a little off its balance, one which has a slightly
squinting brain as its organ, will often prove fertile
in suggestions. Vulgar, cynical, contemptuous listeners fly at all its weaknesses, and please themselves
with making light of its often futile ingenuities, when
a wiser audience would gladly accept a hint which
perhaps could be developed in some profitable direction, or so interpret an erratic thought that it should
prove good sense in disguise. That is the way Number Five was in the habit of dealing with the ex-
plosions of Number Seven. Do you think she did not
see the ridiculous element in a silly speech, or the
absurdity of an outrageously extravagant assertion?
Then you never heard her laugh when she could give
way to her sense of the ludicrous without wounding
the feelings of any other person. But her kind heart
never would forget itself, and so Number Seven had a
champion who was always ready to see that his flashes
of intelligence, fitful as they were, and liable to be
streaked with half-crazy fancies, always found one
willing recipient of what light there was in them.

Number Five, I have found, is a true lover of music, and has a right to claim a real knowledge of its higher and deeper mysteries. But she accepted very cordially what our light-headed companion said about the songs he used to listen to.

"There is no doubt," she remarked, "that the tears which used to be shed over 'Oft in the stilly night,' or 'Auld Robin Gray,' or 'A place in thy memory, dearest,' were honest tears, coming from the true sources of emotion. There was no affectation about them; those songs came home to the sensibilities of young people, — of all who had any sensibilities to be acted upon. And on the other hand, there is a great amount of affectation in the apparent enthusiasm of many persons in admiring and applauding music of which they have not the least real appreciation. They do not know whether it is good or bad, the work of a first-rate or a fifth-rate composer; whether there are coherent elements in it, or whether it is nothing more than 'a concourse of sweet sounds' with no organic connections. One must be educated, no doubt, to understand the more complex and difficult kinds of musical composition. Go to the great concerts where you know that the music is good, and that you ought to like it whether you do or not. Take a music-bath once or twice a week for a few seasons, and you will find that it is to the soul what the water-bath is to the body. I would n't trouble myself about the affectations of people who go to this or that series of concerts chiefly because it is fashionable. Some of these people whom we think so silly and hold so cheap will perhaps find, sooner or later, that they have a dormant faculty which is at last waking up, and that they who came because others came, and began by staring at the audience, are listening with a newly found delight. Every one of us has a harp under bodice or waistcoat, and if it can only once get properly strung and tuned it will respond to all outside harmonies."

The Professor has some ideas about music, which I believe he has given to the world in one form or another ; but the world is growing old and forgetful, and needs to be reminded now and then of what one has formerly told it.

"I have had glimpses," the Professor said, "of the conditions into which music is capable of bringing a sensitive nature. Glimpses, I say, because I cannot pretend that I am capable of sounding all the depths or reaching all the heights to which music may transport our mortal consciousness. Let me remind you of a curious fact with reference to the seat of the musical sense. Far down below the great masses of thinking marrow and its secondary agents, just as the brain is about to merge in the spinal cord, the roots of the nerve of hearing spread their white filaments out into the sentient matter, where they report what the external organs of hearing tell them. This sentient matter is in remote connection only with the mental organs, far more remote than the centres of the sense of vision and that of smell. In a word, the musical faculty might be said to have a little brain of its own. It has a special world and a private language all to itself. How can one explain its significance to those whose musical faculties are in a rudimentary state of development, or who have never had them trained? Can you describe in intelligible language the smell of a rose as compared with that of a violet? No, — music can be translated only by music. Just so far as it suggests worded thought, it falls short of its highest office. Pure emotional movements of the spiritual nature, — that is what I ask of music. Music will be the universal language, — the *Volapük* of spiritual being."

"Angels sit down with their harps and play at each other, I suppose," said Number Seven. "Must have an atmosphere up there if they have harps, or they would n't get any music. Wonder if angels breathe like mortals? If they do, they must have lungs and air passages, of course. Think of an angel with the influenza, and nothing but a cloud for a handkerchief!"

— This is a good instance of the way in which Number Seven's squinting brain works. You will now and then meet just such brains in heads you know very well. Their owners are much given to asking unanswerable questions. A physicist may settle it for us whether there is an atmosphere about a planet or not, but it takes a brain with an extra fissure in it to ask these unexpected questions, — questions which the natural philosopher cannot answer, and which the theologian never thinks of asking.

The company at our table do not keep always in the same places. The first thing I noticed, the other evening, was that the Tutor was sitting between the two Annexes, and the Counsellor was next to Number Five. Something ought to come of this arrangement. One of those two young ladies must certainly captivate and perhaps capture the Tutor. They are just the age to be falling in love and to be fallen in love with. The Tutor is good looking, intellectual, suspected of writing poetry, but a little shy, it appears to me. I am glad to see him between the two girls. If there

were only one, she might be shy too, and then there
would be less chance for a romance such as I am on
the lookout for; but these young persons lend courage
to each other, and between them, if he does not wake
up like Cymon at the sight of Iphigenia, I shall be
disappointed.   As for the Counsellor and Number
Five, they will soon find each other out.   Yes, it is all
pretty clear in my mind, — except that there is always
an x in a problem where sentiments are involved. No,
not so clear about the Tutor.   Predestined, I venture
my guess, to one or the other, but to *which?*   I will
suspend my opinion for the present.

I have found out that the Counsellor is a childless
widower.   I am told that the Tutor is unmarried, and
so far as known not engaged.   There is no use in
denying it, — a company without the possibility of a
love-match between two of its circle is like a champagne bottle with the cork out for some hours as compared to one with its pop yet in reserve.   However, if
there should be any love-making, it need not break up
our conversations.   Most of it will be carried on away
from our tea-table.

Some of us have been attending certain lectures on
Egypt and its antiquities.   I have never been on the
Nile.   If in any future state there shall be vacations
in which we may have liberty to revisit our old home,
equipped with a complete brand-new set of mortal
senses as our travelling outfit, I think one of the first
places I should go to, after my birthplace, the old gam-
brel-roofed house, — the place where it stood, rather,
— would be that mighty, awe-inspiring river.   I do
not suppose we shall ever know half of what we owe
to the wise and wonderful people who confront us with

the overpowering monuments of a past which flows
out of the unfathomable darkness as the great river
streams from sources even as yet but imperfectly ex-
plored.

I have thought a good deal about Egypt, lately, with
reference to our historical monuments. How did the
great unknown masters who fixed the two leading
forms of their monumental records arrive at those
admirable and eternal types, the pyramid and the obelisk? How did they get their model of the pyramid?

Here is an hour-glass, not inappropriately filled
with sand from the great Egyptian desert. I turn it,
and watch the sand as it accumulates in the lower half
of the glass. How symmetrically, how beautifully,
how inevitably, the little particles pile up the cone,
which is ever building and unbuilding itself, always
aiming at the stability which is found only at a certain
fixed angle! The Egyptian children playing in the
sand must have noticed this as they let the grains fall
from their hands, and the sloping sides of the minia-
ture pyramid must have been among the familiar
sights to the little boys and girls for whom the sand
furnished their earliest playthings. Nature taught
her children through the working of the laws of grav-
itation how to build so that her forces should act in
harmony with art, to preserve the integrity of a structure meant to reach a far-off posterity. The pyramid
is only the cone in which Nature arranges her heaped
and sliding fragments ; the cone with flattened surfaces, as it is prefigured in certain well-known crystal-
line forms. The obelisk is from another of Nature's
patterns ; it is only a gigantic acicular crystal.

The Egyptians knew what a monument should be,
simple, noble, durable. It seems to me that we

Americans might take a lesson from those early archi-
tects. Our cemeteries are crowded with monuments
which are very far from simple, anything but noble,
and stand a small chance of being permanent. The
pyramid is rarely seen, perhaps because it takes up so
much room, and when built on a small scale seems
insignificant as we think of it, dwarfed by the vast
structures of antiquity. The obelisk is very common,
and when in just proportions and of respectable dimensions is unobjectionable.

But the gigantic obelisks like that on Bunker Hill,
and especially the Washington monument at the national capital, are open to critical animadversion. Let
us contrast the last mentioned of these great piles
with the obelisk as the Egyptian conceived and exe-
cuted it. The new Pharaoh ordered a memorial of
some important personage or event. In the first
place, a mighty stone was dislodged from its connections, and lifted, unbroken, from the quarry. This
was a feat from which our modern stone-workers
shrink dismayed. The Egyptians appear to have
handled these huge monoliths as our artisans handle
hearthstones and doorsteps, for the land actually bris-
tled with such giant columns. They were shaped and
finished as nicely as if they were breastpins for the
Titans to wear, and on their polished surfaces were
engraved in imperishable characters the records they
were erected to preserve.

Europe and America borrow these noble productions of African art and power, and find them hard
enough to handle after they have succeeded in trans-
porting them to Rome, or London, or New York.
Their simplicity, grandeur, imperishability, speaking
symbolism, shame all the pretentious and fragile

works of human art around them. The obelisk has
no joints for the destructive agencies of nature to
attack; the pyramid has no masses hanging in unsta-
ble equilibrium, and threatening to fall by their own
weight in the course of a thousand or two years.

America says the Father of his Country must have
a monument worthy of his exalted place in history.
What shall it be? A temple such as Athens might
have been proud to rear upon her Acropolis? An
obelisk such as Thebes might have pointed out with
pride to the strangers who found admission through
her hundred gates? After long meditation and the
rejection of the hybrid monstrosities with which the
nation was menaced, an obelisk is at last decided
upon. How can it be made grand and dignified
enough to be equal to the office assigned it? We
dare not attempt to carve a single stone from the living rock, — all our modern appliances fail to make
the task as easy to us as it seems to have been to the
early Egyptians. No artistic skill is required in giving a four-square tapering figure to a stone column.
If we cannot shape a solid obelisk of the proper dimensions, we can build one of separate blocks. How
can we give it the distinction we demand for it? The
nation which can brag that it has "the biggest show
on earth" cannot boast a great deal in the way of
architecture, but it can do one thing, — it can build
an obelisk that shall be taller than any structure now
standing which the hand of man has raised. *Build
an obelisk!* How different the idea of such a structure from that of the unbroken, unjointed prismatic
shaft, one perfect whole, as complete in itself, as fitly
shaped and consolidated to defy the elements, as the
towering palm or the tapering pine! Well, we had

the satisfaction for a time of claiming the tallest
structure in the world; and now that the new Tower
of Babel which has sprung up in Paris has killed that
pretention, I think we shall feel and speak more
modestly about our stone hyperbole, our materializa-
tion of the American love of the superlative. We
have the higher civilization among us, and we must try
to keep down the forthputting instincts of the lower.
We do not want to see our national monument pla-
carded as "the greatest show on earth," — perhaps it
is well that it is taken down from that bad eminence.

I do not think that this speech of mine was very well
received. It appeared to jar somewhat on the nerves
of the American Annex. There was a smile on the lips
of the other Annex, — the English girl, — which she
tried to keep quiet, but it was too plain that she enjoyed my diatribe.

It must be remembered that I and the other Teacups, in common with the rest of our fellow-citizens,
have had our sensibilities greatly worked upon, our
patriotism chilled, our local pride outraged, by the
monstrosities which have been allowed to deform our
beautiful public grounds. We have to be very careful in conducting a visitor, say from his marble-fronted
hotel to the City Hall. — Keep pretty straight along
after entering the Garden, — you will not care to in-
spect the little figure of the military gentleman to your
right. — Yes, the Cochituate water is drinkable, but I
think I would not turn aside to visit that small fabric
which makes believe it is a temple, and is a weak-eyed
fountain feebly weeping over its own insignificance.
About that other stone misfortune, cruelly reminding
us of the "Boston Massacre," we will not discourse;
it is not imposing, and is rarely spoken of.

What a mortification to the inhabitants of a city
with some hereditary and contemporary claims to cul-
tivation; which has noble edifices, grand libraries,
educational institutions of the highest grade, an art-
gallery filled with the finest models and rich in paintings and statuary, — a stately city that stretches
both arms across the Charles to clasp the hands of
Harvard, her twin-sister, each lending lustre to the
other like double stars, — what a pity that she should
be so disfigured by crude attempts to adorn her and
commemorate her past that her most loving children
blush for her artificial deformities amidst the wealth
of her natural beauties !   One hardly knows which to
groan over most sadly, — the tearing down of old
monuments, the shelling of the Parthenon, the over-
throw of the pillared temples of Rome, and in a humbler way the destruction of the old Hancock house, or
the erection of monuments which are to be a perpetual
eyesore to ourselves and our descendants.

We got talking on the subject of *realism*, of which
so much has been said of late.

It seems to me, I said, that the great additions which
have been made by realism to the territory of literature consist largely in swampy, malarious, ill-smelling
patches of soil which had previously been left to reptiles and vermin.   It is perfectly easy to be original
by violating the laws of decency and the canons of
good taste.   The general consent of civilized people
was supposed to have banished certain subjects from
the conversation of well-bred people and the pages of
respectable literature.   There is no subject, or hardly
any, which may not be treated of at the proper time,
in the proper place, by the fitting person, for the right

kind of listener or reader. But when the poet or the story-teller invades the province of the man of science, he is on dangerous ground. I need say nothing of the blunders he is pretty sure to make. The imaginative writer is after effects. The scientific man is after truth. Science is decent, modest; does not try to startle, but to instruct. The same scenes and objects which outrage every sense of delicacy in the story-teller's highly colored paragraphs can be read without giving offence in the chaste language of the physiologist or the physician. .

There is a very celebrated novel, "Madame Bovary," the work of M. Flaubert, which is noted for having been the subject of prosecution as an immoral work. That it has a serious lesson there is no doubt, if one will drink down to the bottom of the cup. But the honey of sensuous description is spread so deeply over the surface of the goblet that a large proportion of its readers never think of its holding anything else. All the phases of unhallowed passion are described in full detail. That is what the book is bought and read for, by the great majority of its purchasers, as all but simpletons very well know. That is what makes it sell and brought it into the courts of justice. This book is famous for its realism; in fact, it is recognized as one of the earliest and most brilliant examples of that modern style of novel which, beginning where Balzac left off, attempted to do for literature what the photograph has done for art. For those who take the trouble to drink out of the cup below the rim of honey, there is a scene where realism is carried to its extreme, — surpassed in horror by no writer, unless it be the one whose name must be looked for at the bottom of the alphabet, as if its natural place were as low down in the dregs of realism as it could find itself. This is the death-bed scene, where Madame Bovary expires in convulsions. The author must have visited the hospitals for the purpose of watching the terrible agonies he was to depict, tramping from one bed to another until he reached the one where the cries and contortions were the most frightful. Such a scene he has reproduced. No hospital physician would have pictured the struggle in such colors. In the same way, that other realist, M. Zola, has painted a patient suffering from delirium tremens, the disease known to common speech as " the horrors." In describing this case he does all that language can do to make it more horrible than the reality. He gives us, not realism, but super-realism, if such a term does not contradict itself.

In this matter of the literal reproduction of sights and scenes which our natural instinct and our better informed taste and judgment teach us to avoid, art has been far in advance of literature. It is three hundred years since Joseph Ribera, more commonly known as Spagnoletto, was born in the province Valencia, in Spain. We had the misfortune of seeing a painting of his in a collection belonging to one of the French princes, and exhibited at the Art Museum. It was that of a man performing upon himself the operation known to the Japanese as hara-kiri. Many persons who looked upon this revolting picture will never get rid of its remembrance, and will regret the day when their eyes fell upon it. I should share the offence of the painter if I ventured to describe it. Ribera was fond of depicting just such odious and frightful subjects. " Saint Lawrence writhing on his gridiron, Saint Sebastian full of arrows, were equally a source

of delight to him. Even in subjects which had no
such elements of horror he finds the materials for the
delectation of his ferocious pencil ; he makes up for
the defect by rendering with a brutal realism deform-
ity and ugliness."

The first great mistake made by the ultra-realists,
like Flaubert and Zola, is, as I have said, their ignor-
ing the line of distinction between imaginative art
and science. We can find realism enough in books
of anatomy, surgery, and medicine. In studying the
human figure, we want to see it clothed with its natural integuments. It is well for the artist to study the
écorché in the dissecting-room, but we do not want the
Apollo or the Venus to leave their skins behind them
when they go into the gallery for exhibition. Lan-
cisi's figures show us how the great statues look when
divested of their natural covering. It is instructive,
but useful chiefly as a means to aid in the true artistic
reproduction of nature. When the hospitals are in-
vaded by the novelist, he should learn something from
the physician as well as from the patients. Science
delineates in monochrome. She never uses high tints
and strontian lights to astonish lookers-on. Such
scenes as Flaubert and Zola describe would be reproduced in their essential characters, but not dressed up
in picturesque phrases. That is the first stumbling-
block in the way of the reader of such realistic stories
as those to which I have referred. There are subjects
which must be investigated by scientific men which
most educated persons would be glad to know nothing
about. When a realistic writer like Zola surprises
his reader into a kind of knowledge he never thought
of wishing for, he sometimes harms him more than he
has any idea of doing. He wants to produce a sensa-

tion, and he leaves a permanent disgust not to be got rid of. Who does not remember odious images that can never be washed out from the consciousness which they have stained? A man's vocabulary is terribly retentive of evil words, and the images they present cling to his memory and will not loose their hold. One who has had the mischance to soil his mind by reading certain poems of Swift will never cleanse it to its original whiteness. Expressions and thoughts of a certain character stain the fibre of the thinking organ, and in some degree affect the hue of every idea that passes through the discolored tissues.

This is the gravest accusation to bring against realism, old or recent, whether in the brutal paintings of Spagnoletto or in the unclean revelations of Zola. Leave the description of the drains and cesspools to the hygienic specialist, the painful facts of disease to the physician, the details of the laundry to the washer-woman. If we are to have realism in its tedious descriptions of unimportant particulars, let it be of particulars which do not excite disgust. Such is the description of the vegetables in Zola's " Ventre de Paris," where, if one wishes to see the apotheosis of turnips, beets, and cabbages, he can find them glorified as supremely as if they had been symbols of so many deities; their forms, their colors, their expression, worked upon until they seem as if they were made to be looked at and worshipped rather than to be boiled and eaten.

I am pleased to find a French critic of M. Flaubert expressing ideas with which many of my own entirely coincide. " The great mistake of the realists, " he says, " is that they profess to tell the truth because they tell everything. This puerile hunting after details, this cold and cynical inventory of all the wretched conditions in the midst of which poor humanity vegetates, not only do not help us to understand it better, but, on the contrary, the effect on the spectators is a kind of dazzled confusion mingled with fatigue and disgust. The material truthfulness to which the school of M. Flaubert more especially pretends misses its aim in going beyond it. Truth is lost in its own excess."

I return to my thoughts on the relations of imaginative art in all its forms with science. The subject which in the hands of the scientific student is handled decorously, — reverently, we might almost say, — becomes repulsive, shameful, and debasing in the unscrupulous manipulations of the low-bred man of letters.

I confess that I am a little jealous of certain tendencies in our own American literature, which led one of the severest and most outspoken of our satirical fellow-countrymen, no longer living to be called to account for it, to say, in a moment of bitterness, that the mission of America was to vulgarize mankind. I myself have sometimes wondered at the pleasure some Old World critics have professed to find in the most lawless freaks of New World literature. I have questioned whether their delight was not like that of the Spartans in the drunken antics of their Helots. But I suppose I belong to another age, and must not attempt to judge the present by my old-fashioned standards.

The company listened very civilly to these remarks, whether they agreed with them or not. I am not sure that I want all the young people to think just as I do in matters of critical judgment. New wine does not go well into old bottles, but if an old cask has held good wine, it may improve a crude juice to stand awhile upon the lees of that which once filled it.

I thought the company had had about enough of this disquisition. They listened very decorously, and the Professor, who agrees very well with me, as I happen to know, in my views on this business of realism, thanked me for giving them the benefit of my opinion.

The silence that followed was broken by Number Seven's suddenly exclaiming, —

"I should like to boss creation for a week!"

This expression was an outbreak suggested by some train of thought which Number Seven had been following while I was discoursing. I do not think one of the company looked as if he or she were shocked by it as an irreligious or even profane speech. It is a better way always, in dealing with one of those squinting brains, to let it follow out its own thought. It will keep to it for a while; then it will quit the rail, so to speak, and run to any side-track which may present itself.

"What is the first thing you would do?" asked Number Five in a pleasant, easy way.

"The first thing? Pick out a few thousand of the best specimens of the best races, and drown the rest like so many blind puppies."

"Why," said she, "that was tried once, and does not seem to have worked very well."

"Very likely. You mean Noah's flood, I suppose. More people nowadays, and a better lot to pick from than Noah had."

"Do tell us whom you would take with you," said Number Five.

"You, if you would go," he answered, and I thought I saw a slight flush on his cheek. "But I did n't say that I should go aboard the new ark myself. I am not sure that I should. No, I am pretty sure that I should n't. I don't believe, on the whole, it would pay me to save myself. I ain't of much account: But I could pick out some that were."

And just now he was saying that he should like to boss the universe! All this has nothing very wonderful about it. Every one of us is subject to alternations of overvaluation and undervaluation of ourselves. Do you not remember soliloquies something like this? "Was there ever such a senseless, stupid creature as I am? How have I managed to keep so long out of the idiot asylum? Undertook to write a poem, and stuck fast at the first verse. Had a call from a friend who had just been round the world. Did n't ask him one word about what he had seen or heard, but gave him full details of my private history, I having never been off my own hearth-rug for more than an hour or two at a time, while he was circumnavigating and circumrailroading the globe. Yes, if anybody can claim the title, I am certainly the prize idiot." I am afraid that we all say such things as this to ourselves at times. Do we not use more emphatic words than these in our self-depreciation? I cannot say how it is with others, but my vocabulary of self-reproach and humiliation is so rich in energetic expressions that I should be sorry to have an interviewer present at an outburst of one of its raging geysers, its savage soliloquies. A man is a kind of inverted thermometer, the bulb uppermost, and the column of self-valuation is all the time going up and down. Number Seven is very much like other people in this respect, — very much like you and me.

This train of reflections must not carry me away from Number Seven.

"If I can't get a chance to boss this planet for a week or so," he began again, "I think I could write its history, — yes, the history of the world, in less compass than any one who has tried it so far."

"You know Sir Walter Raleigh's 'History of the World,' of course?" said the Professor.

"More or less, — more or less," said Number Seven prudently. "But I don't care who has written it before me. I will agree to write the story of *two* worlds, this and the next, in such a compact way that you can commit them both to memory in less time than you can learn the answer to the first question in the Catechism."

What he had got into his head we could not guess, but there was no little curiosity to discover the particular bee which was buzzing in his bonnet. He evidently enjoyed our curiosity, and meant to keep us waiting awhile before revealing the great secret.

"How many words do you think I shall want?"

It is a formula, I suppose, I said, and I will grant you a hundred words.

"Twenty," said the Professor. "That was more than the wise men of Greece wanted for their grand utterances."

The two Annexes whispered together, and the American Annex gave their joint result. One thousand was the number they had fixed on. They were used to hearing lectures, and could hardly conceive that any subject could be treated without taking up a good part of an hour.

"Less than ten," said Number Five. "If there are to be more than ten, I don't believe that Number

Seven would think the surprise would be up to our expectations."

"Guess as much as you like," said Number Seven. "The answer will keep. I don't mean to say what it is until we are ready to leave the table." He took a blank card from his pocket-book, wrote something on it, or appeared, at any rate, to write, and handed it, face down, to the Mistress. What was on the card will be found near the end of this paper. I wonder if anybody will be curious enough to look further along to find out what it was before she reads the next paragraph?

In the mean time there is a train of thought suggested by Number Seven and his whims. If you want to know how to account for yourself, study the characters of your relations. *All* of our brains squint more or less. There is not one in a hundred, certainly, that does not sometimes see things distorted by double refraction, out of plumb or out of focus, or with colors which do not belong to it, or in some way betraying that the two halves of the brain are not acting in harmony with each other. You wonder at the eccentricities of this or that connection of your own. Watch yourself, and you will find impulses which, but for the restraints you put upon them, would make you do the same foolish things which you laugh at in that cousin of yours. I once lived in the same house with the near relative of a very distinguished person, whose name is still honored and revered among us. His brain was an active one, like that of his famous relative, but it was full of random ideas, unconnected trains of thought, whims, crotchets, erratic suggestions. Knowing him, I could interpret the mental characteristics of the whole family connection in the light of its exaggerated peculiarities as exhibited in my odd fellow-boarder. Squinting brains are a great deal more common than we should at first sight believe. Here is a great book, a solid octavo of five hundred pages, full of the vagaries of this class of organizations. I hope to refer to this work hereafter, but just now I will only say that, after reading till one is tired the strange fancies of the squarers of the circle, the inventors of perpetual motion, and the rest of the moonstruck dreamers, most persons will confess to themselves that they have had notions as wild, conceptions as extravagant, theories as baseless, as the least rational of those which are here recorded.

Some day I want to talk about my library. It is such a curious collection of old and new books, such a mosaic of learning and fancies and follies, that a glance over it would interest the company. Perhaps I may hereafter give you a talk about books, but while I am saying a few passing words upon the subject the greatest bibliographical event that ever happened in the book-market of the New World is taking place under our eyes. Here is Mr. Bernard Quaritch just come from his well-known habitat, No. 15 Piccadilly, with such a collection of rare, beautiful, and somewhat expensive volumes as the Western Continent never saw before on the shelves of a bibliopole.

We bookworms are all of us now and then betrayed into an extravagance. The keen tradesmen who tempt us are like the fishermen who dangle a minnow, a frog, or a worm before the perch or pickerel who may be on the lookout for his breakfast. But Mr. Quaritch

comes among us like that formidable angler of whom
it is said, —

> His hook he baited with a dragon's tail,
> And sat upon a rock and bobbed for whale.

The two catalogues which herald his coming are themselves interesting literary documents.   One can go
out with a few shillings in his pocket, and venture
among the books of the first of these catalogues without being ashamed to show himself with no larger
furnishing of the means for indulging his tastes, — he
will find books enough at comparatively modest prices.
But if one feels *very* rich, so rich that it requires a
good deal to frighten him, let him take the other catalogue and see how many books he proposes to add to
his library at the prices affixed.   Here is a Latin
Psalter with the Canticles, from the press of Fust and
Schoeffer, the second book issued from their press, the
second book printed with a date, that date being
1459.   There are only eight copies of this work
known to exist; you can have one of them, if so disposed, and if you have change enough in your pocket.
Twenty-six thousand two hundred and fifty dollars
will make you the happy owner of this precious volume.   If this is more than you want to pay, you can
have the Gold Gospels of Henry VIII., on purple
vellum, for about half the money.   There are pages
on pages of titles of works any one of which would
be a snug little property if turned into money at its
catalogue price.

Why will not our multimillionaires look over this
catalogue of Mr. Quaritch, and detain some of its
treasures on this side of the Atlantic for some of
our public libraries?   We decant the choicest wines
of Europe into our cellars; we ought to be always

decanting the precious treasures of her libraries and galleries into our own, as we have opportunity and means. As to the means, there are so many rich people who hardly know what to do with their money that it is well to suggest to them any new useful end to which their superfluity may contribute. I am not in alliance with Mr. Quaritch; in fact, I am afraid of him, for if I stayed a single hour in his library, where I never was but once, and then for fifteen minutes only, I should leave it so much poorer than I entered it that I should be reminded of the picture in the title-page of Fuller's "Historie of the Holy Warre:" "We went out full. We returned empty."

— After the teacups were all emptied, the card containing Number Seven's abridged history of two worlds, this and the next, was handed round.

This was all it held : —

$$! \over ?$$

After all had looked at it, it was passed back to me. "Let The Dictator interpret it," they all said.

This is what I announced as my interpretation : —

Two worlds, the higher and the lower, separated by the thinnest of partitions. The lower world is that of questions; the upper world is that of answers. Endless doubt and unrest here below; wondering, admiring, adoring certainty above. — Am I not right?

"You are right," answered Number Seven solemnly. "That is my revelation."

The following poem was found in the sugar-bowl. I read it to the company.

There was much whispering and there were many
conjectures as to its authorship, but every Teacup
looked innocent, and we separated each with his or
her private conviction. I had mine, but I will not
mention it.

THE ROSE AND THE FERN.

Lady, life's sweetest lesson wouldst thou learn,
  Come thou with me to Love's enchanted bower:
High overhead the trellised roses burn ;
Beneath thy feet behold the feathery fern, —
    A leaf without a flower.

What though the rose leaves fall ?   They still are sweet,
  And have been lovely in their beauteous prime,
While the bare frond seems ever to repeat,
"For us no bud, no blossom, wakes to greet
    The joyous flowering time ! "

Heed thou the lesson.   Life has leaves to tread
  And flowers to cherish ; summer round thee glows ;
Wait not till autumn's fading robes are shed,
But while its petals still are burning red
    Gather life's full-blown rose !

VI

OF course the reading of the poem at the end of the last paper has left a deep impression. I strongly suspect that something very much like love-making is going on at our table. A peep under the lid of the sugar-bowl has shown me that there is another poem ready for the company. That receptacle is looked upon with an almost tremulous excitement by more than one of The Teacups. The two Annexes turn towards the mystic urn as if the lots which were to determine their destiny were shut up in it. Number Five, quieter, and not betraying more curiosity than belongs to the sex at all ages, glances at the sugar-bowl now and then; looking so like a clairvoyant that sometimes I cannot help thinking she must be one. There is a sly look about that young Doctor's eyes, which might imply that he knows something about what the silver vessel holds, or is going to hold. The Tutor naturally falls under suspicion, as he is known to have written and published poems. I suppose the Professor and myself have hardly been suspected of writing love-poems; but there is no telling, — there is no telling. Why may not some one of the lady Teacups have played the part of a masculine lover? George Sand, George Eliot, Charles Egbert Craddock, made pretty good men in print. The authoress of "Jane Eyre" was taken for a man by many persons. Can Number Five be masquerading in verse? Or is one of the two Annexes the make-believe lover? Or did these girls lay their heads together, and send the poem we had at our last sitting to puzzle the company? It is certain that the Mistress did not write the poem. It is evident that Number Seven, who is so severe in his talk about rhymesters, would not, if he could, make such a fool of himself as to set up for a "poet." Why should not the Counsellor fall in love and write verses? A good many lawyers have been " poets."

Perhaps the next poem, which may be looked for in its proper place, may help us to form a judgment. We may have several verse-writers among us, and if so there will be a good opportunity for the exercise of judgment in distributing their productions among the legitimate claimants. In the mean time, we must not let the love-making and the song-writing interfere with the more serious matters which these papers are expected to contain.

Number Seven's compendious and comprehensive symbolism proved suggestive, as his whimsical notions often do. It always pleases me to take some hint from anything he says when I can, and carry it out in a direction not unlike that of his own remark. I reminded the company of his enigmatical symbol.

You can divide mankind in the same way, I said. Two words, each of two letters, will serve to distinguish two classes of human beings who constitute the principal divisions of mankind. Can any of you tell what those two words are?

" Give me five letters," cried Number Seven, "and I can solve your problem! F-o-o-l-s, — those five letters will give you the first and largest half. For the other fraction "—

Oh, but, said I, I restrict you absolutely to *two* letters. If you are going to take five, you may as well take twenty or a hundred.

After a few attempts, the company gave it up. The nearest approach to the correct answer was Number Five's guess of *Oh* and *Ah: Oh* signifying eternal striving after an ideal, which belongs to one kind of nature; and *Ah* the satisfaction of the other kind of nature, which rests at ease in what it has attained.

Good! I said to Number Five, but not the answer I am after. The great division between human beings is into the *Ifs* and the *Ases.*

"Is the last word to be spelt with one or two s's?" asked the young Doctor.

The company laughed feebly at this question. I answered it soberly. With one *s.* There are more foolish people among the *Ifs* than there are among the *Ases.*

The company looked puzzled, and asked for an explanation.

This is the meaning of those two words as I interpret them: —

If it were, — *if* it might be, — *if* it could be, — *if* it had been. One portion of mankind go through life always regretting, always whining, always imagining. These are the people whose backbones remain cartilaginous all their lives long, as do those of certain other vertebrate animals, — the sturgeons, for instance. A good many poets must be classed with this group of vertebrates.

As it is, — this is the way in which the other class of people look at the conditions in which they find themselves. They may be optimists or pessimists, — they are very largely optimists, — but, taking things just as they find them, they adjust the facts to their wishes if they can ; and if they cannot, then they adjust themselves to the facts. I venture to say that if one should count the *Ifs* and the *Ases* in the conversation of his acquaintances, he would find the more able and important persons among them — statesmen, generals, men of business — among the *Ases*, and the majority of the conspicuous failures among the *Ifs*. I don't know but this would be as good a test as that of Gideon, — lapping the water or taking it up in the hand. I have a poetical friend whose conversation is starred as thick with *ifs* as a boiled ham is with cloves. But another friend of mine, a business man, whom I trust in making my investments, would not let me meddle with a certain stock which I fancied, because, as he said, " there are too many *ifs* in it. *As* it looks now, I would n't touch it."

I noticed, the other evening, that some private conversation was going on between the Counsellor and the two Annexes. There was a mischievous look about the little group, and I thought they were hatching some plot among them. I did not hear what the English Annex said, but the American girl's voice was sharper, and I overheard what sounded to me like, " It is time to stir up that young Doctor." The Counsellor looked very knowing, and said that he would find a chance before long. I was rather amused to see how readily he entered into the project of the young people. The fact is, the Counsellor is young for his time of life; for he already betrays some signs of the change referred to in that once familiar street song, which my friend, the great American surgeon, inquired for at the music-shops under the title, as he got it from the Italian minstrel,

"Silva tredi mondi goo."

I saw, soon after this, that the Counsellor was watching his chance to "stir up the young Doctor."

It does not follow, because our young Doctor's bald spot is slower in coming than he could have wished, that he has not had time to form many sound conclusions in the calling to which he has devoted himself. Vesalius, the father of modern descriptive anatomy, published his great work on that subject before he was thirty. Bichat, the great anatomist and physiologist, who died near the beginning of this century, published his treatise, which made a revolution in anatomy and pathology, at about the same age; dying soon after he had reached the age of thirty. So, possibly the Counsellor may find that he has "stirred up" a young man who can take care of his own head, in case of aggressive movements in its direction.

"Well, Doctor," the Counsellor began, "how are stocks in the measles market about these times? Any corner in bronchitis? Any syndicate in the vaccination business?" All this playfully.

"I can't say how it is with other people's patients; most of my families are doing very well without my help, at this time."

"Do tell me, Doctor, how many families you own. I have heard it said that some of our fellow-citizens have two distinct families, but you speak as if you had a dozen."

"I have, but not so large a number as I should like. I could take care of fifteen or twenty more without having to work too hard."

"Why, Doctor, you are as bad as a Mormon. What do you mean by calling certain families *yours?*"

"Don't you speak about *my* client? Don't your

clients call you *their* lawyer?   Does n't your baker, does n't your butcher, speak of the families he supplies as *his* families?"

"To be sure, yes, of course they do; but I had a notion that a man had as many doctors as he had organs to be doctored."

"Well, there is some truth in that; but did you think the old-fashioned family doctor was extinct, — a fossil like the megatherium?"

"Why, yes, after the recent experience of a friend of mine, I did begin to think that there would soon be no such personage left as that same old-fashioned family doctor.   Shall I tell you what that experience was?"

The young Doctor said he should be mightily pleased to hear it.   He was going to be one of those old-fogy practitioners himself.

"I don't know," the Counsellor said, "whether my friend got all the professional terms of his story correctly, nor whether I have got them from him without making any mistakes; but if I do make blunders in some of the queer names, you can correct me.   This is my friend's story: —

"'My family doctor,' he said, 'was a very sensible man, educated at a school where they professed to teach all the specialties, but not confining himself to any one branch of *medical* practice.   Surgical practice he did not profess to meddle with, and there were some classes of patients whom he was willing to leave to the female physician.   But throughout the range of diseases not requiring exceptionally skilled manual interference, his education had authorized him to consider himself, and he did consider himself, qualified to undertake the treatment of all ordinary cases.   It so

happened that my young wife was one of those uneasy
persons who are never long contented with their habitual comforts and blessings, but always trying to find
something a little better, something newer, at any rate.
I was getting to be near fifty years old, and it happened to me, as it not rarely does to people at about
that time of life, that my hair began to fall out. I
spoke of it to my doctor, who smiled, said it was a part
of the process of reversed evolution, but might be re-
tarded a little, and gave me a prescription. I did not
find any great effect from it, and my wife would have
me go to a noted dermatologist. The distinguished
specialist examined my denuded scalp with great care.
He looked at it through a strong magnifier. He examined the bulb of a fallen hair in a powerful microscope. He deliberated for a while, and then said,
" This is a case of *alopecia*. It may perhaps be partially remedied. I will give you a prescription."
Which he did, and told me to call again in a fortnight. At the end of three months I had called six
times, and each time got a new recipe, and detected
no difference in the course of my "alopecia." After
I had got through my treatment, I showed my recipes
to my family physician ; and we found that three of
them were the same he had used, familiar, old-fashioned remedies, and the others were taken from a list
of new and little-tried prescriptions mentioned in one
of the last medical journals, which was lying on the old
doctor's table. I might as well have got no better under his charge, and should have got off much cheaper.

" ' The next trouble I had was a little redness of the
eyes, for which my doctor gave me a wash ; but my
wife would have it that I must see an oculist. So I
made four visits to an oculist, and at the last visit the

redness was nearly gone, — as it ought to have been
by that time.   The specialist called my complaint *con-
junctivitis*, but that did not make it feel any better
nor get well any quicker.   If I had had a cataract or
any grave disease of the eye, requiring a nice operation on that delicate organ, of course I should have
properly sought the aid of an expert, whose eye, hand,
and judgment were trained to that special business ;
but in this case I don't doubt that my family doctor
would have done just as well as the expert.   However, I had to obey orders, and my wife would have it
that I should entrust my precious person only to the
most skilful specialist in each department of medical
practice.

    " ' In the course of the year I experienced a variety
of slight indispositions.   For these I was auriscoped
by an aurist, laryngoscoped by a laryngologist, aus-
culted by a stethoscopist, and so on, until a complete
inventory of my organs was made out, and I found
that if I believed all these searching inquirers professed to have detected in my unfortunate person, I
could repeat with too literal truth the words of the
General Confession, "And there is no health in us."
I never heard so many hard names in all my life.   I
proved to be the subject of a long catalogue of diseases, and what maladies I was not manifestly guilty
of I was at least ,suspected of harboring.   I was
handed along all the way from *alopecia*, which used
to be called baldness, to *zoster*, which used to be
known as shingles.   I was the patient of more than a
dozen specialists.   Very pleasant persons, many of
them, but what a fuss they made about my trifling
incommodities !   Please look at that photograph.   See
if there is a minute elevation under one eye.'

"'On which side?' I asked him, for I could not be sure there was anything different on one side from what I saw on the other.

"'Under the left eye. I called it a pimple; the specialist called it *acne*. Now look at this photograph. It was taken after my acne had been three months under treatment. It shows a little more distinctly than in the first photograph, does n't it?'

"'I think it does,' I answered. 'It does n't seem to me that you gained a great deal by leaving your customary adviser for the specialist.'

"'Well,' my friend continued, 'following my wife's urgent counsel, I kept on, as I told you, for a whole year with my specialists, going from head to foot, and tapering off with a chiropodist. I got a deal of amusement out of their contrivances and experiments. Some of them lighted up my internal surfaces with electrical or other illuminating apparatus. Thermometers, dynamometers, exploring-tubes, little mirrors that went half-way down to my stomach, tuning-forks, ophthalmoscopes, percussion-hammers, single and double stethoscopes, speculums, sphygmometers, — such a battery of detective instruments I had never imagined. All useful, I don't doubt; but at the end of the year I began to question whether I should n't have done about as well to stick to my long-tried practitioner. When the bills for "professional services" came in, and the new carpet had to be given up, and the old bonnet trimmed over again, and the sealskin sack remained a vision, we both agreed, my wife and I, that we would try to get along without consulting specialists, except in such cases as our family physician considered to be beyond his skill.'"

The Counsellor's story of his friend's experiences seemed to please the young Doctor very much. It "stirred him up," but in an agreeable way; for, as he said, he meant to devote himself to family practice, and not to adopt any limited class of cases as a specialty. I liked his views so well that I should have been ready to adopt them as my own, if they had been challenged.

The young Doctor discourses.

"I am very glad," he said, "that we have a number of practitioners among us who confine themselves to the care of single organs and their functions. I want to be able to consult an oculist who has done nothing but attend to eyes long enough to know all that is known about their diseases and their treatment, — skilful enough to be trusted with the manipulation of that delicate and most precious organ. I want an aurist who knows all about the ear and what can be done for its disorders. The maladies of the larynx are very ticklish things to handle, and nobody should be trusted to go behind the epiglottis who has not the *tactus eruditus*. And so of certain other particular classes of complaints. A great city must have a limited number of experts, each a final authority, to be appealed to in cases where the family physician finds himself in doubt. There are operations which no surgeon should be willing to undertake unless he has paid a particular, if not an exclusive, attention to the cases demanding such operations. All this I willingly grant.

"But it must not be supposed that we can return to the methods of the old Egyptians — who, if my memory serves me correctly, had a special physician for every part of the body — without falling into certain errors and incurring certain liabilities.

" The specialist is much like other people engaged in lucrative business. He is apt to magnify his calling, to make much of any symptom which will bring a patient within range of his battery of remedies. I found a case in one of our medical journals, a couple of years ago, which illustrates what I mean. Dr. ——, of Philadelphia, had a female patient with a crooked nose, — deviated *septum*, if our young scholars like that better. She was suffering from what the doctor called reflex headache. She had been to an oculist, who found that the trouble was in her eyes. She went from him to a gynecologist, who considered her headache as owing to causes for which his specialty had the remedies. How many more specialists would have appropriated her, if she had gone the rounds of them all, I dare not guess ; but you remember the old story of the siege, in which each artisan proposed means of defence which he himself was ready to furnish. Then a shoemaker said, ' Hang your walls with new boots.'

" Human nature is the same with medical specialists as it was with ancient cordwainers, and it is too possible that a hungry practitioner may be warped by his interest in fastening on a patient who, as he persuades himself, comes under his medical jurisdiction. The specialist has but one fang with which to seize and hold his prey, but that fang is a fearfully long and sharp canine. Being confined to a narrow field of observation and practice, he is apt to give much of his time to curious study, which may be *magnifique*, but is not exactly *la guerre* against the patient's malady. He divides and subdivides, and gets many varieties of diseases, in most respects similar. These he equips with new names, and thus we have those terrific nomenclatures which are enough to frighten the medical student, to say nothing of the sufferers staggering under this long catalogue of local infirmities. The 'old-fogy' doctor, who knows the family tendencies of his patient, who 'understands his constitution,' will often treat him better than the famous specialist, who sees him for the first time, and has to guess at many things 'the old doctor' knows from his previous experience with the same patient and the family to which he belongs.

"It is a great luxury to practise as a specialist in almost any class of diseases. The special practitioner has his own hours, hardly needs a night-bell, can have his residence out of the town in which he exercises his calling, — in short, lives like a gentleman ; while the hard-worked general practitioner submits to a servitude more exacting than that of the man who is employed in his stable or in his kitchen. That is the kind of life I have made up my mind to."

The teaspoons tinkled all round the table. This was the usual sign of approbation, instead of the clapping of hands.

The young Doctor paused, and looked round among The Teacups. "I beg your pardon," he said, "for taking up so much of your time with medicine. It is a subject that a good many persons, especially ladies, take an interest in and have a curiosity about, but I have no right to turn this tea-table into a lecture platform."

" We should like to hear you talk longer about it," said the English Annex. "One of us has thought of devoting herself to the practice of medicine. Would you lecture to us, if you were a professor in one of the great medical schools?"

"Lecture to students of your sex? Why not, I should like to know? I don't think it is the calling for which the average woman is especially adapted, but my teacher got a part of his medical education from a lady, Madame Lachapelle; and I don't see why, if one can learn from a woman, he may not teach a woman, if he knows enough."

"We all like a little medical talk now and then," said Number Five, "and we are much obliged to you for your discourse. You are specialist enough to take care of a sprained ankle, I suppose, are you not?"

"I hope I should be equal to that emergency," answered the young Doctor; "but I trust you are not suffering from any such accident?"

"No," said Number Five, "but there is no telling what may happen. I might slip, and get a sprain or break a sinew, or something, and I should like to know that there is a practitioner at hand to take care of my injury. I think I would risk myself in your hands, although you are not a specialist. Would you venture to take charge of the case?"

"Ah, my dear lady," he answered gallantly, "the risk would be in the other direction. I am afraid it would be safer for your doctor if he were an older man than I am."

This is the first clearly, indisputably sentimental outbreak which has happened in conversation at our table. I tremble to think what will come of it; for we have several inflammable elements in our circle, and a spark like this is liable to light on any one or two of them.

I was not sorry that this medical episode came in to vary the usual course of talk at our table. I like to have one of an intelligent company, who knows anything thoroughly, hold the floor for a time, and discourse upon the subject which chiefly engages his daily thoughts and furnishes his habitual occupation. It is a privilege to meet such a person now and then, and let him have his full swing. But because there are " professionals " to whom we are willing to listen as oracles, I do not want to see everybody who is not a " professional " silenced or snubbed, if he ventures into any field of knowledge which he has not made especially his own. I like to read Montaigne's remarks about doctors, though he never took a medical degree. I can even enjoy the truth in the sharp satire of Voltaire on the medical profession. I frequently prefer the remarks I hear from the pew after the sermon to those I have just been hearing from the pulpit. There are a great many things which I never expect to comprehend, but which I desire very much to apprehend. Suppose that our circle of Teacups were made up of specialists, — experts in various departments. I should be very willing that each one should have his innings at the proper time, when the company were ready for him. But the time is coming when everybody will know something about everything. How can one have the illustrated magazines, the "Popular Science Monthly," the psychological journals, the theological periodicals, books on all subjects, forced on his attention, in their own persons, so to speak, or in the reviews which analyze and pass judgment upon them, without getting some ideas which belong to many provinces of human intelligence? The air we breathe is made up of four elements, at

least : oxygen, nitrogen, carbonic acid gas, and know-)
ledge.   There is something quite delightful to witness
in the absorption and devotion of a genuine specialist.
There is a certain sublimity in that picture of the
dying scholar in Browning's " A Grammarian's Funeral : " —

> " So with the throttling hands of death at strife,
>   Ground he at grammar ;
>   Still, through the rattle, parts of speech were rife ;
>   While he could stammer
>   He settled *Hoti's* business — let it be —
>   Properly based *Oun* —
>   Gave us the doctrine of the enclitic *De*,
>   Dead from the waist down."

A genuine enthusiasm, which will never be satisfied
until it has pumped the well dry at the bottom of
which truth is lying, always excites our interest, if not
our admiration.

One of the pleasantest of our American writers,
whom we all remember as Ik Marvel, and greet in
his more recent appearance as Donald Grant Mitchell,
speaks of the awkwardness which he feels in offering
to the public a " panoramic view of British writers in
these days of specialists, — when students devote half
a lifetime to the analysis of the works of a single
author, and to the proper study of a single period."

He need not have feared that his connected sketches
of " English Lands, Letters and Kings " would be
any less welcome because they do not pretend to fill
up all the details or cover all the incidents they hint
in vivid outline.   How many of us ever read or ever
will read Drayton's " Poly-Olbion ? "   Twenty thousand long Alexandrines are filled with admirable
descriptions of scenery, natural productions, and historical events, but how many of us in these days have

time to read and inwardly digest twenty thousand Alexandrine verses? I fear that the specialist is apt to hold his intelligent reader or hearer too cheap. So far as I have observed in medical specialties, what he knows in addition to the knowledge of the well-taught general practitioner is very largely curious rather than important. Having exhausted all that is practical, the specialist is naturally tempted to amuse himself with the natural history of the organ or function he deals with; to feel as a writing-master does when he sets a copy, — not content to shape the letters properly, but he must add flourishes and fancy figures, to let off his spare energy.

I am beginning to be frightened. When I began these papers, my idea was a very simple and innocent one. Here was a mixed company, of various conditions, as I have already told my readers, who came together regularly, and before they were aware of it formed something like a club or association. As I was the patriarch among them, they gave me the name some of you may need to be reminded of; for as these reports are published at intervals, you may not remember the fact that I am what The Teacups have seen fit to call The Dictator.

Now, what did I expect when I began these papers, and what is it that has begun to frighten me?

I expected to report grave conversations and light colloquial passages of arms among the members of the circle. I expected to hear, perhaps to read, a paper now and then. I expected to have, from time to time, a poem from some one of The Teacups, for I felt sure there must be among them one or more poets, — Teacups of the finer and rarer translucent kind of porce-

ain, to speak metaphorically.   Out of these conversations and written contributions I thought I might
make up a readable series of papers ; a not wholly
unwelcome string of recollections, anticipations, suggestions, too often perhaps repetitions, that would be
the twilight to what my earlier series had been to the
morning.

I hoped also that I should come into personal relations with my old constituency, if I may call my
nearer friends, and those more distant ones who belong to my reading parish, by that name.   It is time
that I should.   I received this blessed morning — I
am telling the literal truth — a highly flattering obituary of myself in the shape of an extract from " Le
National " of the 10th of February last.   This is a
bi-weekly newspaper, published in French, in the city
of Plattsburg, Clinton County, New York.   I am
occasionally reminded by my unknown friends that I
must hurry up their autograph, or make haste to copy
that poem they wish to have in the author's own handwriting, or it will be too late; but I have never before been huddled out of the world in this way.   I
take this rather premature obituary as a hint that,
unless I come to some arrangement with my well-
meaning but insatiable correspondents, it would be as
well to leave it in type, for I cannot bear much longer
the load they lay upon me.   I will explain myself on
this point after I have told my readers what has
frightened me.

I am beginning to think this room where we take
our tea is more like a tinder-box than a quiet and safe
place for " a party in a parlor."   It is true that there
are at least two or three incombustibles at our table,
but it looks to me as if the company might pair off

before the season is over, like the crew of Her Majesty's ship the Mantelpiece, — three or four weddings
clear our whole table of all but one or two of the im-
pregnables.   The poem we found in the sugar-bowl
last week first opened my eyes to the probable state of
things.   Now, the idea of having to tell a love-story,
— perhaps two or three love-stories, — when I set out
with the intention of repeating instructive, useful, or
entertaining discussions, naturally alarms me.   It is
quite true that many things which look to me suspi-
cious may be simply playful.   Young people (and we
have several such among The Teacups) are fond of
make-believe courting when they cannot have the real
thing, — " flirting," as it used to be practised in the
days of Arcadian innocence, not the more modern and
more questionable recreation which has reached us
from the home of the *cicisbeo*.   Whatever comes of it,
I shall tell what I see, and take the consequences.

But I am at this moment going to talk in my own
proper person to my own particular public, which, as
I find by my correspondence, is a very considerable
one, and with which I consider myself in exceptionally
pleasant relations.

I have read recently that Mr. Gladstone receives
six hundred letters a day.   Perhaps he does not receive six hundred letters every day, but if he gets anything like half that number daily, what can he do with
them?   There was a time when he was said to answer
all his correspondents.   It is understood, I think, that
he has given up doing so in these later days.

I do not pretend that I receive six hundred or even
sixty letters a day, but I do receive a good many, and
have told the public of the fact from time to time,

under the pressure of their constantly increasing exactions. As it is extremely onerous, and is soon going to be impossible, for me to keep up the wide range of correspondence which has become a large part of my occupation, and tends to absorb all the vital force which is left me, I wish to enter into a final explanation with the well-meaning but merciless taskmasters who have now for many years been levying their daily tax upon me. I have preserved thousands of their letters, and destroyed a very large number, after answering most of them. A few interesting chapters might be made out of the letters I have kept, — not only such as are signed by the names of well-known personages, but many from unknown friends, of whom I had never heard before and have never heard since. A great deal of the best writing the languages of the world have ever known has been committed to leaves that withered out of sight before a second sunlight had fallen upon them. I have had many letters I should have liked to give the public, had their nature admitted of their being offered to the world. What struggles of young ambition, finding no place for its energies, or feeling its incapacity to reach the ideal towards which it was striving! What longings of disappointed, defeated fellow-mortals, trying to find a new home for themselves in the heart of one whom they have amiably idealized! And oh, what hopeless efforts of mediocrities and inferiorities, believing in themselves as superiorities, and stumbling on through limping disappointments to prostrate failure! Poverty comes pleading, not for charity, for the most part, but imploring us to find a purchaser for its unmarketable wares. The unreadable author particularly requests us to make a critical examination of his book, and report to him whatever may be our verdict, — as if he wanted anything but our praise, and that very often to be used in his publisher's advertisements.

But what does not one have to submit to who has become the martyr — the Saint Sebastian — of a literary correspondence! I will not dwell on the possible impression produced on a sensitive nature by reading one's own premature obituary, as I have told you has been my recent experience. I will not stop to think whether the urgent request for an autograph by return post, in view of the possible contingencies which might render it the last one was ever to write, is pleasing or not. At threescore and twenty one must expect such hints of what is like to happen before long. I suppose, if some near friend were to watch one who was looking over such a pressing letter, he might possibly see a slight shadow flit over the reader's features, and some such dialogue might follow as that between Othello and Iago, after "this honest creature" has been giving breath to his suspicions about Desdemona : —

" I see this hath a little dash'd your spirits.
" Not a jot, not a jot.

            .   .   .   .   .   .

'My lord, I see you 're moved."

And a little later the reader might, like Othello, complain, —

" I have a pain upon my forehead here."

Nothing more likely. But, for myself, I have grown callous to all such allusions. The repetition of the Scriptural phrase for the natural term of life is so frequent that it wears out one's sensibilities.

But how many charming and refreshing letters I have received! How often I have felt their encouragement in moments of doubt and depression, such as the happiest temperaments must sometimes experience! If the time comes when to answer all my kind unknown friends, even by dictation, is impossible, or more than I feel equal to, I wish to refer any of those who may feel disappointed at not receiving an answer to the following general acknowledgments : —

I. I am always grateful for any attention which shows me that I am kindly remembered. — II. Your pleasant message has been read to me, and has been thankfully listened to. — III. Your book (your essay) (your poem) has reached me safely, and has received all the respectful attention to which it seemed entitled. It would take more than all the time I have at my disposal to read all the printed matter and all the manuscripts which are sent to me, and you would not ask me to attempt the impossible. You will not, therefore, expect me to express a critical opinion of your work. — IV. I am deeply sensible to your expressions of personal attachment to me as the author of certain writings which have brought me very near to you, in virtue of some affinity in our ways of thought and moods of feeling. Although I cannot keep up correspondences with many of my readers who seem to be thoroughly congenial with myself, let them be assured that their letters have been read or heard with peculiar gratification, and are preserved as precious treasures.

I trust that after this notice no correspondent will be surprised to find his or her letter thus answered by anticipation ; and that if one of the above formulæ is the only answer he receives, the unknown friend will

remember that he or she is one of a great many whose
incessant demands have entirely outrun my power of
answering them as fully as the applicants might wish
and perhaps expect.

I could make a very interesting volume of the letters I have received from correspondents unknown to
the world of authorship, but writing from an instinctive impulse, which many of them say they have long
felt and resisted.   One must not allow himself to be
flattered into an overestimate of his powers because he
gets many letters expressing a peculiar attraction towards his books, and a preference of them to those
with which he would not have dared to compare his
own.   Still, if the *homo unius libri* — the man of one
book — choose to select one of our own writing as his
favorite volume, it means *something*, — not much, perhaps ; but if one has unlocked the door to the secret
entrance of one heart, it is not unlikely that his key
may fit the locks of others.   What if nature has lent
him a master key ?   He has found the wards and slid
back the bolt of one lock ; perhaps he may have
learned the secret of others.   One success is an encouragement to try again.   Let the writer of a truly
loving letter, such as greets one from time to time,
remember that, though he never hears a word from it,
it may prove one of the best rewards of an anxious
and laborious past, and the stimulus of a still aspiring
future.

Among the letters I have recently received, none is
more interesting than the following.   The story of
Helen Keller, who wrote it, is told in the well-known
illustrated magazine called " The Wide Awake," in
the number for July, 1888.   For the account of this
little girl, now between nine and ten years old, and

other letters of her writing, I must refer to the article
I have mentioned. It is enough to say that she is
deaf and dumb and totally blind. She was seven
years old when her teacher, Miss Sullivan, under the
direction of Mr. Anagnos, at the Blind Asylum at
South Boston, began her education. A child fuller
of life and happiness it would be hard to find. It
seems as if her soul was flooded with light and
filled with music that had found entrance to it through
avenues closed to other mortals. It is hard to understand how she has learned to deal with abstract ideas,
and so far to supplement the blanks left by the senses
of sight and hearing that one would hardly think of
her as wanting in any human faculty. Remember
Milton's pathetic picture of himself, suffering from
only one of poor little Helen's deprivations : —

> " Not to me returns
> Day, or the sweet approach of even or morn,
> Or sight of vernal bloom, or summer's rose,
> Or flocks, or herds, or human face divine ;
> But cloud instead, and ever-during dark
> Surrounds me, from the cheerful ways of men
> Cut off, and for the book of knowledge fair
> Presented with a universal blank
> Of Nature's works, to me expunged and rased,
> And wisdom at one entrance quite shut out."

Surely for this loving and lovely child does

> " the celestial Light
> Shine inward."

Anthropologist, metaphysician, most of all theologian,
here is a lesson which can teach you much that you
will not find in your primers and catechisms. Why
should I call her " poor little Helen " ? Where can
you find a happier child ?

SOUTH BOSTON, MASS., *March* 1, 1890.

DEAR KIND POET, — I have thought of you many times since that bright Sunday when I bade you good-bye, and I am going to write you a letter because I love you. I am sorry that you have no little children to play with sometimes, but I think you are very happy with your books, and your many, many friends. On Washington's Birthday a great many people came here to see the little blind children, and I read for them from your poems, and showed them some beautiful shells which came from a little island near Palos. I am reading a very sad story called " Little Jakey." Jakey was the sweetest little fellow you can imagine, but he was poor and blind. I used to think, when I was small and before I could read, that everybody was always happy, and at first it made me very sad to know about pain and great sorrow ; but now I know that we could never learn to be brave and patient, if there were only joy in the world. I am studying about insects in Zoölogy, and I have learned many things about butterflies. They do not make honey for us, like the bees, but many of them are as beautiful as the flowers they light upon, and they always delight the hearts of little children. They live a gay life, flitting from flower to flower, sipping the drops of honey-dew, without a thought for the morrow. They are just like little boys and girls when they forget books and studies, and run away to the woods and the fields to gather wild-flowers, or wade in the ponds for fragrant lilies, happy in the bright sunshine. If my little sister comes to Boston next June, will you let me bring her to see you ? She is a lovely baby and I am sure you will love [her]. Now I must tell my gentle poet good-bye, for I have a letter to write home before I go to bed. From your loving little friend,

HELEN A. KELLER.

The reading of this letter made many eyes glisten, and a dead silence hushed the whole circle. All at once Delilah, our pretty table-maid, forgot her place, — what business had she to be listening to our conversation and reading? — and began sobbing, just as if she had been a lady. She could n't help it, she explained afterwards, — she had a little blind sister at the asylum, who had told her about Helen's reading to the children.

It was very awkward, this breaking-down of our pretty Delilah, for one girl crying will sometimes set off a whole row of others, — it is as hazardous as lighting one cracker in a bunch. The two Annexes hurried out their pocket-handkerchiefs, and I almost expected a semi-hysteric cataclysm. At this critical moment Number Five called Delilah to her, looked into her face with those calm eyes of hers, and spoke a few soft words. Was Number Five forgetful, too? Did she not remember the difference of their position? I suppose so. But she quieted the poor hand-maiden as simply and easily as a nursing mother quiets her unweaned baby. Why are we not all in love with Number Five? Perhaps we are. At any rate, I suspect the Professor. When we all get quiet, I will touch him up about that visit she promised to make to his laboratory.

I got a chance at last to speak privately with him.

" Did Number Five go to meet you in your laboratory, as she talked of doing ? "

"Oh, yes, of course she did, — why, she *said* she would!"

"Oh, to be sure. Do tell me what she wanted in your laboratory."

"She wanted me to burn a diamond for her."

"*Burn a diamond!* What was that for? Because Cleopatra swallowed a pearl?"

"No, nothing of that kind. It was a small stone, and had a flaw in it. Number Five said she did n't want a diamond with a flaw in it, and that she did want to see how a diamond would burn."

"Was that all that happened?"

"That was all. She brought the two Annexes with her, and I gave my three visitors a lecture on carbon, which they seemed to enjoy very much."

I looked steadily in the Professor's face during the reading of the following poem. I saw no questionable look upon it, — but he has a remarkable command of his features. Number Five read it with a certain archness of expression, as if she saw all its meaning, which I think some of the company did not quite take in. They said they must read it slowly and carefully. Somehow, "I like you" and "I love you" got a little mixed, as they heard it. It was not Number Five's fault, for she read it beautifully, as we all agreed, and as I knew she would when I handed it to her.

I LIKE YOU AND I LOVE YOU.

I LIKE YOU met I LOVE YOU, face to face ;
  The path was narrow, and they could not pass.
I LIKE YOU smiled ; I LOVE YOU cried, Alas !
And so they halted for a little space.

"Turn thou and go before," I LOVE YOU said,
  " Down the green pathway, bright with many a flower ;
  Deep in the valley, lo ! my bridal bower
Awaits thee."   But I LIKE YOU shook his head.

Then while they lingered on the span-wide shelf
  That shaped a pathway round the rocky ledge,
  I LIKE YOU bared his icy dagger's edge,
And first he slew I LOVE YOU, — then himself.

VII

THERE is no use in burdening my table with those letters of inquiry as to where our meetings are held, and what are the names of the persons designated by numbers, or spoken of under the titles of the Professor, the Tutor, and so forth. It is enough that you are aware who I am, and that I am known at the tea-table as The Dictator. Theatrical "asides" are apt to be whispered in a pretty loud voice, and the persons who ought not to have any idea of what is said are expected to be reasonably hard of hearing. If I named all The Teacups, some of them might be offended. If any of my readers happen to be able to identify any one Teacup by some accidental circumstance, — say, for instance, Number Five, by the incident of her burning the diamond, — I hope they will keep quiet about it. Number Five does n't want to be pointed out in the street as the extravagant person who makes use of such expensive fuel, for the story would soon grow to a statement that she always uses diamonds, instead of cheaper forms of carbon, to heat her coffee with. So with other members of the circle. The "cracked Teacup," Number Seven, would not, perhaps, be pleased to recognize himself under that title. I repeat it, therefore, *Do not try to identify the individual Teacups.* You will not get them right; or, if you do, you may too probably make trouble. How is it possible that I can keep up my freedom of intercourse with you all if you insist on bellowing my " asides " through a speaking-trumpet? Besides, you cannot have failed to see that there are strong symptoms of the springing up of delicate relations between some of our number. I told you how it would be. It did not require a prophet to foresee that the saucy intruder who, as Mr. Willis wrote, and the dear dead girls used to sing, in our young days,

> " Taketh every form of air,
> And every shape of earth,
> And comes unbidden everywhere,
> Like thought's mysterious birth,"

would pop his little curly head up between one or more pairs of Teacups. If you will stop these questions, then, I will go on with my reports of what was said and done at our meetings over the teacups.

Of all things beautiful in this fair world, there is nothing so enchanting to look upon, to dream about, as the first opening of the flower of young love. How closely the calyx has hidden the glowing leaves in its quiet green mantle! Side by side, two buds have been tossing jauntily in the breeze, often brought very near to each other, sometimes touching for a moment, with a secret thrill in their close-folded heart-leaves, it may be, but still the cool green sepals shutting tight over the burning secret within. All at once a morning ray touches one of the two buds, and the point of a blushing petal betrays the imprisoned and swelling blossom.

— Oh, no, I did not promise a love-story. There may be a little sentiment now and then, but these papers are devoted chiefly to the opinions, prejudices, fancies, whims, of myself, The Dictator, and others of The Teacups who have talked or written for the general benefit of the company.

Here are some of the remarks I made the other evening on the subject of *Intellectual Over-Feeding* and its consequence, *Mental Dyspepsia.*

There is something positively appalling in the amount of printed matter yearly, monthly, weekly, daily, secreted by that great gland of the civilized organism, the press. I need not dilate upon this point, for it is brought home to every one of you who ever looks into a bookstore or a public library. So large is the variety of literary products continually coming forward, forced upon the attention of the reader by stimulating and suggestive titles, commended to his notice by famous names, recasting old subjects and developing and illustrating new ones, that the mind is liable to be urged into a kind of unnatural hunger, leading to a repletion which is often followed by disgust and disturbed nervous conditions as its natural consequence.

It has long been a favorite rule with me, a rule which I have never lost sight of, however imperfectly I have carried it out : Try to know enough of a wide range of subjects to profit by the conversation of intelligent persons of different callings and various intellectual gifts and acquisitions. The cynic will paraphrase this into a shorter formula : Get a smattering in every sort of knowledge. I must therefore add a second piece of advice : Learn to hold as of small account the comments of the cynic. He is often amusing, sometimes really witty, occasionally, without meaning it, instructive ; but his talk is to profitable conversation what the stone is to the pulp of the peach, what the cob is to the kernels on an ear of Indian corn. Once more : Do not be bullied out of your common sense by the specialist ; two to one, he

is a pedant, with all his knowledge and valuable qualities, and will " cavil on the ninth part of a hair," if
it will give him a chance to show off his idle erudition.

I saw attributed to me, the other day, the saying,
" Know something about everything, and everything
about something." I am afraid it does not belong to
me, but I will treat it as I used to treat a stray boat
which came through my meadow, floating down the
Housatonic, — get hold of it and draw it ashore, and
hold on to it until the owner turns up.   If this precept
is used discreetly, it is very serviceable ; but it is as
well to recognize the fact that you cannot know something about everything in days like these of intellectual activity, of literary and scientific production. We
all feel this.   It makes us nervous to see the shelves
of new books, many of which we feel as if we ought to
read, and some among them to study.   We must adopt
some principle of selection among the books outside of
any particular branch which we may have selected for
study.   I have often been asked what books I would
recommend for a course of reading.   I have always
answered that I had a great deal rather take advice
than give it.   Fortunately, a number of scholars have
furnished lists of books to which the inquirer may be
directed.   But the worst of it is that each student is
in need of a little library specially adapted to his
wants.   Here is a young man writing to me from a
Western college, and wants me to send him a list of
the books which I think would be most useful to him.
He does not send me his intellectual measurements ;
and he might as well have sent to a Boston tailor for
a coat, without any hint of his dimensions in length,
breadth, and thickness.

But instead of laying down rules for reading, and

furnishing lists of the books which should be read in order, I will undertake the much humbler task of giving a little *quasi*-medical advice to persons, young or old, suffering from book-hunger, book-surfeit, book-nervousness, book-indigestion, book-nausea, and all other maladies which, directly or indirectly, may be traced to books, and to which I could give Greek or Latin names if I thought it worth while.

I have a picture hanging in my library, a lithograph, of which many of my readers may have seen copies. It represents a gray-haired old book-lover at the top of a long flight of steps. He finds himself in clover, so to speak, among rare old editions, books he has longed to look upon and never seen before, rarities, precious old volumes, *incunabula*, cradle-books, printed while the art was in its infancy, — its glorious infancy, for it was born a giant. The old bookworm is so intoxicated with the sight and handling of the priceless treasures that he cannot bear to put one of the volumes back after he has taken it from the shelf. So there he stands, — one book open in his hands, a volume under each arm, and one or more between his legs, — loaded with as many as he can possibly hold at the same time.

Now, that is just the way in which the extreme form of book-hunger shows itself in the reader whose appetite has become over-developed. He wants to read so many books that he over-crams himself with the crude materials of knowledge, which become knowledge only when the mental digestion has time to assimilate them. I never can go into that famous " Corner Bookstore " and look over the new books in the row before me, as I enter the door, without seeing half a dozen which I want to read, or at least to know something about. I cannot empty my purse of its contents, and crowd my bookshelves with all those volumes. The titles of many of them interest me. I look into one or two, perhaps. I have sometimes picked up a line or a sentence, in these momentary glances between the uncut leaves of a new book, which I have never forgotten. As a trivial but *bona fide* example, one day I opened a book on duelling. I remember only these words: "*Conservons-la, cette noble institution.*" I had never before seen duelling called a noble institution, and I wish I had taken the name of the book. Book-*tasting* is not necessarily profitless, but it is very stimulating, and makes one hungry for more than he needs for the nourishment of his thinking-marrow. To feed this insatiable hunger, the abstracts, the reviews, do their best. But these, again, have grown so numerous and so crowded with matter that it is hard to find time to master their contents. We are accustomed, therefore, to look for analyses of these periodicals, and at last we have placed before us a formidable-looking monthly, "The Review of Reviews." After the analyses comes the newspaper notice; and there is still room for the epigram, which sometimes makes short work with all that has gone before on the same subject.

It is just as well to recognize the fact that if one should read day and night, confining himself to his own language, he could not pretend to keep up with the press. He might as well try to race with a locomotive. The first discipline, therefore, is that of despair. If you could stick to your reading day and night for fifty years, what a learned idiot you would become long before the half-century was over! Well, then, there is no use in gorging one's self with knowledge, and no need of self-reproach because one is content to remain more or less ignorant of many things which interest his fellow-creatures. We gain a good deal of knowledge through the atmosphere; we learn a great deal by accidental hearsay, provided we have the *mordant* in our own consciousness which makes the wise remark, the significant fact, the instructive incident, take hold upon it. After the stage of despair comes the period of consolation. We soon find that we are not so much worse off than most of our neighbors as we supposed. The fractional value of the wisest shows a small numerator divided by an infinite denominator of knowledge.

I made some explanations to The Teacups, the other evening, which they received very intelligently and graciously, as I have no doubt the readers of these reports of mine will receive them. If the reader will turn back to the end of the fourth number of these papers, he will find certain lines entitled, " *Cacoethes Scribendi.*" They were said to have been taken from the usual receptacle of the verses which are contributed by The Teacups, and, though the fact was not mentioned, were of my own composition. I found them in manuscript in my drawer, and as my subject had naturally suggested the train of thought they carried out into extravagance, I printed them. At the same time they sounded very natural, as we say, and I felt as if I had published them somewhere or other before; but I could find no evidence of it, and so I ventured to have them put in type.

And here I wish to take breath for a short, separate paragraph. I have often felt, after writing a line which pleased me more than common, that it was not new, and perhaps was not my own. I have very rarely, however, found such a coincidence in ideas or expression as would be enough to justify an accusation of unconscious plagiarism, — *conscious* plagiarism is not my particular failing. I therefore say my say, set down my thought, print my line, and do not heed the suspicion that I may not be as original as I supposed, in the passage I have been writing. My experience may be worth something to a modest young writer, and so I have interrupted what I was about to say by intercalating this paragraph.

In this instance my telltale suspicion had not been at fault. I *had* printed those same lines, years ago, in " The Contributors' Club," to which I have rarely sent any of my prose or verse. Nobody but the editor has noticed the fact, so far as I know. This is consoling, or mortifying, I hardly know which. I suppose one has a right to plagiarize from himself, but he does not want to present his work as fresh from the workshop when it has been long standing in his neighbor's shop-window.

But I have just received a letter from a brother of the late Henry Howard Brownell, the poet of the Bay Fight and the River Fight, in which he quotes a passage from an old book, " A Heroine, Adventures of Cherubina," which might well have suggested my own lines, if I had ever seen it. I have not the slightest recollection of the book or the passage. I think its liveliness and " local color " will make it please the reader, as it pleases me, more than my own more prosaic extravagances : —

LINES TO A PRETTY LITTLE MAID OF MAMMA'S.

"If Black Sea, Red Sea, White Sea, ran
  One tide of ink to Ispahan,
  If all the geese in Lincoln fens
  Produced spontaneous well-made **pens**,
  If Holland old and Holland new
  One wondrous sheet of paper **grew**,
  And could I sing but half the **grace**
  Of half a freckle in thy face,
  Each syllable I wrote would **reach**
  From Inverness to Bognor's beach, —
  Each hair-stroke be a river Rhine,
  Each verse an equinoctial line!"

"The immediate dismissal of the 'little maid' was the consequence."

I may as well say that our Delilah was not in the room when the last sentence was read.

Readers must be either very good-natured or very careless. I have laid myself open to criticism by more than one piece of negligence, which has been passed over without invidious comment by the readers of my papers. How could I, for instance, have written in my original "copy" for the printer about the fisherman baiting his hook with a *giant's* tail instead of a dragon's? It is the automatic fellow, — Me-Number-Two of our dual personality, — who does these things, who forgets the message Me - Number - One sends down to him from the cerebral convolutions, and substitutes a wrong word for the right one. I suppose Me - Number - Two will "sass back," and swear that "giant's" was the message which came down from headquarters. He is always doing the wrong thing and excusing himself. Who blows out the gas instead of shutting it off? Who puts the key in the desk and fastens it tight with the spring lock? Do you mean to say that the upper Me, the Me of the true thinking-marrow, the convolutions of the brain, does not know better? Of course he does, and Me - Number - Two is a careless servant, who remembers some old direction, and follows that instead of the one just given.

Number Seven demurred to this, and I am not sure that he is wrong in so doing. He maintains that the automatic fellow always does just what he is told to do. Number Five is disposed to agree with him. We will talk over the question.

But come, now, why should not a giant have a tail as well as a dragon? Linnæus admitted the *homo caudatus* into his anthropological catalogue. The human embryo has a very well marked caudal append-age; that is, the vertebral column appears prolonged, just as it is in a young quadruped. During the late session of the Medical Congress at Washington, my friend Dr. Priestley, a distinguished London physician, of the highest character and standing, showed me the photograph of a small boy, some three or four years old, who had a very respectable little tail, which would have passed muster on a pig, and would have made a frog or a toad ashamed of himself. I have never heard what became of the little boy, nor have I looked in the books or journals to find out if there are similar cases on record, but I have no doubt that there are others. And if boys may have this additional orna-ment to their vertebral columns, why not men? And if men, why not giants? So I may not have made a very bad blunder, after all, and my reader has learned something about the *homo caudatus* as spoken of by Linnæus, and as shown me in photograph by Dr. Priestley. This child is a candidate for the vacant place of Missing Link.

In accounting for the blunders, and even gross blunders, which, sooner or later, one who writes much is pretty sure to commit, I must not forget the part played by the blind spot or idiotic area in the brain, which I have already described.

The most knowing persons we meet with are sometimes at fault. *Non omnia possumus omnes* is not a new nor profound axiom, but it is well to remember it as a counterpoise to that other truly American saying of the late Mr. Samuel Patch, " Some things can be done as well as others." Yes, *some* things, but not all things. We all know men and women who hate to admit their ignorance of anything. Like Talkative in " Pilgrim's Progress, " they are ready to converse of " things heavenly or things earthly ; things moral or things evangelical ; things sacred or things profane ; things past or things to come ; things foreign or things at home ; things more essential or things circumstantial."

Talkative is apt to be a shallow fellow, and to say foolish things about matters he only half understands, and yet he has his place in society. The specialists would grow to be intolerable, were they not counterpoised to some degree by the people of general intelligence. The man who knows *too much* about one particular subject is liable to become a terrible social infliction. Some of the worst bores (to use plain language) we ever meet with are recognized as experts of high grade in their respective departments. Beware of making so much as a pinhole in the dam that holds back their knowledge. They ride their hobbies without bit or bridle. A poet on Pegasus, reciting his own verses, is hardly more to be dreaded than a mounted specialist.

One of the best offices which women perform for men is that of tasting books for them. They may or may not be profound students, — some of them are; but we do not expect to meet women like Mrs. Somerville, or Caroline Herschel, or Maria Mitchell at every dinner-table or afternoon tea. But give your elect lady a pile of books to look over for you, and she will tell you what they have for her and for you in less time than you would have wasted in stupefying yourself over a single volume.

One of the encouraging signs of the times is the condensed and abbreviated form in which knowledge is presented to the general reader. The short biographies of historic personages, of which within the past few years many have been published, have been a great relief to the large class of readers who want to know something, but not too much, about them.

What refuge is there for the victim who is oppressed with the feeling that there are a thousand new books he ought to read, while life is only long enough for him to attempt to read a hundred?

Many readers remember what old Rogers, the poet, said: " When I hear a new book talked about or have it pressed upon me, I read an old one." Happy the man who finds his rest in the pages of some favorite classic! I know no reader more to be envied than that friend of mine who for many years has given his days and nights to the loving study of Horace. After a certain period in life, it is always with an effort that we admit a new author into the inner circle of our intimates. The Parisian omnibuses, as I remember them half a century ago, — they may still keep to the same habit, for aught that I know, — used to put up the sign " *Complet* " as soon as they were full. Our public conveyances are never full until the natural atmospheric pressure of sixteen pounds to the square inch is doubled, in the close packing of the human sardines that fill the all-accommodating vehicles. A new-comer, however well mannered and well dressed, is not very welcome under these circumstances. In the same way, our tables are full of books half read and books we feel that we must read. And here come in two thick volumes, with uncut leaves, in small type, with many pages, and many lines to a page, — a book that must be read and ought to be read at once. What a relief to hand it over to the lovely keeper of your literary conscience, who will tell you all that you will most care to know about it, and leave you free to plunge into your beloved volume, in which you are ever finding new beauties, and from which you rise refreshed, as if you had just come from the cool waters of Hippocrene! The stream of modern literature represented by the books and periodicals on the crowded counters is a turbulent and clamorous torrent, dashing along among the rocks of criticism, over the pebbles of the world's daily events; trying to make itself seen and heard amidst the hoarse cries of the politicians and the rumbling wheels of traffic. The classic is a still lakelet, a mountain tarn, fed by springs that never fail, its surface never ruffled by storms, — always the same, always smiling a welcome to its visitor. Such is Horace to my friend. To his eye " *Lydia, dic per omnes* " is as familiar as " *Pater noster qui es in cœlis* " to that of a pious Catholic. " *Integer vitœ*," which he has put into manly English, his Horace opens to as Watt's hymn-book opens to " From all that dwell below the skies." The more he reads, the more he studies his author, the richer are the treasures he finds. And what Horace is to him, Homer, or Virgil, or Dante is to many a quiet reader, sick to death of the unending train of bookmakers.

I have some curious books in my library, a few of which I should like to say something about to The Teacups, when they have no more immediately pressing subjects before them. A library of a few thousand volumes ought always to have some books in it which the owner almost never opens, yet with whose backs he is so well acquainted that he feels as if he knew something of their contents. They are like those persons whom we meet in our daily walks, with whose faces and figures, whose summer and winter garments, whose walking-sticks and umbrellas even, we feel acquainted, and yet whose names, whose business, whose residences, we know nothing about. Some of these books are so formidable in their dimensions, so rusty and crabbed in their aspect, that it takes a considerable amount of courage to attack them.

I will ask Delilah to bring down from my library a very thick, stout volume, bound in parchment, and standing on the lower shelf, next the fireplace. The pretty handmaid knows my books almost as if she were my librarian, and I don't doubt she would have found it if I had given only the name on the back.

Delilah returned presently, with the heavy quarto in her arms. It was a pleasing sight, — the old book in the embrace of the fresh young damsel. I felt, on looking at them, as I did when I followed the slip of a girl who conducted us in the Temple, that ancient building in the heart of London. The long-enduring monuments of the dead do so mock the fleeting presence of the living!

Is n't this book enough to scare any of you ? I said,

as Delilah dumped it down upon the table. The
teacups jumped from their saucers as it thumped on
the board. *Danielis Georgii Morhofii Polyhistor,
Literarius, Philosophicus et Poeticus. Lubecæ
MDCCXXXIII.* Perhaps I should not have ventured to ask you to look at this old volume, if it had
not been for the fact that Dr. Johnson mentions Morhof as the author to whom he was specially indebted,
— more, I think, than to any other. It is a grand
old encyclopædic summary of all· the author knew
about pretty nearly everything, full of curious interest, but so strangely mediæval, so utterly antiquated
in most departments of knowledge, that it is hard to
believe the volume came from the press at a time
when persons whom I well remember were living. Is
it possible that the books which have been for me
what Morhof was for Dr. Johnson can look like that
to the student of the year 1990?

Morhof was a believer in magic and the transmutation of metals. There was always something fascinating to me in the old books of alchemy. I have felt
that the poetry of science lost its wings when the last
powder of projection had been cast into the crucible,
and the fire of the last transmutation furnace went
out. Perhaps I am wrong in implying that alchemy
is an extinct folly. It existed in New England's early
days, as we learn from the Winthrop papers, and I see
no reason why gold-making should not have its votaries
as well as other popular delusions.

Among the essays of Morhof is one on the " Paradoxes of the Senses." That title brought to mind the
recollection of another work I have been meaning to
say something about, at some time when you were in
the listening mood. The book I refer to is " A

Budget of Paradoxes," by Augustus De Morgan.   De
Morgan is well remembered as a very distinguished
mathematician, whose works have kept his name in
high honor to the present time.   The book I am
speaking of was published by his widow, and is largely
made up of letters received by him and his comments
upon them.   Few persons ever read it through.   Few
intelligent readers ever took it up and laid it down
without taking a long draught of its singular and interesting contents.   The letters are mostly from that
class of persons whom we call "cranks," in our familiar language.

At this point Number Seven interrupted me by
calling out, "Give us some of those cranks' letters.
A crank is a man who does his own thinking.   I had
a relation who was called a crank.   I believe I have
been spoken of as one myself.   That is what you have
to expect if you invent anything that puts an old machine out of fashion, or solve a problem that has puzzled all the world up to your time.   There never was
a religion founded but its Messiah was called a crank.
There never was an idea started that woke up men
out of their stupid indifference but its originator was
spoken of as a crank.   Do you want to know why
that name is given to the men who do most for the
world's progress?   I will tell you.   It is because
cranks make all the wheels in all the machinery of
the world go round.   What would a steam-engine be
without a crank?   I suppose the first fool that looked
on the first crank that was ever made asked what that
crooked, queer-looking thing was good for.   When
the wheels got moving he found out.   Tell us something about that book which has so much to say concerning cranks."

Hereupon I requested Delilah to carry back Mor-hof, and replace him in the wide gap he had left in the bookshelf. She was then to find and bring down the volume I had been speaking of.

Delilah took the wisdom of the seventeenth century in her arms, and departed on her errand. The book she brought down was given me some years ago by a gentleman who had sagaciously foreseen that it was just one of those works which I might hesitate about buying, but should be well pleased to own. He guessed well; the book has been a great source of instruction and entertainment to me. I wonder that so much time and cost should have been expended upon a work which might have borne a title like the Encomium Moriæ of Erasmus; and yet it is such a wonderful museum of the productions of the squinting brains belonging to the class of persons commonly known as cranks that we could hardly spare one of its five hundred octavo pages.

Those of us who are in the habit of receiving let-ters from all sorts of would-be-literary people — letters of inquiry, many of them with reference to matters we are supposed to understand — can readily see how it was that Mr. De Morgan, never too busy to be good-natured with the people who pestered — or amused — him with their queer fancies, received such a number of letters from persons who thought they had made great discoveries, from those who felt that they and their inventions and contrivances had been overlooked, and who sought in his large charity of disposition and great receptiveness a balm for their wounded feelings and a ray of hope for their darkened prospects.

The book before us is made up from papers pub-

lished in "The Athenæum," with additions by the
author. Soon after opening it we come to names with
which we are familiar, the first of these, that of Cor-
nelius Agrippa, being connected with the occult and
mystic doctrines dealt with by many of De Morgan's
correspondents. But the name most likely to arrest
us is that of Giordano Bruno, the same philosopher,
heretic, and martyr whose statue has recently been
erected in Rome, to the great horror of the Pope and
his prelates in the Old World and in the New. De
Morgan's pithy account of him will interest the company : "Giordano Bruno was all paradox. He was,
as has been said, a vorticist before Descartes, an optimist before Leibnitz, a Copernican before Galileo. It
would be easy to collect a hundred strange opinions of
his. He was born about 1550, and was roasted alive
at Rome, February 17, 1600, for the maintenance and
defence of the Holy Church, and the rights and liber-
ties of the same."

Number Seven could not contain himself when the
reading had reached this point. He rose from his
chair, and tinkled his spoon against the side of his
teacup. It may have been a fancy, but I thought it
returned a sound which Mr. Richard Briggs would
have recognized as implying an organic defect. But
Number Seven did not seem to notice it, or, if he did,
to mind it.

"Why did n't we all have a chance to help erect
that statue?" he cried. "A murdered heretic at the
beginning of the seventeenth century, a hero of knowledge in the nineteenth, — I drink to the memory of
the roasted crank, Giordano Bruno!"

Number Seven lifted his teacup to his lips, and
most of us followed his example.

After this outburst of emotion and eloquence had
subsided, and the teaspoons lay quietly in their saucers, I went on with my extract from the book I had
in hand.

I think, I said, that the passage which follows will
be new and instructive to most of the company. De
Morgan's interpretation of the cabalistic sentence,
made up as you will find it, is about as ingenious a
piece of fanciful exposition as you will be likely to
meet with anywhere in any book, new or old. I am
the more willing to mention it as it suggests a puzzle
which some of the company may like to work upon.
Observe the character and position of the two distinguished philosophers who did not think their time
thrown away in laboring at this seemingly puerile
task.

"There is a kind of Cabbala Alphabetica which
the investigators of the numerals in words would do
well to take up; it is the formation of sentences which
contain all the letters of the alphabet, and each only
once. No one has done it with *v* and *j* treated as consonants; but you and I can do it. Dr. Whewell and
I amused ourselves some years ago with attempts.
He could not make sense, though he joined words:
he gave me Phiz, styx, wrong, buck, flame, quiz.

"I gave him the following, which he agreed was
'admirable sense,'— I certainly think the words
would never have come together except in this way:
I quartz pyx who fling muck beds. I long thought
that no human being could say this under any circumstances. At last I happened to be reading a religious
writer, — as he thought himself, — who threw asper-
sions on his opponents thick and threefold. Heyday!

came into my head; this fellow flings muck beds; he must be a quartz pyx. And then I remembered that a pyx is a sacred vessel, and quartz is a hard stone, — as hard as the heart of a religious foe-curser. So that the line is the motto of the ferocious sectarian who turns his religious vessels into mud-holders, for the benefit of those who will not see what he sees."

There are several other sentences given, in which all the letters (except *v* and *j* as consonants) are employed, of which "the following is the best: Get nymph; quiz sad brow; fix luck, — which in more sober English would be, Marry; be cheerful; watch your business. There is more edification, more religion, in this than in all the 666 interpretations put together."

There is something very pleasant in the thought of these two sages playing at jackstraws with the letters of the alphabet. The task which De Morgan and Dr. Whewell, "the omniscient," set themselves would not be unworthy of our own ingenious scholars, and it might be worth while for some one of our popular periodicals to offer a prize for the best sentence using up the whole alphabet, under the same conditions as those submitted to by our two philosophers.

This whole book of De Morgan's seems to me full of instruction. There is too much of it, no doubt; yet one can put up with the redundancy for the sake of the multiplicity of shades of credulity and self-deception it displays in broad daylight. I suspect many of us are conscious of a second personality in our complex nature, which has many traits resembling those found in the writers of the letters addressed to Mr. De Morgan.

I have not ventured very often nor very deeply into

the field of metaphysics, but if I were disposed to make any claim in that direction, it would be the recognition of the squinting brain, the introduction of the term " cerebricity " corresponding to electricity, the idiotic area in the brain or thinking-marrow, and my studies of the second member in the partnership of I-My-Self & Co. I add the Co. with especial reference to a very interesting article in a late Scribner, by my friend Mr. William James. In this article the reader will find a full exposition of the doctrine of plural personality illustrated by striking cases. I have long ago noticed and referred to the fact of the stratification of the currents of thought in three layers, one over the other. I have recognized that where there are two individuals talking together there are really six personalities engaged in the conversation. But the distinct, separable, independent individualities, taking up conscious life one after the other, are brought out by Mr. James and the authorities to which he refers as I have not elsewhere seen them developed.

Whether we shall ever find the exact position of the idiotic centre or area in the brain (if such a spot exists) is uncertain. We know exactly where the blind-spot of the eye is situated, and can demonstrate it anatomically and physiologically. But we have only analogy to lead us to infer the possible or even probable existence of an insensible spot in the thinking-centre. If there is a focal point where consciousness is at its highest development, it would not be strange if near by there should prove to be an anæsthetic district or limited space where no report from the senses was intelligently interpreted. But all this is mere hypothesis.

Notwithstanding the fact that I am nominally the

head personage of the circle of Teacups, I do not pretend or wish to deny that we all look to Number Five as our chief adviser in all the literary questions that come before us. She reads more and better than any of us. She is always ready to welcome the first sign of genius, or of talent which approaches genius. She makes short work with all the pretenders whose only excuse for appealing to the public is that they "want to be famous." She is one of the very few persons to whom I am willing to read any one of my own productions while it is yet in manuscript, unpublished. I know she is disposed to make more of it than it deserves; but, on the other hand, there are degrees in her scale of judgment, and I can distinguish very easily what delights her from what pleases only, or is, except for her kindly feeling to the writer, indifferent, or open to severe comment. What is curious is that she seems to have no literary aspirations, no desire to be known as a writer. Yet Number Five has more *esprit*, more sparkle, more sense in her talk, than many a famous authoress from whom we should expect brilliant conversation.

There are mysteries about Number Five. I am not going to describe her personally. Whether she belongs naturally among the bright young people, or in the company of the maturer persons, who have had a good deal of experience of the world, and have reached the wisdom of the riper decades without losing the graces of the earlier ones, it would be hard to say. The men and women, young and old, who throng about her forget their own ages. "There is no such thing as time in her presence," said the Professor, the other day, in speaking of her. Whether the Professor is in love with her or not is more than I can say, but

I am sure that he goes to her for literary sympathy and counsel, just as I do. The reader may remember what Number Five said about the possibility of her getting a sprained ankle, and her asking the young Doctor whether he felt equal to taking charge of her if she did. I would not for the world insinuate that he wishes she would slip and twist her foot a little, — just a little, you know, but so that it would have to be laid on a pillow in a chair, and inspected, and bandaged, and delicately manipulated. There was a banana-skin which she might naturally have trodden on, in her way to the tea-table. Nobody can suppose that it was there except by the most innocent of accidents. There are people who will suspect everybody. The idea of the Doctor's putting that banana-skin there! People love to talk in that silly way about doctors.

Number Five had promised to read us a narrative which she thought would interest some of the company. Who wrote it she did not tell us, but I inferred from various circumstances that she had known the writer. She read the story most effectively in her rich, musical voice. I noticed that when it came to the sounds of the striking clock, the ringing of the notes was so like that which reaches us from some far-off cathedral tower that we wanted to bow our heads, as if we had just heard a summons to the Angelus. This was the short story that Number Five read to The Teacups: —

I have somewhere read this anecdote. Louis the Fourteenth was looking out, one day, from a window of his palace of Saint-Germain. It was a beautiful landscape which spread out before him, and the mon-

arch, exulting in health, strength, and the splendors
of his exalted position, felt his bosom swell with emotions of pride and happiness. Presently he noticed
the towers of a church in the distance, above the tree-
tops. "What building is that?" he asked. "May
it please your Majesty, that is the Church of St. Denis,
where your royal ancestors have been buried for many
generations." The answer did *not* "please his Royal
Majesty." There, then, was the place where he too
was to lie and moulder in the dust. He turned, sick
at heart, from the window, and was uneasy until he
had built him another palace, from which he could
never be appalled by that fatal prospect.

Something like the experience of Louis the Fourteenth was that of the owner of

THE TERRIBLE CLOCK.

I give the story as transcribed from the original
manuscript : —

The clock was bequeathed to me by an old friend
who had recently died. His mind had been a good
deal disordered in the later period of his life. This
clock, I am told, seemed to have a strange fascination
for him. His eyes were fastened on it during the last
hours of his life. He died just at midnight. The
clock struck twelve, the nurse told me, as he drew
his last breath, and then, without any known cause,
stopped, with both hands upon the hour.

It is a complex and costly piece of mechanism. The
escapement is in front, so that every tooth is seen as
it frees itself. It shows the phases of the moon, the
month of the year, the day of the month, and the day
of the week, as well as the hour and minute of the
day.

I had not owned it a week before I began to perceive the same kind of fascination as that which its former owner had experienced. This gradually grew upon me, and presently led to trains of thought which became at first unwelcome, then worrying, and at last unendurable. I began by taking offence at the moon. I did not like to see that " something large and smooth and round," so like the skull which little Peterkin picked up on the field of Blenheim. " How many times," I kept saying to myself, " is that wicked old moon coming up to stare at me ? " I could not stand it. I stopped a part of the machinery, and the moon went into permanent eclipse. By and by the sounds of the infernal machine began to trouble and pursue me. They *talked* to me ; more and more their language became that of articulately speaking men. They twitted me with the rapid flight of time. They hurried me, as if I had not a moment to lose. Quick ! Quick ! Quick ! as each tooth released itself from the escapement. And as I looked and listened there could not be any mistake about it. I heard Quick ! Quick ! Quick ! as plainly, at least, as I ever heard a word from the phonograph. I stood watching the dial one day, — it was near one o'clock, — and a strange attraction held me fastened to the spot. Presently something appeared to trip or stumble inside of the infernal mechanism. I waited for the sound I knew was to follow. How nervous I got ! It seemed to me that it would never strike. At last the minute-hand reached the highest point of the dial. Then there was a little stir among the works, as there is in a congregation as it rises to receive the benediction. It was no form of blessing which rung out those deep, almost sepulchral tones. But the word they uttered could not be mistaken. I can hear its prolonged, solemn vibrations as if I were standing before the clock at this moment.

Gone! Yes, I said to myself, gone, — its record made up to be opened in eternity.

I stood still, staring vaguely at the dial as in a trance. And as the next hour creeps stealthily up, it starts all at once, and cries aloud, Gone! — Gone! The sun sinks lower, the hour-hand creeps downward with it, until I hear the thrice-repeated monosyllable, Gone! — Gone! — Gone! So on through the darkening hours, until at the dead of night the long roll is called, and with the last Gone! the latest of the long procession that filled the day follows its ghostly companions into the stillness and darkness of the past.

I silenced the striking part of the works. Still the escapement kept repeating, Quick! Quick! Quick! Still the long minute-hand, like the dart in the grasp of Death, as we see it in Roubillac's monument to Mrs. Nightingale, among the tombs of Westminster Abbey, stretched itself out, ready to transfix each hour as it passed, and make it my last. I sat by the clock to watch the leap from one day of the week to the next. Then would come, in natural order, the long stride from one month to the following one.

I could endure it no longer. "*Take that clock away!*" I said. They took it away. They took me away, too, — they thought I needed country air. The sounds and motions still pursued me in imagination. I was very nervous when I came here. The walks are pleasant, but the walls seem to me unnecessarily high. The boarders are numerous; a little miscellaneous, I think. But we have the Queen, and the President of the United States, and several other distinguished

persons, if we may trust what they tell about themselves.

After we had listened to Number Five's story, I was
requested to read a couple of verses written by me
when the guest of my friends, whose name is hinted
by the title prefixed to my lines.

LA MAISON D'OR.

(BAR HARBOR.)

From this fair home behold on either side
   The restful mountains or the restless sea:
So the warm sheltering walls of life divide
   Time and its tides from still eternity.

Look on the waves : their stormy voices teach
   That not on earth may toil and struggle cease.
Look on the mountains : better far than speech
   Their silent promise of eternal peace.

VIII.

I had intended to devote this particular report to an account of my replies to certain questions which have been addressed to me, — questions which I have a right to suppose interest the public, and which, therefore, I was justified in bringing before The Teacups, and presenting to the readers of these articles.

Some may care for one of these questions, and some for another. A good many young people think nothing about life as it presents itself in the far horizon, bounded by the snowy ridges of threescore and the dim peaks beyond that remote barrier. Again, there are numbers of persons who know nothing at all about the Jews; while, on the other hand, there are those who can, or think they can, detect the Israelitish blood in many of their acquaintances who believe themselves of the purest Japhetic origin, and are full of prejudices about the Semitic race.

I do not mean to be cheated out of my intentions. I propose to answer my questioners on the two points just referred to, but I find myself so much interested in the personal affairs of The Teacups that I must deal with them before attacking those less exciting subjects. There is no use, let me say here, in addressing to me letters marked " personal, " " private, " " confidential, " and so forth, asking me how I came to know what happened in certain conversations of which I shall give a partial account. If there is a very sensi-

tive phonograph lying about here and there in unsus-
pected corners, that might account for some part of
my revelations. If Delilah, whose hearing is of almost
supernatural delicacy, reports to me what .she over-
hears, it might explain a part of the mystery. I do
not want to accuse Delilah, but a young person who
assures me she can hear my watch ticking in my
pocket, when I am in the next room, might undoubt-
edly tell many secrets, if so disposed. Number Five
is pretty nearly omniscient, and she and I are on the
best terms with each other. These are all the hints I
shall give you at present.

The Teacups of whom the least has been heard at
our table are the Tutor and the Musician. The Tutor
is a modest young man, kept down a little, I think, by
the presence of older persons, like the Professor and
myself. I have met him several times, of late, walking with different lady Teacups: once with the American Annex; twice with the English Annex; once
with the two Annexes together; once with Number
Five.

I have mentioned the fact that the Tutor is a poet
as among his claims to our attention. I must add that
I do not think any the worse of him for expressing his
emotions and experiences in verse. For though rhyming is often a bad sign in a young man, especially if
he is already out of his teens, there are those to whom
it is as natural, one might almost say as necessary, as
it is to a young bird to fly. One does not care to see
barnyard fowls tumbling about in trying to use their
wings. They have a pair of good, stout drumsticks,
and had better keep to them, for the most part. But
that feeling does not apply to young eagles, or even to
young swallows and sparrows. The Tutor is by no

means one of those ignorant, silly, conceited phrase-
tinklers, who live on the music of their own jingling
syllables and the flattery of their foolish friends. I
think Number Five must appreciate him. He is sincere, warm-hearted, — his poetry shows that, — not in
haste to be famous, and he looks to me as if he only
wanted *love* to steady him. With one of those two
young girls he ought certainly to be captivated, if he
is not already. *Twice* walking with the English Annex, I met him, and they were so deeply absorbed in
conversation they hardly noticed me. He has been
talking over the matter with Number Five, who is
just the kind of person for a confidante.

"I know I feel very lonely," he was saying, "and
I only wish I felt sure that I could make another person happy. My life would be transfigured if I could
find such a one, whom I could love well enough to
give my life to her, — for her, if that were needful, —
and who felt an affinity for me, if any one could."

"And why not your English maiden?" said Number Five.

"What makes you think I care more for her than
for her American friend?" said the Tutor.

"Why, have n't I met you walking with her, and
did n't you both seem greatly interested in the subject
you were discussing? I thought, of course, it was
something more or less sentimental that you were
talking about."

"I was explaining that 'enclitic de' in Browning's
Grammarian's Funeral. I don't think there was anything very sentimental about that. She is an inquisitive creature, that English girl. She is very fond of
asking me questions, — in fact, both of them are.
There is one curious difference between them: the

English girl settles down into her answers and is quiet; the American girl is never satisfied with yesterday's conclusions; she is always reopening old questions in the light of some new fact or some novel idea.   I suppose that people bred from childhood to lean their backs against the wall of the Creed and the church catechism find it hard to sit up straight on the republican stool, which obliges them to stiffen their own backs.   Which of these two girls would be the safest choice for a young man?   I should really like to hear what answer you would make if I consulted you seriously, with a view to my own choice, — on the supposition that there was a fair chance that either of them might be won."

"The one you are in love with," answered Number Five.

"But what if it were a case of 'How happy could I be with either'?   Which offers the best chance of happiness, — a marriage between two persons of the same country, or a marriage where one of the parties is of foreign birth?   Everything else being equal, which is best for an American to marry, an American or an English girl?   We need not confine the question to those two young persons, but put it more generally."

"There are reasons on both sides," answered Number Five.   "I have often talked this matter over with The Dictator.   This is the way he speaks about it. — English blood is apt to tell well on the stock upon which it is engrafted.   Over and over again he has noticed finely grown specimens of human beings, and on inquiry has found that one or both of the parents or grandparents were of British origin.   The chances are that the descendants of the imported stock will be of a richer organization, more florid, more muscular, with mellower voices, than the native whose blood has been unmingled with that of new emigrants since the earlier colonial times. — So talks The Dictator. — I myself think the American will find his English wife concentrates herself more readily and more exclusively on her husband, — for the obvious reason that she is obliged to live mainly in him. I remember hearing an old friend of my early days say, ' A woman does not bear transplanting.' It does not do to trust these old sayings, and yet they almost always have some foundation in the experience of mankind, which has repeated them from generation to generation. Happy is the married woman of foreign birth who can say to her husband, as Andromache said to Hector, after enumerating all the dear relatives she had lost, —

> ' Yet while my Hector still survives, I see
> My father, mother, brethren, all in thee ! '

How many a sorrowing wife, exiled from her native country, dreams of the mother she shall see no more ! How many a widow, in a strange land, wishes that her poor, worn-out body could be laid among her kinsfolk, in the little churchyard where she used to gather daisies in her childhood ! It takes a great deal of love to keep down the ' climbing sorrow ' that swells up in a woman's throat when such memories seize upon her, in her moments of desolation. But if a foreign-born woman does willingly give up all for a man, and never looks backward, like Lot's wife, she is a prize that it is worth running a risk to gain, — that is, if she has the making of a good woman in her; and a few years will go far towards naturalizing her."

The Tutor listened to Number Five with much apparent interest. "And now," he said, "what do you think of her companion?"

"A charming girl for a man of a quiet, easy temperament. The great trouble is with her voice. It is pitched a full note too high. It is aggressive, disturbing, and would wear out a nervous man without his ever knowing what was the matter with him. A good many crazy Northern people would recover their reason if they could live for a year or two among the blacks of the Southern States. But the penetrating, perturbing quality of the voices of many of our Northern women has a great deal to answer for in the way of determining love and friendship. You remember that dear friend of ours who left us not long since? If there were more voices like hers, the world would be a different place to live in. I do not believe any man or woman ever came within the range of those sweet, tranquil tones without being hushed, captivated, entranced I might almost say, by their calming, soothing influence. Can you not imagine the tones in which those words, 'Peace, be still,' were spoken? Such was the effect of the voice to which but a few weeks ago we were listening. It is hard to believe that it has died out of human consciousness. Can such a voice be spared from that world of happiness to which we fondly look forward, where we love to dream, if we do not believe with assured conviction, that whatever is loveliest in this our mortal condition shall be with us again as an undying possession? Your English friend has a very agreeable voice, round, mellow, cheery, and her articulation is charming. Other things being equal, I think you, who are, perhaps, oversensitive, would live from two to three years longer with her than with the other. I suppose a man who lived within hearing of a murmuring brook would find his life shortened if a sawmill were set up within earshot of his dwelling."

"And so you advise me to make love to the English girl, do you?" asked the Tutor.

Number Five laughed. It was not a loud laugh, — she never laughed noisily; it was not a very hearty laugh; the idea did not seem to amuse her much.

"No," she said, "I won't take the responsibility. Perhaps this is a case in which the true reading of Gay's line would be

How happy could I be with *neither.*

There are several young women in the world besides our two Annexes."

I question whether the Tutor had asked those questions very seriously, and I doubt if Number Five thought he was very much in earnest.

One of The Teacups reminded me that I had promised to say something of my answers to certain questions. So I began at once: —

I have given the name of *brain - tappers* to the literary operatives who address persons whose names are well known to the public, asking their opinions or their experiences on subjects which are at the time of general interest. They expect a literary man or a scientific expert to furnish them materials for symposia and similar articles, to be used by them for their own special purposes. Sometimes they expect to pay for the information furnished them; at other times, the honor of being included in a list of noted personages who have received similar requests is thought sufficient compensation. The object with which the

brain-tapper puts his questions may be a purely be-
nevolent and entirely disinterested one. Such was the
object of some of those questions which I have received
and answered. There are other cases, in which the
brain-tapper is acting much as those persons do who
stop a physician in the street to talk with him about
their livers or stomachs, or other internal arrangements, instead of going to his office and consulting
him, expecting to pay for his advice. Others are
more like those busy women who, having the generous intention of making a handsome present to their
pastor, at as little expense as may be, send to all their
neighbors and acquaintances for scraps of various materials, out of which the imposing " bedspread " or
counterpane is to be elaborated.

That is all very well so long as old pieces of stuff
are all they call for, but it is a different matter to ask
for clippings out of new and uncut rolls of cloth. So
it is one thing to ask an author for liberty to use extracts from his published writings, and it is a very
different thing to expect him to write expressly for
the editor's or compiler's piece of literary patchwork.

I have received many questions within the last year
or two, some of which I am willing to answer, but
prefer to answer at my own time, in my own way,
through my customary channel of communication with
the public. I hope I shall not be misunderstood as
implying any reproach against the inquirers who, in
order to get at facts which ought to be known, apply
to all whom they can reach for information. Their
inquisitiveness is not always agreeable or welcome,
but we ought to be glad that there are mousing fact-
hunters to worry us with queries to which, for the
sake of the public, we are bound to give our attention. Let me begin with my brain-tappers.

And first, as the papers have given publicity to the fact that I, The Dictator of this tea-table, have reached the age of threescore years and twenty, I am requested to give information as to how I managed to do it, and to explain just how they can go and do likewise. I think I can lay down a few rules that will help them to the desired result. There is no certainty in these biological problems, but there are reasonable probabilities upon which it is safe to act.

The first thing to be done is, some years before birth, to advertise for a couple of parents both belonging to long-lived families. Especially let the mother come of a race in which octogenarians and nonagenarians are very common phenomena. There are practical difficulties in following out this suggestion, but possibly the forethought of your progenitors, or that concurrence of circumstances which we call accident, may have arranged this for you.

Do not think that a robust organization is any warrant of long life, nor that a frail and slight bodily constitution necessarily means scanty length of days. Many a strong-limbed young man and many a blooming young woman have I seen failing and dropping away in or before middle life, and many a delicate and slightly constituted person outliving the athletes and the beauties of their generation. Whether the excessive development of the muscular system is compatible with the best condition of general health is, I think, more than doubtful. The muscles are great sponges that suck up and make use of large quantities of blood, and the other organs must be liable to suffer for want of their share.

One of the Seven Wise Men of Greece boiled his wisdom down into two words, μηδὲν ἄγαν, — nothing too much. It is a rule which will apply to food, exercise, labor, sleep, and, in short, to every part of life. This is not so very difficult a matter if one begins in good season and forms regular habits. But what if I should lay down the rule, Be cheerful; take all the troubles and trials of life with perfect equanimity and a smiling countenance? Admirable directions! Your friend, the curly-haired blonde, with florid complexion, round cheeks, the best possible digestion and respiration, the stomach of an ostrich and the lungs of a pearl-diver, finds it perfectly easy to carry them into practice. You, of leaden complexion, with black and lank hair, lean, hollow-eyed, dyspeptic, nervous, find it not so easy to be always hilarious and happy. The truth is that the persons of that buoyant disposition which comes always heralded by a smile, as a yacht driven by a favoring breeze carries a wreath of sparkling foam before her, are born with their happiness ready made. They cannot help being cheerful any more than their saturnine fellow-mortal can help seeing everything through the cloud he carries with him. I give you the precept, then, *Be cheerful*, for just what it is worth, as I would recommend to you to be six feet, or at least five feet ten, in stature. You cannot settle that matter for yourself, but you can stand up straight, and give your five feet five its full value. You can help along a little by wearing high-heeled shoes. So you can do something to encourage yourself in serenity of aspect and demeanor, keeping your infirmities and troubles in the background instead of making them the staple of your conversation. This piece of advice, if followed, may be worth from three to five years of the fourscore which you hope to attain.

If, on the other hand, instead of going about cheerily in society, making the best of everything and as far as possible forgetting your troubles, you can make up your mind to economize all your stores of vital energy, to hoard your life as a miser hoards his money, you will stand a fair chance of living until you are tired of life, — fortunate if everybody is not tired of you.

One of my prescriptions for longevity may startle you somewhat. It is this: *Become the subject of a mortal disease.* Let half a dozen doctors thump you, and knead you, and test you in every possible way, and render their verdict that you have an internal complaint; they don't know exactly what it is, but it will certainly kill you by and by. Then bid farewell to the world and shut yourself up for an invalid. If you are threescore years old when you begin this mode of life, you may very probably last twenty years, and there you are, — an octogenarian. In the mean time, your friends outside have been dropping off, one after another, until you find yourself almost alone, nursing your mortal complaint as if it were your baby, hugging it and kept alive by it, — if to exist is to live. Who has not seen cases like this, — a man or a woman shutting himself or herself up, visited by a doctor or a succession of doctors (I remember that once, in my earlier experience, I was the twenty-seventh physician who had been consulted), always taking medicine, until everybody was reminded of that impatient speech of a relative of one of these invalid vampires who live on the blood of tired-out attendants, "I do wish she would get well — *or something*"? Persons who are shut up in that way, confined to their chambers, sometimes to their beds, have a very small

amount of vital expenditure, and wear out very little
of their living substance.   They are like lamps with
half their wicks picked down, and will continue to
burn when other lamps have used up all their oil.   An
insurance office might make money by taking no risks
except on lives of persons suffering from mortal disease.   It is on this principle of economizing the
powers of life that a very eminent American physician,
— Dr. Weir Mitchell, a man of genius, — has founded
his treatment of certain cases of nervous exhaustion.

What have I got to say about temperance, the use
of animal food, and so forth?   These are questions
asked me.   Nature has proved a wise teacher, as I
think, in my own case.   The older I grow, the less
use I make of alcoholic stimulants.   In fact, I hardly
meddle with them at all, except a glass or two of
champagne occasionally.   I find that by far the best
borne of all drinks containing alcohol.   I do not suppose my experience can be the foundation of a universal rule.   Dr. Holyoke, who lived to be a hundred,
used habitually, in moderate quantities, a mixture of
cider, water, and rum.   I think, as one grows older,
less food, especially less animal food, is required.   But
old people have a right to be epicures, if they can afford it.   The pleasures of the palate are among the
last gratifications of the senses allowed them.   We
begin life as little cannibals, — feeding on the flesh
and blood of our mothers.   We range through all the
vegetable and animal products of nature, and I suppose, if the second childhood could return to the food
of the first, it might prove a wholesome diet.

What do I say to smoking?   I cannot grudge an
old man his pipe, but I think tobacco often does a
good deal of harm to the health, — to the eyes espe-

cially, to the nervous system generally, producing headache, palpitation, and trembling. I myself gave it up
many years ago. Philosophically speaking, I think
self-narcotization and self-alcoholization are rather ignoble substitutes for undisturbed self-consciousness
and unfettered self-control.

Here is another of those brain-tapping letters, of
similar character, which I have no objection to answering at my own time and in the place which best suits
me. As the questions must be supposed to be asked
with a purely scientific and philanthropic purpose, it
can make little difference when and where they are
answered. For myself, I prefer our own tea-table to
the symposia to which I am often invited. I do not
quarrel with those who invite their friends to a ban-
quet to which many strangers are expected to contribute. It is a very easy and pleasant way of giving an
entertainment at little cost and with no responsibility.
Somebody has been writing to me about "Oatmeal
and Literature," and somebody else wants to know
whether I have found character influenced by diet;
also whether, in my opinion, oatmeal is preferable to
pie as an American national food.

In answer to these questions, I should say that I have
my beliefs and prejudices ; but if I were pressed hard
for my proofs of their correctness, I should make but a
poor show in the witness-box. Most assuredly I do
believe that body and mind are much influenced by
the kind of food habitually depended upon. I am
persuaded that a too exclusively porcine diet gives a
bristly character to the beard and hair, which is borrowed from the animal whose tissues these stiff-bearded
compatriots of ours have too largely assimilated. I

can never stray among the village people of our windy
capes without now and then coming upon a human being who looks as if he had been split, salted, and
dried, like the salt-fish which has built up his arid organism.   If the body is modified by the food which
nourishes it, the mind and character very certainly will
be modified by it also.   We know enough of their
close connection with each other to be sure of that,
without any statistical observations to prove it.

Do you really want to know "whether oatmeal is
preferable to pie as an American national food"?   I
suppose the best answer I can give to your question is
to tell you what is my own practice.   Oatmeal in the
morning, as an architect lays a bed of concrete to form
a base for his superstructure.   Pie when I can get it;
that is, of the genuine sort, for I am not patriotic
enough to think very highly of the article named after
the Father of his Country, who was first in war, first
in peace, — not first in pies, according to my standard.

There is a very odd prejudice against pie as an article of diet.   It is common to hear every form of
bodily degeneracy and infirmity attributed to this particular favorite food.   I see no reason or sense in it.
Mr. Emerson believed in pie, and was almost indig-
nant when a fellow-traveller refused the slice he offered him.   "Why, Mr. ——," said he, "*what is pie
made for!*"   If every Green Mountain boy has not
eaten a thousand times his weight in apple, pumpkin,
squash, and mince pie, call me a dumpling.   And
Colonel Ethan Allen was one of them, — Ethan Allen,
who, as they used to say, could wrench off the head of
a wrought nail with his teeth.

If you mean to keep as well as possible, the less
you think about your health the better. You know

enough not to eat or drink what you have found does
not agree with you. You ought to know enough not
to expose yourself needlessly to draughts.   If you
take a " constitutional," walk with the wind when you
can, and take a closed car against it if you can get
one.   Walking against the wind is one of the most
dangerous kinds of exposure, if you are sensitive to
cold.   But except a few simple rules such as I have
just given, let your health take care of itself so long
as it behaves decently.   If you want to be sure *not*
to reach threescore and twenty, get a little box of
homœopathic pellets and a little book of homœopathic
prescriptions.   I had a poor friend who fell into that
way, and became at last a regular Hahnemaniac.   He
left a box of his little jokers, which at last came into
my hands.   The poor fellow had cultivated symptoms
as other people cultivate roses or chrysanthemums.
What a luxury of choice his imagination presented to
him !   When one watches for symptoms, every organ
in the body is ready to put in its claim.   By and by
a real illness attacked him, and the box of little pellets was shut up, to minister to his fancied evils no
longer.

Let me tell you one thing.   I think if patients and
physicians were in the habit of recognizing the fact I
am going to mention, both would be gainers.   The
law I refer to must be familiar to all observing physicians, and to all intelligent persons who have observed
their own bodily and mental conditions.   This is the
curve of health.   It is a mistake to suppose that the
normal state of health is represented by a straight
horizontal line.   Independently of the well-known
causes which se or depress the standard of vitality,
there seems be, — I think I may venture to say

there is,— a rhythmic undulation in the flow of the vital
force. The "dynamo" which furnishes the working
powers of consciousness and action has its annual, its
monthly, its diurnal waves, even its momentary rip-
ples, in the current it furnishes. There are greater
and lesser curves in the movement of every day's life,
— a series of ascending and descending movements, a
periodicity depending on the very nature of the force
at work in the living organism. Thus we have our
good seasons and our bad seasons, our good days and
our bad days, life climbing and descending in long or
short undulations, which I have called the curve of
health.

From this fact spring a great proportion of the
errors of medical practice. On it are based the delusions of the various shadowy systems which impose
themselves on the ignorant and half-learned public as
branches or "schools" of science. A remedy taken
at the time of the ascent in the curve of health is
found successful. The same remedy taken while the
curve is in its downward movement proves a failure.

So long as this biological law exists, so long the
charlatan will keep his hold on the ignorant public.
So long as it exists, the wisest practitioner will be liable to deceive himself about the effect of what he calls
and loves to think are his *remedies*. Long-continued
and sagacious observation will to some extent unde-
ceive him; but were it not for the happy illusion that
his useless or even deleterious drugs were doing good
service, many a practitioner would give up his calling
for one in which he could be more certain that he was
really being useful to the subjects of his professional
dealings. For myself, I should prefer a physician of
a sanguine temperament, who had a firm belief in him-

self and his methods. I do not wonder at all that the
public support a whole community of pretenders who
show the portraits of the patients they have " cured."
The best physicians will tell you that, though many
patients get well under their treatment, they rarely
cure anybody. If you are told also that the best physician has many more patients die on his hands than
the worst of his fellow-practitioners, you may add
these two statements to your bundle of paradoxes, and
if they puzzle you I will explain them at some future
time.

[I take this opportunity of correcting a statement
now going the rounds of the medical and probably
other periodicals. In " The Journal of the American
Medical Association," dated April 26, 1890, published
at Chicago, I am reported, in quotation marks, as
saying, —

" Give me opium, wine, and milk, and I will cure
all diseases to which flesh is heir."

In the first place, I never said I will cure, or can
cure, or would or could cure, or had cured any disease.
My venerated instructor, Dr. James Jackson, taught
me never to use that expression. *Curo* means, I take
care of, he used to say, and in that sense, if you mean
nothing more, it is properly employed. So, in the
amphitheatre of the Ecole de Médecine, I used to
read the words of Ambroise Paré, — " Je le pansay,
Dieu le guarist." (I dressed his wound, and God
cured him.) Next, I am not in the habit of talking
about " the diseases to which flesh is heir." The expression has become rather too familiar for repetition,
and belongs to the rhetoric of other latitudes. And,
lastly, I have said some plain things, perhaps some

sharp ones, about the abuse of drugs and the limited number of vitally important remedies, but I am not so ignorantly presumptuous as to make the foolish statement falsely attributed to me.]

I paused a minute or two, and as no one spoke out, I put a question to the Counsellor.

Are you quite sure that you wish to live to be three-score and twenty years old?

"Most certainly I do. Don't they say that Theophrastus lived to his hundred and seventh year, and did n't he complain of the shortness of life? At eighty a man has had just about time to get warmly settled in his nest. Do you suppose he does n't enjoy the quiet of that resting-place? No more haggard responsibility to keep him awake nights, — unless he prefers to retain his hold on offices and duties from which he can be excused if he chooses. No more goading ambitions, — he knows he has done his best. No more jealousies, if he were weak enough to feel such ignoble stirrings in his more active season. An octogenarian with a good record, and free from annoying or distressing infirmities, ought to be the happiest of men. Everybody treats him with deference. Everybody wants to help him. He is the ward of the generations that have grown up since he was in the vigor of maturity. Yes, let me live to be fourscore years, and then I will tell you whether I should like a few more years or not."

You carry the feelings of middle age, I said, in imagination, over into the period of senility, and then reason and dream about it as if its whole mode of being were like that of the earlier period of life. But how many things there are in old age which you must live into if you would expect to have any "realizing sense" of their significance! In the first place, you have no coevals, or next to none. At fifty, your vessel is stanch, and you are on deck with the rest, in all weathers. At sixty, the vessel still floats, and you are in the cabin. At seventy, you, with a few fellow-passengers, are on a raft. At eighty, you are on a spar, to which, possibly, one, or two, or three friends of about your own age are still clinging. After that, you must expect soon to find yourself alone, if you are still floating, with only a life-preserver to keep your old white-bearded chin above the water.

Kindness? Yes, *pitying* kindness, which is a bitter sweet in which the amiable ingredient can hardly be said to predominate. How pleasant do you think it is to have an arm offered to you when you are walking on a level surface, where there is no chance to trip? How agreeable do you suppose it is to have your well-meaning friends shout and screech at you, as if you were deaf as an adder, instead of only being, as you insist, somewhat hard of hearing? I was a little over twenty years old when I wrote the lines which some of you may have met with, for they have been often reprinted : —

> The mossy marbles rest
> On the lips that he has prest
>   In their bloom,
> And the names he loved to hear
> Have been carved for many a year
>   On the tomb.

The world was a garden to me then ; it is a churchyard now.

"I thought you were one of those who looked upon old age cheerfully, and welcomed it as a season of peace and contented enjoyment."

I *am* one of those who so regard it. Those are not bitter or scalding tears that fall from my eyes upon "the mossy marbles." The young who left my side early in my life's journey are still with me in the unchanged freshness and beauty of youth. Those who have long kept company with me live on after their seeming departure, were it only by the mere force of habit; their images are all around me, as if every surface had been a sensitive film that photographed them; their voices echo about me, as if they had been recorded on those unforgetting cylinders which bring back to us the tones and accents that have imprinted them, as the hardened sands show us the tracks of extinct animals. The melancholy of old age has a divine tenderness in it, which only the sad experiences of life can lend a human soul. But there is a lower level, — that of tranquil contentment and easy acquiescence in the conditions in which we find ourselves; a lower level, in which old age trudges patiently when it is not using its wings. I say its wings, for no period of life is so imaginative as that which looks to younger people the most prosaic. The atmosphere of memory is one in which imagination flies more easily and feels itself more at home than in the thinner ether of youthful anticipation. I have told you some of the drawbacks of age; I would not have you forget its privileges. When it comes down from its aerial excursions, it has much left to enjoy on the humble plane of being. And so you think you would like to become an octogenarian?

"I should," said the Counsellor, now a man in the high noon of bodily and mental vigor. "Four more — yes, five more — decades would not be too much, I think. And how much I should live to see in that time! I am glad you have laid down some rules by which a man may reasonably expect to leap the eight-barred gate. I won't promise to obey them all, though."

Among the questions addressed to me, as to a large number of other persons, are the following. I take them from "The American Hebrew" of April 4, 1890. I cannot pretend to answer them all, but I can say something about one or two of them.

"I. Can you, of your own personal experience, find any justification whatever for the entertainment of prejudice towards individuals solely because they are Jews?

"II. Is this prejudice not due largely to the religious instruction that is given by the church and Sunday-school? For instance, the teachings that the Jews crucified Jesus; that they rejected him, and can only secure salvation by belief in him, and similar matters that are calculated to excite in the impressionable mind of the child an aversion, if not a loathing, for members of 'the despised race.'

"III. Have you observed in the social or business life of the Jew, so far as your personal experience has gone, any different standard of conduct than prevails among Christians of the same social status?

"IV. Can you suggest what should be done to dispel the existing prejudice?"

As to the first question, I have had very slight acquaintance with the children of Israel. I shared more or less the prevailing prejudices against the persecuted race. I used to read in my hymn-book, — I hope I quote correctly, —

> " See what a living stone
>   The builders did refuse ¡

Yet God has built his church thereon,
In spite of envious Jews."

I grew up inheriting the traditional idea that they
were a race lying under a curse for their obstinacy in
refusing the gospel.   Like other children of New England birth, I walked in the narrow path of Puritan
exclusiveness.   The great historical church of Christendom was presented to me as Bunyan depicted it:
one of the two giants sitting at the door of their caves,
with the bones of pilgrims scattered about them, and
grinning at the travellers whom they could no longer
devour.   In the nurseries of old-fashioned Orthodoxy
there was one religion in the world, — one religion,
and a multitude of detestable, literally damnable im-
positions, believed in by uncounted millions, who were
doomed to perdition for so believing.   The Jews were
the believers in one of these false religions.   It had
been true once, but was now a pernicious and abomi-
nable lie.   The principal use of the Jews seemed to be
to lend money, and to fulfil the predictions of the old
prophets of their race.

No doubt the individual sons of Abraham whom we
found in our ill-favored and ill-flavored streets were
apt to be unpleasing specimens of the race.   It was
against the most adverse influences of legislation, of
religious feeling, of social repugnance, that the great
names of Jewish origin made themselves illustrious;
that the philosophers, the musicians, the financiers,
the statesmen, of the last centuries forced the world
to recognize and accept them.   Benjamin, the son of
Isaac, a son of Israel, as his family name makes obvious, has shown how largely Jewish blood has been
represented in the great men and women of modern
days.

There are two virtues which Christians have found
it very hard to exemplify in practice. These are modesty and civility. The Founder of the Christian religion appeared among a people accustomed to look
for a Messiah, — a special ambassador from heaven,
with an authoritative message. They were intimately
acquainted with every expression having reference to
this divine messenger. They had a religion of their
own, about which Christianity agrees with Judaism in
asserting that it was of divine origin. It is a serious
fact, to which we do not give all the attention it deserves, that this divinely instructed people were not
satisfied with the evidence that the young Rabbi who
came to overthow their ancient church and found a
new one was a supernatural being. "We think he
was a great Doctor," said a Jewish companion with
whom I was conversing. He meant a great Teacher,
I presume, though healing the sick was one of his
special offices. Instead of remembering that they
were entitled to form their own judgment of the new
Teacher, as they had judged of Hillel and other great
instructors, Christians, as they called themselves, have
insulted, calumniated, oppressed, abased, outraged,
"the chosen race" during the long succession of centuries since the Jewish contemporaries of the Founder
of Christianity made up their minds that he did not
meet the conditions required by the subject of the predictions of their Scriptures. The course of the argument against them is very briefly and effectively stated
by Mr. Emerson : —

"This was Jehovah come down out of heaven. I
will kill you if you say he was a man."

It seems as if there should be certain laws of etiquette regulating the relation of different religions to

each other.   It is not civil for a follower of Mahomet
to call his neighbor of another creed a "Christian
dog."   Still more, there should be something like po-
liteness in the bearing of Christian sects toward each
other, and of believers in the new dispensation toward
those who still adhere to the old.   We are in the habit
of allowing a certain arrogant assumption to our Roman Catholic brethren.   We have got used to their
pretensions.   They may call us " heretics," if they
like.   They may speak of us as " infidels," if they
choose, especially if they say it in Latin.   So long as
there is no inquisition, so long as there is no *auto da
fé*, we do not mind the hard words much ; and we
have as good phrases to give them back : the Man of
Sin and the Scarlet Woman will serve for examples.
But it is better to be civil to each other all round.   I
doubt if a convert to the religion of Mahomet was
ever made by calling a man a Christian dog.   I doubt
if a Hebrew ever became a good Christian if the baptismal rite was performed by spitting on his Jewish
gabardine.   I have often thought of the advance in
comity and true charity shown in the title of my late
honored friend James Freeman Clarke's book, "The
Ten Great Religions."   If the creeds of mankind try
to understand each other before attempting mutual
extermination, they will be sure to find a meaning in
beliefs which are different from their own.   The
old Calvinistic spirit was almost savagely exclusive.
While the author of the " Ten Great Religions " was
growing up in Boston under the benignant, large-
minded teachings of the Rev. James Freeman, the famous Dr. John M. Mason, at New York, was fiercely
attacking the noble humanity of " The Universal
Prayer."   " In preaching," says his biographer, " he

once quoted Pope's lines as to God's being adored alike ' by saint, by savage, and by sage,' and pronounced it (in his deepest guttural) ' the most damnable lie.' "

What could the Hebrew expect when a Christian preacher could use such language about a petition breathing the very soul of humanity? Happily, the true human spirit is encroaching on that arrogant and narrow-minded form of selfishness which called itself Christianity.

The golden rule should govern us in dealing with those whom we call unbelievers, with heathen, and with all who do not accept our religious views. The Jews are with us as a perpetual lesson to teach us modesty and civility. The religion we profess is not self-evident. It did not convince the people to whom it was sent. We have no claim to take it for granted that we are all right, and they are all wrong. And, therefore, in the midst of all the triumphs of Christianity, it is well that the stately synagogue should lift its walls by the side of the aspiring cathedral, a perpetual reminder that there are many mansions in the Father's earthly house as well as in the heavenly one; that civilized humanity, longer in time and broader in space than any historical form of belief, is mightier than any one institution or organization it includes.

Many years ago I argued with myself the proposition which my Hebrew correspondent has suggested. Recognizing the fact that I was born to a birthright of national and social prejudices against " the chosen people," — chosen as the object of contumely and abuse by the rest of the world, — I pictured my own inherited feelings of aversion in all their intensity, and the strain of thought under the influence of which

those prejudices gave way to a more human, a more
truly Christian feeling of brotherhood. I must ask
your indulgence while I quote a few verses from a
poem of my own, printed long ago under the title " At
the Pantomime."

I was crowded between two children of Israel, and
gave free inward expression to my feelings. All at
once I happened to look more closely at one of my
neighbors, and saw that the youth was the very ideal
of the Son of Mary.

> A fresh young cheek whose olive hue
> The mantling blood shows faintly through;
> Locks dark as midnight, that divide
> And shade the neck on either side;
> Soft, gentle, loving eyes that gleam
> Clear as a starlit mountain stream ;
> So looked that other child of Shem,
> The Maiden's Boy of Bethlehem !
>
> — And thou couldst scorn the peerless blood
> That flows unmingled from the Flood, —
> Thy scutcheon spotted with the stains
> Of Norman thieves and pirate Danes !
> The New World's foundling, in thy pride
> Scowl on the Hebrew at thy side,
> And lo ! the very semblance there
> The Lord of Glory deigned to wear !
>
> I see that radiant image rise,
> The flowing hair, the pitying eyes,
> The faintly crimsoned cheek that shows
> The blush of Sharon's opening rose, —
> Thy hands would clasp his hallowed feet
> Whose brethren soil thy Christian seat,
> Thy lips would press his garment's hem
> That curl in wrathful scorn for them !
>
> A sudden mist, a watery screen,
> Dropped like a veil before the scene ;

The shadow floated from my soul,
And to my lips a whisper stole : —
"Thy prophets caught the Spirit's flame,
From thee the Son of Mary came,
With thee the Father deigned to dwell, —
Peace be upon thee, Israel ! "

It is not to be expected that intimate relations will be established between Jewish and Christian communities until both become so far rationalized and humanized that their differences are comparatively unimportant. But already there is an evident approximation in the extreme left of what is called liberal Christianity and the representatives of modern Judaism. The life of a man like the late Sir Moses Montefiore reads a lesson from the Old Testament which might well have been inspired by the noblest teachings of the Christian Gospels.

Delilah, and how she got her name.

Est-elle bien gentille, cette petite? I said one day to Number Five, as our pretty Delilah put her arm between us with a bunch of those tender early radishes that so recall the ῥοδοδάκτυλος Ἠώς, the rosy-fingered morning of Homer. The little hand which held the radishes would not have shamed Aurora. That hand has never known drudgery, I feel sure.

When I spoke those French words our little Delilah gave a slight, seemingly involuntary start, and her cheeks grew of as bright a red as her radishes. Ah, said I to myself, does that young girl understand French? It may be worth while to be careful what one says before her.

There is a mystery about this girl. She seems to know her place perfectly, — except, perhaps, when

she burst out crying, the other day, which was against
all the rules of table-maiden's etiquette, — and yet she
looks as if she had been born to be waited on, and
not to perform that humble service for others. We
know that once in a while girls with education and
well connected take it into their heads to go into service for a few weeks or months. Sometimes it is from
economic motives, — to procure means for their education, or to help members of their families who need
assistance. At any rate, they undertake the lighter
menial duties of some household where they are not
known, and, having stooped — if stooping it is to be
considered — to lowly offices, no born and bred servants are more faithful to all their obligations. You
must not suppose she was christened Delilah. Any
of our ministers would hesitate to give such a heathen
name to a Christian child.

The way she came to get it was this : The Professor
was going to give a lecture before an occasional audience, one evening. When he took his seat with the
other Teacups, the American Annex whispered to the
other Annex, " His hair wants cutting, — it looks like
fury." " Quite so," said the English Annex. " I
wish you would tell him so, — I do, awfully." " I 'll
fix it," said the American girl. So, after the teacups
were emptied and the company had left the table, she
went up to the Professor. " You read this lecture,
don't you, Professor ? " she said. " I do," he answered. " I should think that lock of hair which falls
down over your forehead would trouble you," she
said. " It does sometimes," replied the Professor.
" Let our little maid trim it for you. You 're equal
to that, are n't you ? " turning to the handmaiden.
" I always used to cut my father's hair," she answered.

She brought a pair of glittering shears, and before she would let the Professor go she had trimmed his hair and beard as they had not been dealt with for many a day. Everybody said the Professor looked ten years younger. After that our little handmaiden was always called Delilah, among the talking Teacups.

The Mistress keeps a watchful eye on this young girl. I should not be surprised to find that she was carrying out some ideal, some fancy or whim, — possibly nothing more, but springing from some generous, youthful impulse. Perhaps she is working for that little sister at the Blind Asylum. Where did she learn French? She did certainly blush, and betrayed every sign of understanding the words spoken about her in that language. Sometimes she sings while at her work, and we have all been struck with the pure, musical character of her voice. It is just such a voice as ought to come from that round white throat. We made a discovery about it the other evening.

The Mistress keeps a piano in her room, and we have sometimes had music in the evening. One of The Teacups, to whom I have slightly referred, is an accomplished pianist, and the two Annexes sing very sweetly together, — the American girl having a clear soprano voice, the English girl a mellow contralto. They had sung several tunes, when the Mistress rang for Avis, — for that is our Delilah's real name. She whispered to the young girl, who blushed and trembled. " Don't be frightened," said the Mistress encouragingly. " I have heard you singing ' Too Young for Love,' and I will get our pianist to play it. The young ladies both know it, and you must join in."

The two voices, with the accompaniment, had hardly finished the first line when a pure, ringing, almost

childlike voice joined the vocal duet. The sound of
her own voice seemed to make her forget her fears,
and she warbled as naturally and freely as any young
bird of a May morning. Number Five came in while
she was singing, and when she got through caught her
in her arms and kissed her, as if she were her sister,
and not Delilah, our table-maid. Number Five is apt
to forget herself and those social differences to which
some of us attach so much importance. This is the
song in which the little maid took part : —

TOO YOUNG FOR LOVE.

Too young for love?
Ah, say not so !
Tell reddening rose-buds not to blow !
Wait not for spring to pass away, —
Love's summer months begin with May !
Too young for love ?
Ah, say not so !
Too young ? Too young ?
Ah, no ! no ! no !

Too young for love ?
Ah, say not so,
While daisies bloom and tulips glow !
June soon will come with lengthened day
To practise all love learned in May.
Too oung for love ?
Ah, say not so !
Too young ? Too young ?
Ah, no ! no ! no !

IX

I OFTEN wish that our Number Seven could have known and corresponded with the author of "The Budget of Paradoxes." I think Mr. De Morgan would have found some of his vagaries and fancies not undeserving of a place in his wonderful collection of eccentricities, absurdities, ingenuities, — mental freaks of all sorts. But I think he would have now and then recognized a sound idea, a just comparison, a suggestive hint, a practical notion, which redeemed a page of extravagances and crotchety whims. I confess that I am often pleased with fancies of his, and should be willing to adopt them as my own. I think he has, in the midst of his erratic and tangled conceptions, some perfectly clear and consistent trains of thought.

So when Number Seven spoke of sending us a paper, I welcomed the suggestion. I asked him whether he had any objection to my looking it over before he read it. My proposal rather pleased him, I thought, for, as was observed on a former occasion, he has in connection with a belief in himself another side, — a curious self-distrust. I have no question that he has an obscure sense of some mental deficiency. Thus you may expect from him first a dogma, and presently a doubt. If you fight his dogma, he will do battle for it stoutly ; if you let him alone, he will very probably explain its extravagances, if it has any, and tame it into reasonable limits. Sometimes he is in one mood, sometimes in another.

The first portion of what we listened to shows him at his best; in the latter part I am afraid you will think he gets a little wild.

I proceed to lay before you the paper which Number Seven read to The Teacups. There was something very pleasing in the deference which was shown him. We all feel that there is a crack in the teacup, and are disposed to handle it carefully. I have left out a few things which he said, feeling that they might give offence to some of the company. There were sentences so involved and obscure that I was sure they would not be understood, if indeed he understood them himself. But there are other passages so entirely sane, and as it seems to me so just, that if any reader attributes them to me I shall not think myself wronged by the supposition. You must remember that Number Seven has had a fair education, that he has been a wide reader in many directions, and that he belongs to a family of remarkable intellectual gifts. So it was not surprising that he said some things which pleased the company, as in fact they did. The reader will not be startled to see a certain abruptness in the transition from one subject to another, — it is a characteristic of the squinting brain wherever you find it. Another curious mark rarely wanting in the subjects of mental strabismus is an irregular and often sprawling and deformed handwriting. Many and many a time I have said, after glancing at the back of a letter, " This comes from an insane asylum, or from an eccentric who might well be a candidate for such an institution." Number Seven's manuscript, which showed marks of my corrections here and there, furnished good examples of the chirography of persons with ill-mated cerebral hemispheres. But the earlier portions of the manuscript are of perfectly normal appearance.

Conticuere omnes, as Virgil says. We were all silent as Number Seven began the reading of his paper.

Number Seven reads.

I am the seventh son of a seventh son, as I suppose you all know. It is commonly believed that some extraordinary gifts belong to the fortunate individuals born under these exceptional conditions. However this may be, a peculiar virtue was supposed to dwell in me from my earliest years. My touch was believed to have the influence formerly attributed to that of the kings and queens of England. You may remember that the great Dr. Samuel Johnson, when a child, was carried to be touched by her Majesty Queen Anne for the "king's evil," as scrofula used to be called. Our honored friend The Dictator will tell you that the brother of one of his Andover schoolmates was taken to one of these gifted persons, who touched him, and hung a small bright silver coin, either a "fourpence ha'penny" or a "ninepence," about his neck, which, strange to say, after being worn a certain time, became tarnished, and finally black, — a proof of the poisonous matters which had become eliminated from the system and gathered upon the coin. I remember that at one time I used to carry fourpence ha'pennies with holes bored through them, which I furnished to children or to their mothers, under pledges of secrecy, — receiving a piece of silver of larger dimensions in exchange. I never felt quite sure about any extraordinary endowment being a part of my inheritance in virtue of my special conditions of birth. A phrenologist, who examined my head

when I was a boy, said the two sides were unlike.
My hatter's measurement told me the same thing;
but in looking over more than a bushel of the small
cardboard hat-patterns which give the exact shape of
the head, I have found this is not uncommon. The
phrenologist made all sorts of predictions of what I
should be and do, which proved about as near the
truth as those recorded in Miss Edith Thomas's
charming little poem, " Augury," which some of us
were reading the other day.

I have never been through college, but I had a relative who was famous as a teacher of rhetoric in one of
our universities, and especially for taking the nonsense out of sophomorical young fellows who could
not say anything without rigging it up in showy and
sounding phrases. I think I learned from him to express myself in good old-fashioned English, and without making as much fuss about it as our Fourth of
July orators and political haranguers were in the
habit of making.

I read a good many stories during my boyhood, one
of which left a lasting impression upon me, and which
I have always commended to young people. It is too
late, generally, to try to teach old people, yet one may
profit by it at any period of life before the sight has
become too dim to be of any use. The story I refer
to is in " Evenings at Home," and is called " Eyes and
No Eyes." I ought to have it by me, but it is constantly happening that the best old things get over-
laid by the newest trash ; and though I have never
seen anything of the kind half so good, my table and
shelves are cracking with the weight of involuntary
accessions to my library.

This is the story as I remember it : Two children

walk out, and are questioned when they come home.
One has found nothing to observe, nothing to admire,
nothing to describe, nothing to ask questions about.
The other has found everywhere objects of curiosity
and interest. I advise you, if you are a child anywhere under forty-five, and do not yet wear glasses,
to send at once for " Evenings at Home " and read
that story. For myself, I am always grateful to the
writer of it for calling my attention to common things.
How many people have been waked to a quicker consciousness of life by Wordsworth's simple lines about
the daffodils, and what he says of the thoughts suggested to him by " the meanest flower that blows " !

I was driving with a friend, the other day, through
a somewhat dreary stretch of country, where there
seemed to be very little to attract notice or deserve
remark. Still, the old spirit infused by " Eyes and
No Eyes " was upon me, and I looked for something
to fasten my thought upon, and treat as an artist
treats a study for a picture. The first object to which
my eyes were drawn was an old-fashioned well-sweep.
It did not take much imaginative sensibility to be
stirred by the sight of this most useful, most ancient,
most picturesque, of domestic conveniences. I know
something of the *shadoof* of Egypt, — the same arrangement by which the sacred waters of the Nile
have been lifted, from the days of the Pharaohs to
those of the Khedives. That long forefinger pointing
to heaven was a symbol which spoke to the Puritan
exile as it spoke of old to the enslaved Israelite. Was
there ever any such water as that which we used to
draw from the deep, cold well, in " the old oaken
bucket " ? What memories gather about the well in
all ages ! What love-matches have been made at its

margin, from the times of Jacob and Rachel downward! What fairy legends hover over it, what fearful mysteries has it hidden! The beautiful well-
sweep! It is too rarely that we see it, and as it dies
out and gives place to the odiously convenient pump,
with the last patent on its cast-iron uninterestingness,
does it not seem as if the farmyard aspect had lost
half its attraction? So long as the dairy farm exists,
doubtless there must be every facility for getting
water in abundance; but the loss of the well-sweep
cannot be made up to us even if our milk were diluted
to twice its present attenuation.

The well-sweep had served its turn, and my companion and I relapsed into silence. After a while we
passed another farmyard, with nothing which seemed
deserving of remark except the wreck of an old
wagon.

"Look," I said, "if you want to see one of the
greatest of all the triumphs of human ingenuity, —
one of the most beautiful, as it is one of the most useful, of all the mechanisms which the intelligence of
successive ages has called into being."

"I see nothing," my companion answered, "but an
old broken-down wagon. Why they leave such a
piece of lumbering trash about their place, where people can see it as they pass, is more than I can account
for."

"And yet," said I, "there is one of the most extraordinary products of human genius and skill, — an
object which combines the useful and the beautiful to
an extent which hardly any simple form of mechanism
can pretend to rival. Do you notice how, while everything else has gone to smash, that *wheel* remains sound
and fit for service? Look at it merely for its beauty.

See the perfect circles, the outer and the inner. A circle is in itself a consummate wonder of geometrical symmetry. It is the line in which the omnipotent energy delights to move. There is no fault in it to be amended. The first drawn circle and the last both embody the same complete fulfillment of a perfect design. Then look at the rays which pass from the inner to the outer circle. How beautifully they bring the greater and lesser circles into connection with each other! The flowers know that secret, — the marguerite in the meadow displays it as clearly as the great sun in heaven. How beautiful is this flower of wood and iron, which we were ready to pass by without wasting a look upon it! But its beauty is only the beginning of its wonderful claim upon us for our admiration. Look at that field of flowering grass, the *triticum vulgare*, — see how its waves follow the breeze in satiny alternations of light and shadow. You admire it for its lovely aspect; but when you remember that this flowering grass is *wheat*, the finest food of the highest human races, it gains a dignity, a glory, that its beauty alone could not give it.

"Now look at that exquisite structure lying neglected and disgraced, but essentially unchanged in its perfection, before you. That slight and delicate-looking fabric has stood such a trial as hardly any slender contrivance, excepting always the valves of the heart, was ever subjected to. It has rattled for years over the cobble-stones of a rough city pavement. It has climbed over all the accidental obstructions it met in the highway, and dropped into all the holes and deep ruts that made the heavy farmer sitting over it use his Sunday vocabulary in a week-day form of speech. At one time or another, almost every part of that old wagon has given way. It has had two new pairs of shafts. Twice the axle has broken off close to the hub, or nave. The seat broke when Zekle and Huldy were having what they called ' a ride ' together. The front was kicked in by a vicious mare. The springs gave way and the floor bumped on the axle. Every portion of the wagon became a prey of its special accident, except that most fragile looking of all its parts, the wheel. Who can help admiring the exact distribution of the power of resistance at the least possible expenditure of material which is manifested in this wondrous triumph of human genius and skill? The spokes are planted in the solid hub as strongly as the jaw-teeth of a lion in their deep-sunken sockets. Each spoke has its own territory in the circumference, for which it is responsible. According to the load the vehicle is expected to carry, they are few or many, stout or slender, but they share their joint labor with absolute justice, — not one does more, not one does less, than its just proportion. The outer end of the spokes is received into the deep mortise of the wooden fellies, and the structure appears to be complete. But how long would it take to turn that circle into a polygon, unless some mighty counteracting force should prevent it? See the iron tire brought hot from the furnace and laid around the smoking circumference. Once in place, the workman cools the hot iron ; and as it shrinks with a force that seems like a hand-grasp of the Omnipotent, it clasps the fitted fragments of the structure, and compresses them into a single inseparable whole.

" Was it not worth our while to stop a moment before passing that old broken wagon, and see whether we could not find as much in it as Swift found in his

' Meditations on a Broomstick ' ?   I have been laughed at for making so much of such a common thing as a wheel.   Idiots !   Solomon's court fool would have scoffed at the thought of the young Galilean who dared compare the lilies of the field to his august master.   *Nil admirari* is very well for a North American Indian and his degenerate successor, who has grown too grand to admire anything but himself, and takes a cynical pride in his stolid indifference to everything worth reverencing or honoring."

After calling my companion's attention to the wheel, and discoursing upon it until I thought he was getting sleepy, we jogged along until we came to a running stream.   It was crossed by a stone bridge of a single arch.   There are very few stone arches over the streams in New England country towns, and I always delighted in this one.   It was built in the last century, amidst the doubting predictions of staring rustics, and stands to-day as strong as ever, and seemingly good for centuries to come.

"See there!" said I, — "there is another of my 'Eyes and No Eyes' subjects to meditate upon.   Next to the wheel, the arch is the noblest of those elementary mechanical composites, corresponding to the proximate principles of chemistry.   The beauty of the arch consists first in its curve, commonly a part of the circle, of the perfection of which I have spoken.   But the mind derives another distinct pleasure from the admirable manner in which the several parts, each different from all the others, contribute to a single harmonious effect.   It is a typical example of the *più nel uno*.   An arch cut out of a single stone would not be so beautiful as one of which each individual stone was shaped for its exact position.   Its completion by the

locking of the keystone is a delight to witness and to
contemplate.   And how the arch endures, when its
lateral thrust is met by solid masses of resistance !   In
one of the great temples of Baalbec a keystone has
slipped, but how rare is that occurrence !   One will
hardly find another such example among all the ruins
of antiquity.   Yes, I never get tired of arches.   They
are noble when shaped of solid marble blocks, each
carefully beveled for its position.   They are beautiful
when constructed with the large thin tiles the Romans
were so fond of using.   I noticed some arches built
in this way in the wall of one of the grand houses just
going up on the bank of the river.   They were over
the capstones of the windows, — to take off the pressure from them, no doubt, for now and then a cap-
stone will crack under the weight of the superincum-
bent mass.   How close they fit, and how striking the
effect of their long radiations ! ''

The company listened very well up to this point.
When he began the strain of thoughts which follows,
a curious look went round The Teacups.

What a strange underground life is that which is
led by the organisms we call *trees !*   These great flut-
tering masses of leaves, stems, boughs, trunks, are not
the real trees.   *They* live underground, and what we
see are nothing more nor less than their *tails.*

The Mistress dropped her teaspoon.   Number Five
looked at the Doctor, whose face was very still and
sober.   The two Annexes giggled, or came very near it.

Yes, a tree is an underground creature, with its

tail in the air. All its intelligence is in its roots. All the senses it has are in its roots. Think what sagacity it shows in its search after food and drink! Somehow or other, the rootlets, which are its tentacles, find out that there is a brook at a moderate distance from the trunk of the tree, and they make for it with all their might. They find every crack in the rocks where there are a few grains of the nourishing substance they care for, and insinuate themselves into its deepest recesses. When spring and summer come, they let their tails grow, and delight in whisking them about in the wind, or letting them be whisked about by it; for these tails are poor passive things, with very little will of their own, and bend in whatever direction the wind chooses to make them. The leaves make a deal of noise whispering. I have sometimes thought I could understand them, as they talk with each other, and that they seemed to think they made the wind as they wagged forward and back. Remember what I say. The next time you see a tree waving in the wind, recollect that it is the tail of a great underground, many-armed, polypus-like creature, which is as proud of its caudal appendage, especially in summer-time, as a peacock of his gorgeous expanse of plumage.

Do you think there is anything so very odd about this idea? Once get it well into your heads, and you will find it renders the landscape wonderfully interesting. There are as many kinds of tree-tails as there are of tails to dogs and other quadrupeds. Study them as Daddy Gilpin studied them in his "Forest Scenery," but don't forget that they are only the appendage of the underground vegetable polypus, the true organism to which they belong.

He paused at this point, and we all drew long breaths, wondering what was coming next. There was no denying it, the " cracked Teacup " was clinking a little false, — so it seemed to the company. Yet, after all, the fancy was not delirious, — the mind could follow it well enough ;. let him go on.

What do you say to this? You have heard all sorts of things said in prose and verse about Niagara. Ask our young Doctor there what it reminds him of. Is n't it a giant putting his tongue out? How can you fail to see the resemblance? The continent is a great giant, and the northern half holds the head and shoulders. You can count the pulse of the giant wherever the tide runs up a creek ; but if you want to look at the giant's tongue, you must go to Niagara. If there were such a thing as a cosmic physician, I believe he could tell the state of the country's health, and the prospects of the mortality for the coming season, by careful inspection of the great tongue which Niagara is putting out for him, and has been showing to mankind ever since the first flint-shapers chipped their arrow-heads. You don't think the idea adds to the sublimity and associations of the cataract? I am sorry for that, but I can't help the suggestion. It is just as manifestly a tongue put out for inspection as if it had Nature's own label to that effect hung over it. I don't know whether you can see these things as clearly as I do. There are some people that never see anything, if it is as plain as a hole in a grindstone, until it is pointed out to them ; and some that can't see it then, and won't believe there is any hole till they 've poked their finger through it. I 've got a great many things to thank God for, but perhaps most of all that I can find something to admire, to wonder at, to set my fancy going, and to wind up my enthusiasm pretty much everywhere.

Look here! There are crowds of people whirled through our streets on these new-fashioned cars, with their witch-broomsticks overhead, — if they don't come from Salem, they ought to, — and not more than one in a dozen of these fish-eyed bipeds thinks or cares a nickel's worth about the miracle which is wrought for their convenience. They know that without hands or feet, without horses, without steam, so far as they can see, they are transported from place to place, and that there is nothing to account for it except the witch-broomstick and the iron or copper cobweb which they see stretched above them. What do they know or care about this last revelation of the omnipresent spirit of the material universe? We ought to go down on our knees when one of these mighty caravans, car after car, spins by us, under the mystic impulse which seems to know not whether its train is loaded or empty. We are used to force in the muscles of horses, in the expansive potency of steam, but here we have force stripped stark naked, — nothing but a filament to cover its nudity, — and yet showing its might in efforts that would task the working-beam of a ponderous steam-engine. I am thankful that in an age of cynicism I have not lost my reverence. Perhaps you would wonder to see how some very common sights impress me. I always take off my hat if I stop to speak to a stone-cutter at his work. " Why ? " do you ask me? Because I know that his is the only labor that is likely to endure. A score of centuries has not effaced the marks of the Greek's or the Roman's chisel on his block of marble. And now, before this

new manifestation of that form of cosmic vitality which
we call electricity, I feel like taking the posture of
the peasants listening to the Angelus. How near the
mystic effluence of mechanical energy brings us to the
divine source of all power and motion! In the old
mythology, the right hand of Jove held and sent forth
the lightning. So, in the record of the Hebrew prophets, did the right hand of Jehovah cast forth and
direct it. Was Nahum thinking of our far-off time
when he wrote, " The chariots shall rage in the streets,
they shall justle one against another in the broad ways :
they shall seem like torches, they shall run like the
lightnings " ?.

Number Seven had finished reading his paper. Two
bright spots in his cheeks showed that he had felt a
good deal in writing it, and the flush returned as he
listened to his own thoughts. Poor old fellow! The
" cracked Teacup " of our younger wits, — not yet
come to their full human sensibilities, — the " crank "
of vulgar tongues, the eccentric, the seventh son of a
seventh son, too often made the butt of thoughtless
pleasantry, was, after all, a fellow-creature, with flesh
and blood like the rest of us. The wild freaks of his
fancy did not hurt us, nor did they prevent him from
seeing many things justly, and perhaps sometimes
more vividly and acutely than if he were as sound as
the dullest of us.

The teaspoons tinkled loudly all round the table, as
he finished reading. The Mistress caught her breath.
I was afraid she was going to sob, but she took it out
in vigorous stirring of her tea. Will you believe that
I saw Number Five, with a sweet, approving smile on
her face all the time, brush her cheek with her hand-

kerchief? There must have been a tear stealing from beneath its eyelid. I hope Number Seven saw it. He is one of the two men at our table who most need the tender looks and tones of a woman. The Professor and I are *hors de combat;* the Counsellor is busy with his cases and his ambitions; the Doctor is probably in love with a microscope, and flirting with pathological specimens; but Number Seven and the Tutor are, I fear, both suffering from that worst of all famines, heart-hunger.

Do you remember that Number Seven said he never wrote a line of " poetry " in his life, except once when he was suffering from temporary weakness of body and mind? That is because he is a poet. If he had not been one, he would very certainly have taken to tinkling-rhymes. What should you think of the probable musical genius of a young man who was particularly fond of jingling a set of sleigh-bells? Should you expect him to turn out a Mozart or a Beethoven? Now, I think I recognize the poetical instinct in Number Seven, however imperfect may be its expression, and however he may be run away with at times by fantastic notions that come into his head. If fate had allotted him a helpful companion in the shape of a loving and intelligent wife, he might have been half cured of his eccentricities, and we should not have had to say, in speaking of him, " Poor fellow! " But since this cannot be, I am pleased that he should have been so kindly treated on the occasion of the reading of his paper. If he saw Number Five's tear, he will certainly fall in love with her. No matter if he does. Number Five is a kind of Circe who does not turn the victims of her enchantment into swine, but into lambs. I want to see Number Seven one of her little flock. I say "little." I suspect it is larger than most of us know. Anyhow, she can spare him sympathy and kindness and encouragement enough to keep him contented with himself and with her, and never miss the pulses of her loving life she lends him. It seems to be the errand of some women to give many people as much happiness as they have any right to in this world. If they concentrated their affection on one, they would give him more than any mortal could claim as his share. I saw Number Five watering her flowers, the other day. The watering-pot had one of those perforated heads, through which the water runs in many small streams. Every plant got its share: the proudest lily bent beneath the gentle shower; the lowliest daisy held its little face up for baptism. All were refreshed, none was flooded. Presently she took the perforated head, or "rose," from the neck of the watering-pot, and the full stream poured out in a round, solid column. It was almost too much for the poor geranium on which it fell, and it looked at one minute as if the roots would be laid bare, and perhaps the whole plant be washed out of the soil in which it was planted. What if Number Five should take off the "rose" that sprinkles her affections on so many, and pour them all on one? Can that ever be? If it can, life is worth living for him on whom her love may be lavished.

One of my neighbors, a thorough American, is much concerned about the growth of what he calls the "hard-handed aristocracy." He tells the following story : —

"I was putting up a fence about my yard, and employed a man of whom I knew something, — that he was industrious, temperate, and that he had a wife and children to support, — a worthy man, a native New Englander. I engaged him, I say, to dig some post-holes. My employee bought a new spade and scoop on purpose, and came to my place at the appointed time, and began digging. While he was at work, two men came over from a drinking-saloon, to which my residence is nearer than I could desire. One of them I had known as Mike Fagan, the other as Hans Schleimer. They looked at Hiram, my New Hampshire man, in a contemptuous and threatening way for a minute or so, when Fagan addressed him: —

"'And how much does the man pay yez by the hour?'

"'The gentleman does n't pay me by the hour,' said Hiram.

"'How mosh does he bay you by der vecks?' said Hans.

"'I don' know as that 's any of your business,' answered Hiram.

"'Faith, we 'll make it our business,' said Mike Fagan. 'We 're Knoights of Labor, we 'd have yez to know, and ye can't make yer bargains jist as ye loikes. We manes to know how mony hours ye worrks, and how much ye gets for it.'

"'*Knights* of Labor!' said I. 'Why, that is a kind of title of nobility, is n't it? I thought the laws of our country did n't allow titles of that kind. But if you have a right to be called knights, I suppose I ought to address you as such. Sir Michael, I congratulate you on the dignity you have attained. I hope Lady Fagan is getting on well with my shirts. Sir Hans, I pay my respects to your title. I trust that Lady Schleimer has got through that little difficulty between her ladyship and yourself in which the police court thought it necessary to intervene.'

"The two men looked at me. I weigh about a hundred and eighty pounds, and am well put together. Hiram was noted in his village as a 'rahstler.' But my face is rather pallid and peaked, and Hiram had something of the greenhorn look. The two men, who had been drinking, hardly knew what ground to take. They rather liked the sound of *Sir* Michael and *Sir* Hans. They did not know very well what to make of their wives as 'ladies.' They looked doubtful whether to take what had been said as a *casus belli* or not, but they wanted a pretext of some kind or other. Presently one of them saw a label on the scoop, or long-handled, spoon-like shovel, with which Hiram had been working.

"'Arrah, be jabers!' exclaimed Mike Fagan, 'but has n't he been a-tradin' wid Brown, the hardware fellah, that we boycotted! Grab it, Hans, and we'll carry it off and show it to the brotherhood.'

"The men made a move toward the implement.

"'You let that are scoop-shovel alone,' said Hiram.

"I stepped to his side. The Knights were combative, as their noble predecessors with the same title always were, and it was necessary to come to a *voie de fait.* My straight blow from the shoulder did for Sir Michael. Hiram treated Sir Hans to what is technically known as a cross-buttock.

"'Naow, Dutchman,' said Hiram, 'if you don't want to be planted in that are post-hole, y'd better take y'rself out o' this here piece of private property. "Dangerous passin'," as the sign-posts say, abaout these times.'

"Sir Michael went down half stunned by my expressive gesture; Sir Hans did not know whether his hip was out of joint or he had got a bad sprain; but they were both out of condition for further hostilities. Perhaps it was hardly fair to take advantage of their misfortunes to inflict a discourse upon them, but they had brought it on themselves, and we each of us gave them a piece of our mind.

"'I tell you what it is,' said Hiram, 'I'm a free and independent American citizen, and I an't a-gōn' to hev no man tȳrannize over me, if he doos call himself by one o' them noblemen's titles. Ef I can't work jes' as I choose, fur folks that wants me to work fur 'em and that I want to work fur, I might jes' as well go to Sibery and done with it. My gran'f'ther fit in Bunker Hill battle. I guess if our folks in them days did n't care no great abaout Lord Percy and Sir William Haowe, we an't a-gōn' to be scārt by Sir Michael Fagan and Sir Hans What's-his-name, nor no other fellahs that undertakes to be noblemen, and tells us common folks what we shall dew an' what we sha'n't. No, *sir!*'

"I took the opportunity to explain to Sir Michael and Sir Hans what it was our fathers fought for, and what is the meaning of liberty. If these noblemen did not like the country, they could go elsewhere. If they did n't like the laws, they had the ballot-box, and could choose new legislators. But as long as the laws existed they must obey them. I could not admit that, because they called themselves by the titles the Old World nobility thought so much of, they had a right to interfere in the agreements I entered into with my neighbor. I told Sir Michael that if he would go home and help Lady Fagan to saw and split the wood for her fire, he would be better employed than in med-

dling with my domestic arrangements. I advised Sir
Hans to ask Lady Schleimer for her bottle of spirits
to use as an embrocation for his lame hip. And so
my two visitors with the aristocratic titles staggered
off, and left us plain, untitled citizens, Hiram and myself, to set our posts, and consider the question whether
we lived in a free country or under the authority of a
self-constituted order of *quasi*-nobility."

It is a very curious fact that, with all our boasted
"free and equal" superiority over the communities of
the Old World, our people have the most enormous
appetite for Old World titles of distinction. Sir Michael and Sir Hans belong to one of the most extended
of the aristocratic orders. But we have also "Knights
and Ladies of Honor," and, what is still grander,
"Royal Conclave of Knights and Ladies," "Royal
Arcanum," and "Royal Society of Good Fellows,"
"Supreme Council," "Imperial Court," "Grand Pro-
tector," and "Grand Dictator," and so on. Nothing
less than "Grand" and "Supreme" is good enough
for the dignitaries of our associations of citizens.
Where does all this ambition for names without reali-
ties come from? Because a Knight of the Garter
wears a golden star, why does the worthy cordwainer,
who mends the shoes of his fellow-citizens, want to
wear a tin star, and take a name that had a meaning
as used by the representatives of ancient families, or
the men who had made themselves illustrious by their
achievements?

It appears to be a peculiarly American weakness.
The French republicans of the earlier period thought
the term *citizen* was good enough for anybody. At a
later period, "le Roi Citoyen" — the citizen king —

was a common title given to Louis Philippe. But nothing is too grand for the American, in the way of titles. The proudest of them all signify absolutely nothing. They do not stand for ability, for public service, for social importance, for large possessions; but, on the contrary, are oftenest found in connection with personalities to which they are supremely inapplicable. We can hardly afford to quarrel with a national habit which, if lightly handled, may involve us in serious domestic difficulties. The "Right Worshipful" functionary whose equipage stops at my back gate, and whose services are indispensable to the health and comfort of my household, is a dignitary whom I must not offend. I must speak with proper deference to the lady who is scrubbing my floors, when I remember that her husband, who saws my wood, carries a string of high-sounding titles which would satisfy a Spanish nobleman.

After all, every people must have its own forms of ostentation, pretence, and vulgarity. The ancient Romans had theirs, the English and the French have theirs as well, — why should not we Americans have ours? Educated and refined persons must recognize frequent internal conflicts between the "*Homo sum*" of Terence and the "*Odi ignobile vulgus*" of Horace. The nobler sentiment should be that of every true American, and it is in that direction that our best civilization is constantly tending.

We were waited on by a new girl, the other evening. Our pretty maiden had left us for a visit to some relative, — so the Mistress said. I do sincerely hope she will soon come back, for we all like to see her flitting round the table.

I don't know what to make of it. I had it all laid
out in my mind. With such a company there must
be a love-story. Perhaps there will be, but there may
be new combinations of the elements which are to
make it up, and here is a bud among the full-blown
flowers to which I must devote a little space.

Delilah.

I must call her by the name we gave her after she
had trimmed the Samson locks of our Professor. Delilah is a puzzle to most of us. A pretty creature, —
dangerously pretty to be in a station not guarded by
all the protective arrangements which surround the
maidens of a higher social order. It takes a strong
cage to keep in a tiger or a grizzly bear, but what iron
bars, what barbed wires, can keep out the smooth and
subtle enemy that finds out the cage where beauty is
imprisoned ? Our young Doctor is evidently attracted
by the charming maiden who serves him and us so
modestly and so gracefully. Fortunately, the Mistress
never loses sight of her. If she were her own daughter, she could not be more watchful of all her movements. And yet I do not believe that Delilah needs
all this overlooking. If I am not mistaken, she
knows how to take care of herself, and could be
trusted anywhere, in any company, without a duenna.
She has a history, — I feel sure of it. She has been
trained and taught as young persons of higher position
in life are brought up, and does not belong in the
humble station in which we find her. But inasmuch
as the Mistress says nothing about her antecedents,
we do not like to be too inquisitive. The two Annexes are, it is plain, very curious about her. I cannot wonder. They are both good-looking girls, but

Delilah is prettier than either of them. My sight is not so good as it was, but I can see the way in which the eyes of the young people follow each other about plainly enough to set me thinking as to what is going on in the thinking marrow behind them. The young Doctor's follow Delilah as she glides round the table, — they look into hers whenever they get a chance; but the girl's never betray any consciousness of it, so far as I can see. There is no mistaking the interest with which the two Annexes watch all this. Why should n't they, I should like to know? The Doctor is a bright young fellow, and wants nothing but a bald spot and a wife to find himself in a comfortable family practice. One of the Annexes, as I have said, has had thoughts of becoming a doctress. I don't think the Doctor would want his wife to practise medicine, for reasons which I will not stop to mention. Such a partnership sometimes works wonderfully well, as in one well-known instance where husband and wife are both eminent in the profession ; but our young Doctor has said to me that he had rather see his wife, — if he ever should have one, — at the piano than at the dissecting-table. Of course the Annexes know nothing about this, and they may think, as he professed himself willing to lecture on medicine to women, he might like to take one of his pupils as a helpmeet.

If it were not for our Delilah's humble position, I don't see why she would not be a good match for any young man. But then it is so hard to take a young woman from so very lowly a condition as that of a "waitress" that it would require a deal of courage to venture on such a step. If we could only find out that she is a princess in disguise, so to speak, — that

is, a young person of presentable connections as well
as pleasing looks and manners; that she has had an
education of some kind, as we suspected when she
blushed on hearing herself spoken of as a "*gentille
petite*," why, then everything would be all right, the
young Doctor would have plain sailing, — that is, if
he is in love with her, and if she fancies him, — and I
should find my love-story, — the one I expected, but
not between the parties I had thought would be mat-
ing with each other.

Dear little Delilah! Lily of the valley, growing in
the shade now, — perhaps better there until her petals
drop; and yet if she is all I often fancy she is, how
her youthful presence would illuminate and sweeten a
household! There is not one of us who does not feel
interested in her, — not one of us who would not be
delighted at some Cinderella transformation which
would show her in the setting Nature meant for her
favorite.

The fancy of Number Seven about the witches'
broomsticks suggested to one of us the following
poem : —

THE BROOMSTICK TRAIN; OR, THE RETURN OF THE WITCHES.

Look out! Look out, boys! Clear the track!
The witches are here! They 've all come back!
They hanged them high, — No use! No use!
What cares a witch for a hangman's noose?
They buried them deep, but they would n't lie still,
For cats and witches are hard to kill;
They swore they should n't and would n't die, —
Books said they did, but they lie! they lie!

— A couple of hundred years, or so,
They had knocked about in the world below,
When an Essex Deacon dropped in to call,
And a homesick feeling seized them all ;
For he came from a place they knew full well,
And many a tale he had to tell.
They long to visit the haunts of men,
To see the old dwellings they knew again,
And ride on their broomsticks all around
Their wide domain of unhallowed ground.

In Essex county there 's many a roof
Well known to him of the cloven hoof ;
The small square windows are full in view
Which the midnight hags went sailing through,
On their well-trained broomsticks mounted high,
Seen like shadows against the sky ;
Crossing the track of owls and bats,
Hugging before them their coal-black cats.

Well did they know, those gray old wives,
The sights we see in our daily drives :
Shimmer of lake and shine of sea,
Brown's bare hill with its lonely tree,
(It was n't then as we see it now,
With one scant scalp-lock to shade its brow;)
Dusky nooks in the Essex woods,
Dark, dim, Dante-like solitudes,
Where the tree-toad watches the sinuous snake
Glide through his forests of fern and brake ;
Ipswich River ; its old stone bridge ;
Far off Andover's Indian Ridge,
And many a scene where history tells
Some shadow of bygone terror dwells, —
Of " Norman's Woe " with its tale of dread,
Of the Screeching Woman of Marblehead,
(The fearful story that turns men pale :
Don't bid me tell it, — my speech would fail.)

Who would not, will not, if he can,
Bathe in the breezes of fair Cape Ann, —

Rest in the bowers her bays enfold,
Loved by the sachems and squaws of old ?
Home where the white magnolias bloom,
Sweet with the bayberry's chaste perfume,
Hugged by the woods and kissed by the sea !
Where is the Eden like to thee ?

For that " couple of hundred years, or so,"
There had been no peace in the world below ;
The witches still grumbling, " It is n't fair ;
Come, give us a taste of the upper air !
We 've had enough of your sulphur springs,
And the evil odor that round them clings ;
We long for a drink that is cool and nice, —
Great buckets of water with Wenham ice ;
We 've served you well up-stairs, you know ;
You 're a good old — fellow — come, let us go ! "

I don't feel sure of his being good,
But he happened to be in a pleasant mood, —
As fiends with their skins full sometimes are, —
(He 'd been drinking with " roughs " at a Boston bar.)
So what does he do but up and shout
To a graybeard turnkey, " Let 'em out ! "

To mind his orders was all he knew ;
The gates swung open, and out they flew.
" Where are our broomsticks ? " the beldams cried.
" Here are your broomsticks," an imp replied.
" They 've been in — the place you know — so long
They smell of brimstone uncommon strong ;
But they 've gained by being left alone, —
Just look, and you 'll see how tall they 've grown."
— " And where is my cat ? " a vixen squalled.
" Yes, where are our cats ? " the witches bawled,
And began to call them all by name :
As fast as they called the cats, they came :
There was bob-tailed Tommy and long-tailed Tim,
And wall-eyed Jacky and green-eyed Jim,
And splay-foot Benny and slim-legged Beau,
And Skinny and Squally, and Jerry and Joe,

And many another that came at call, —
It would take too long to count them all.
All black, — one could hardly tell which was which,
But every cat knew his own old witch ;
And she knew hers as hers knew her, —
Ah, did n't they curl their tails and purr !

No sooner the withered hags were free
Than out they swarmed for a midnight spree ;
I could n't tell all they did in rhymes,
But the Essex people had dreadful times.
The Swampscott fishermen still relate
How a strange sea-monster stole their bait ;
How their nets were tangled in loops and knots,
And they found dead crabs in their lobster-pots.
Poor Danvers grieved for her blasted crops,
And Wilmington mourned over mildewed hops.
A blight played havoc with Beverly beans, —
It was all the work of those hateful queans !
A dreadful panic began at " Pride's,"
Where the witches stopped in their midnight rides,
And there rose strange rumors and vague alarms
'Mid the peaceful dwellers at Beverly Farms.

Now when the Boss of the Beldams found
That without his leave they were ramping round,
He called, — they could hear him twenty miles,
From Chelsea beach to the Misery Isles ;
The deafest old granny knew his tone
Without the trick of the telephone.
" Come here, you witches !   Come here ! " says he, —
" At your games of old, without asking me !
I 'll give you a little job to do
That will keep you stirring, you godless crew ! "

They came, of course, at their master's call,
The witches, the broomsticks, the cats, and all ;
He led the hags to a railway train
The horses were trying to drag in vain.
" Now, then," says he, " you 've had your fun,
And here are the cars you 've got to run.

The driver may just unhitch his team,
We don't want horses, we don't want steam ;
You may keep your old black cats to hug,
But the loaded train you 've got to lug."

Since then on many a car you 'll see
A broomstick plain as plain can be ;
On every stick there 's a witch astride, —
The string you see to her leg is tied.
She will do a mischief if she can,
But the string is held by a careful man,
And whenever the evil-minded witch
Would cut some caper, he gives a twitch.
As for the hag, you can't see her,
But hark ! you can hear her black cat's purr,
And now and then, as a car goes by,
You may catch a gleam from her wicked eye.

Often you 've looked on a rushing train,
But just what moved it was not so plain.
It could n't be those wires above,
For they could neither pull nor shove ;
Where was the motor that made it go
You could n't guess, *but now you know.*

Remember my rhymes when you ride again
On the rattling rail by the broomstick train !

X

In my last report of our talks over the teacups I had something to say of the fondness of our people for titles. Where did the anti-republican, anti-democratic passion for swelling names come from, and how long has it been naturalized among us?

A striking instance of it occurred at about the end of the last century. It was at that time there appeared among us one of the most original and singular personages to whom America has given birth. Many of our company, — many of my readers, — are well acquainted with his name, and not wholly ignorant of his history. They will not object to my giving some particulars relating to him, which, if not new to them, will be new to others into whose hands these pages may fall.

Timothy Dexter, the first claimant of a title of nobility among the people of the United States of America, was born in the town of Malden, near Boston. He served an apprenticeship as a leather-dresser, saved some money, got some more with his wife, began trading and speculating, and became at last rich, for those days. His most famous business enterprise was that of sending an invoice of warming-pans to the West Indies. A few tons of ice would have seemed to promise a better return; but in point of fact, he tells us, the warming-pans were found useful in the manufacture of sugar, and brought him in a handsome profit.   His ambition rose with his fortune.   He purchased a large and stately house in Newburyport, and proceeded to embellish and furnish it according to the dictates of his taste and fancy.   In the grounds about his house, he caused to be erected between forty and fifty wooden statues of great men and allegorical figures, together with four lions and one lamb.   Among these images were two statues of Dexter himself, one of which held a label with a characteristic inscription. His house was ornamented with minarets, adorned with golden balls, and surmounted by a large gilt eagle.   He equipped it with costly furniture, with paintings, and a library.   He went so far as to procure the services of a poet laureate, whose business it seems to have been to sing his praises.   Surrounded with splendors like these, the plain title of " Mr." Dexter would have been infinitely too mean and common.   He therefore boldly took the step of self-ennobling, and gave himself forth — as he said, obeying " the voice of the people at large " — as " Lord Timothy Dexter," by which appellation he has ever since been known to the American public.

If to be the pioneer in the introduction of Old World titles into republican America can confer a claim to be remembered by posterity, Lord Timothy Dexter has a right to historic immortality.   If the true American spirit shows itself most clearly in boundless self-assertion, Timothy Dexter is the great original American egotist.   If to throw off the shackles of Old World pedantry, and defy the paltry rules and examples of grammarians and rhetoricians, is the special province and the chartered privilege of the American writer, Timothy Dexter is the founder of a new school, which tramples under foot the conventionalities that hampered and subjugated the faculties of the poets, the dramatists, the historians, essayists, story-tellers, orators, of the worn-out races which have preceded the great American people.

The material traces of the first American nobleman's existence have nearly disappeared. The house is still standing, but the statues, the minarets, the arches, and the memory of the great Lord Timothy Dexter live chiefly in tradition, and in the work which he bequeathed to posterity, and of which I shall say a few words. It is unquestionably a thoroughly original production, and I fear that some readers may think I am trifling with them when I am quoting it literally. I am going to make a strong claim for Lord Timothy as against other candidates for a certain elevated position.

Thomas Jefferson is commonly recognized as the first to proclaim before the world the political independence of America. It is not so generally agreed upon as to who was the first to announce the literary emancipation of our country.

One of Mr. Emerson's biographers has claimed that his Phi Beta Kappa Oration was our Declaration of Literary Independence. But Mr. Emerson did not cut himself loose from all the traditions of Old World scholarship. He spelled his words correctly, he constructed his sentences grammatically. He adhered to the slavish rules of propriety, and observed the reticences which a traditional delicacy has considered inviolable in decent society, European and Oriental alike. When he wrote poetry, he commonly selected subjects which seemed adapted to poetical treatment, — apparently thinking that all things were not equally calculated to inspire the true poet's genius. Once, indeed, he ventured to refer to " the meal in the firkin, the milk in the pan," but he chiefly restricted himself to subjects such as a fastidious conventionalism would approve as having a certain fitness for poetical treatment. He was not always so careful as he might have been in the rhythm and rhyme of his verse, but in the main he recognized the old established laws which have been accepted as regulating both. In short, with all his originality, he worked in Old World harness, and cannot be considered as the creator of a truly American, self-governed, self-centred, absolutely independent style of thinking and writing, knowing no law but its own sovereign will and pleasure.

A stronger claim might be urged for Mr. Whitman. He takes into his hospitable vocabulary words which no English dictionary recognizes as belonging to the language, — words which will be looked for in vain outside of his own pages. He accepts as poetical subjects all things alike, common and unclean, without discrimination, miscellaneous as the contents of the great sheet which Peter saw let down from heaven. He carries the principle of republicanism through the whole world of created objects. He will " thread a thread through [his] poems," he tells us, " that no one thing in the universe is inferior to another thing." No man has ever asserted the surpassing dignity and importance of the American citizen so boldly and freely as Mr. Whitman. He calls himself " teacher of the unquenchable creed, namely, egotism." He begins one of his chants, " I celebrate myself," but he takes us all in as partners in his self-glorification. He believes in America as the new Eden.

" A world primal again, — vistas of glory incessant and branch-
ing,
A new race dominating previous ones and grander far,
New politics — new literature and religious — new inventions
and arts."

Of the new literature he himself has furnished
specimens which certainly have all the originality he
can claim for them. So far as egotism is concerned,
he was clearly anticipated by the titled personage to
whom I have referred, who says of himself, " I am the
first in the East, the first in the West, and the greatest philosopher in the Western world." But while
Mr. Whitman divests himself of a part of his baptismal name, the distinguished New Englander thus
announces his proud position : " Ime the first Lord in
the younited States of A mercary Now of Newburyport. it is the voice of the peopel and I cant Help it."
This extract is from his famous little book called " A
Pickle for the Knowing Ones." As an inventor of
a new American style he goes far beyond Mr. Whitman, who, to be sure, cares little for the dictionary,
and makes his own rules of rhythm, so far as there is
any rhythm in his sentences. But Lord Timothy
spells to suit himself, and in place of employing punctuation as it is commonly used, prints a separate page
of periods, colons, semicolons, commas, notes of inter-
rogation and of admiration, with which the reader is
requested to " peper and soolt " the book as he pleases.

I am afraid that Mr. Emerson and Mr. Whitman
must yield the claim of declaring American literary
independence to Lord Timothy Dexter, who not only
taught his countrymen that they need not go to the
Heralds' College to authenticate their titles of nobility, but also that they were at perfect liberty to spell

just as they liked, and to write without troubling themselves about stops of any kind. In writing what I suppose he intended for poetry, he did not even take the pains to break up his lines into lengths to make them look like verse, as may be seen by the following specimen : —

WONDER OF WONDERS !

How great the soul is ! Do not you all wonder and admire to see and behold and hear ? Can you all believe half the truth, and admire to hear the wonders how great the soul is — only behold — past finding out ! Only see how large the soul is ! that if a man is drowned in the sea what a great bubble comes up out of the top of the water. . . . The bubble is the soul.

I confess that I am not in sympathy with some of the movements that accompany the manifestations of American social and literary independence. I do not like the assumption of titles of Lords and Knights by plain citizens of a country which prides itself on recognizing simple manhood and womanhood as sufficiently entitled to respect without these unnecessary additions. I do not like any better the familiar, and as it seems to me rude, way of speaking of our fellow-citizens who are entitled to the common courtesies of civilized society. I never thought it dignified or even proper for a President of the United States to call himself, or to be called by others, "Frank" Pierce. In the first place I had to look in a biographical dictionary to find out whether his baptismal name was Franklin, or Francis, or simply Frank, for I think children are sometimes christened with this abbreviated name. But it is too much in the style of Cowper's unpleasant acquaintance : —

> " The man who hails you Tom or Jack,
> And proves by thumping on your back
> How he esteems your merit."

I should not like to hear our past chief magistrates spoken of as Jack Adams or Jim Madison, and it would have been only as a political partisan that I should have reconciled myself to "Tom" Jefferson.   So, in spite of " Ben " Jonson, " Tom " Moore, and " Jack " Sheppard, I prefer to speak of a fellow-citizen already venerable by his years, entitled to respect by useful services to his country, and recognized by many as the prophet of a new poetical dispensation, with the customary title of adults rather than by the free and easy school-boy abbreviation with which he introduced himself many years ago to the public.   As for his rhapsodies, Number Seven, our " cracked Teacup, " says they sound to him like " fugues played on a big organ which has been struck by lightning."   So far as concerns literary independence, if we understand by that term the getting rid of our subjection to British criticism, such as it was in the days when the question was asked, " Who reads an American book ? " we may consider it pretty well established.   If it means dispensing with punctuation, coining words at will, self-revelation unrestrained by a sense of what is decorous, declamations in which everything is glorified without being idealized, "poetry" in which the reader must make the rhythms which the poet has not made for him, then I think we had better continue literary colonists.   I shrink from a lawless independence to which all the virile energy and trampling audacity of Mr. Whitman fail to reconcile me.   But there is room for everybody and everything in our huge hemisphere. Young America is like a three-year-old colt with his

saddle and bridle just taken off. The first thing he
wants to do is to *roll*. He is a droll object, sprawling
in the grass with his four hoofs in the air; but he
likes it, and it won't harm us. So let him roll, — let
him roll!

Of all The Teacups around our table, Number Five
is the one who is the object of the greatest interest.
Everybody wants to be her friend, and she has room
enough in her hospitable nature to find a place for
every one who is worthy of the privilege. The difficulty is that it is so hard to be her friend without becoming her lover. I have said before that she turns
the subjects of her Circe-like enchantment, not into
swine, but into lambs. The Professor and I move
round among her lambs, the docile and amiable flock
that come and go at her bidding, that follow her footsteps, and are content to live in the sunshine of her
smile and within reach of the music of her voice. I
like to get her away from their amiable bleatings; I
love to talk with her about life, of which she has seen
a great deal, for she knows what it is to be an idol in
society and the centre of her social circle. It might
be a question whether women or men most admire and
love her. With her own sex she is always helpful,
sympathizing, tender, charitable, sharing their griefs
as well as taking part in their pleasures. With men
it has seemed to make little difference whether they
were young or old: all have found her the same sweet,
generous, unaffected companion; fresh enough in feeling for the youngest, deep enough in the wisdom of
the heart for the oldest. She does not pretend to be
youthful, nor does she trouble herself that she has seen
the roses of more Junes than many of the younger

women who gather round her.   She has not had to
say,

Comme je regrette
Mon bras si dodu,

for her arm has never lost its roundness, and her face
is one of those that cannot be cheated of their charm
even if they live long enough to look upon the grown
up grandchildren of their coevals.

It is a wonder how Number Five can find the time
to be so much to so many friends of both sexes, in
spite of the fact that she is one of the most insatiable
of readers.   She not only reads, but she remembers;
she not only remembers, but she records, for her own
use and pleasure, and for the delight and profit of
those who are privileged to look over her note-books.
Number Five, as I think I have said before, has not
the ambition to figure as an authoress.   That she
could write most agreeably is certain.   I have seen
letters of hers to friends which prove that clearly
enough.   Whether she would find prose or verse the
most natural mode of expression I cannot say, but I
know she is passionately fond of poetry, and I should
not be surprised if, laid away among the pressed pan-
sies and roses of past summers, there were poems, —
songs, perhaps, of her own, which she sings to herself
with her fingers touching the piano; for to that she
tells her secrets in tones sweet as the ring-dove's call
to her mate.

I am afraid it may be suggested that I am drawing
Number Five's portrait too nearly after some model
who is unconsciously sitting for it; but have n't I told
you that you must not look for flesh and blood personalities behind or beneath my Teacups?   I am not
going to make these so lifelike that you will be saying,

This is Mr., or Miss, or Mrs. So-and-So. My readers must remember that there are very many pretty, sweet, amiable girls and women sitting at their pianos, and finding chords to the music of their heart-strings. If I have pictured Number Five as one of her lambs might do it, I have succeeded in what I wanted to accomplish. Why don't I describe her person? If I do, some gossip or other will be sure to say, "Oh, he means *her*, of course," and find a name to match the pronoun.

It is strange to see how we are all coming to depend upon the friendly aid of Number Five in our various perplexities. The Counsellor asked her opinion in one of those cases where a divorce was too probable, but a reconciliation was possible. It takes a woman to sound a woman's heart, and she found there was still love enough under the ruffled waters to warrant the hope of peace and tranquillity. The young Doctor went to her for counsel in the case of a hysteric girl possessed with the idea that she was a born poetess, and covering whole pages of foolscap with senseless outbursts, which she wrote in paroxysms of wild excitement, and read with a rapture of self-admiration which there was nothing in her verses to justify or account for. How sweetly Number Five dealt with that poor deluded sister in her talk with the Doctor! "Yes," she said to him, "nothing can be fuller of vanity, self-worship, and self-deception. But we must be very gentle with her. I knew a young girl tormented with aspirations, and possessed by a belief that she was meant for a higher place than that which fate had assigned her, who needed wholesome advice, just as this poor young thing does. She did not ask for it, and it was not offered. Alas, alas! 'no man

cared for her soul,'—no man nor woman either. She
was in her early teens, and the thought of her earthly
future, as it stretched out before her, was more than
she could bear, and she sought the presence of her
Maker to ask the meaning of her abortive existence.
— We will talk it over. I will help you take care of
this child."

The Doctor was thankful to have her assistance in
a case with which he would have found it difficult to
deal if he had been left to his unaided judgment,
and between them the young girl was safely piloted
through the perilous straits in which she came near
shipwreck.

I know that it is commonly said of her that every
male friend of hers must become her lover unless he
is already lassoed by another. *Il faut passer par là.*
The young Doctor is, I think, safe, for I am convinced
that he is bewitched with Delilah. Since she has left
us, he has seemed rather dejected ; I feel sure that he
misses her. We all do, but he more seriously than
the rest of us. I have said that I cannot tell whether
the Counsellor is to be counted as one of Number
Five's lambs or not, but he evidently admires her, and
if he is not fascinated, looks as if he were very near
that condition.

It was a more delicate matter about which the
Tutor talked with her. Something which she had
pleasantly said to him about the two Annexes led him
to ask her, more or less seriously, it may be remembered, about the fitness of either of them to be the
wife of a young man in his position. She talked so
sensibly, as it seemed to him, about it that he continued the conversation, and, shy as he was, became quite
easy and confidential in her company. The Tutor is

not only a poet, but is a great reader of the poetry of many languages. It so happened that Number Five was puzzled, one day, in reading a sonnet of Petrarch, and had recourse to the Tutor to explain the difficult passage. She found him so thoroughly instructed, so clear, so much interested, so ready to impart knowledge, and so happy in his way of doing it, that she asked him if he would not allow her the privilege of reading an Italian author under his guidance, now and then.

The Tutor found Number Five an apt scholar, and something more than that; for while, as a linguist, he was, of course, her master, her intelligent comments brought out the beauties of an author in a way to make the text seem like a different version. They did not always confine themselves to the book they were reading. Number Five showed some curiosity about the Tutor's relations with the two Annexes. She suggested whether it would not be well to ask one or both of them in to take part in their readings. The Tutor blushed and hesitated. "Perhaps *you* would like to ask one of them," said Number Five. "Which one shall it be?" "It makes no difference to me which," he answered, "but I do not see that we need either." Number Five did not press the matter further. So the young Tutor and Number Five read together pretty regularly, and came to depend upon their meeting over a book as one of their stated seasons of enjoyment. He is so many years younger than she is that I do not suppose he will have to pass *par là*, as most of her male friends have done. I tell her sometimes that she reminds me of my Alma Mater, always young, always fresh in her attractions, with her scholars all round her, many of them graduates, or to graduate sooner or later.

What do I mean by graduates? Why, that they have made love to her, and would be entitled to her diploma, if she gave a parchment to each one of them who had had the courage to face the inevitable. About the Counsellor I am, as I have said, in doubt. Who wrote that " I Like You and I Love You," which we found in the sugar - bowl the other day? Was it a graduate who had felt the " icy dagger," or only a candidate for graduation who was afraid of it? So completely does she subjugate those who come under her influence that I believe she looks upon it as a mat- ter of course that the fateful question will certainly come, often after a brief acquaintance. She confessed as much to me, who am in her confidence, and not a candidate for graduation from her academy. Her graduates — her lambs I called them — are commonly faithful to her, and though now and then one may have gone off and sulked in solitude, most of them feel kindly to her, and to those who have shared the common fate of her suitors. I do really believe that some of them would be glad to see her captured by any one, if such there can be, who is worthy of her. She is the best of friends, they say, but can she *love* anybody, as so many other women do, or seem to? Why should n't our Musician, who is evidently fond of her company, and sings and plays duets with her, steal her heart as Piozzi stole that of the pretty and bright Mrs. Thrale, as so many music-teachers have run away with their pupils' hearts? At present she seems to be getting along very placidly and content- edly with her young friend the Tutor. There is some- thing quite charming in their relations with each other. He knows many things she does not, for he is reck- oned one of the most learned in his literary specialty

of all the young men of his time; and it can be a
question of only a few years when some first-class pro-
fessorship will be offered him. She, on the other hand,
has so much more experience, so much more practical wisdom, than he has that he consults her on many
every-day questions, as he did, or made believe do,
about that of making love to one of the two Annexes.
I had thought, when we first sat round the tea-table,
that she was good for the bit of romance I wanted;
but since she has undertaken to be a kind of half-
maternal friend to the young Tutor, I am afraid I
shall have to give her up as the heroine of a romantic
episode. It would be a pity if there were nothing to
commend these papers to those who take up this periodical but essays, more or less significant, on subjects
more or less interesting to the jaded and impatient
readers of the numberless stories and entertaining
articles which crowd the magazines of this prolific
period. A whole year of a tea-table as large as ours
without a single love passage in it would be discredit-
able to the company. We must find one, or make
one, before the tea-things are taken away and the
table is no longer spread.

The Dictator turns preacher.

We have so many light and playful talks over the
teacups that some readers may be surprised to find us
taking up the most serious and solemn subject which
can occupy a human intelligence. The sudden appearance among our New England Protestants of the
doctrine of purgatory as a possibility, or even proba-
bility, has startled the descendants of the Puritans.
It has naturally led to a reconsideration of the doctrine of eternal punishment. It is on that subject

that Number Five and I have talked together. I love
to listen to her, for she talks from the promptings of
a true woman's heart. I love to talk to her, for I
learn my own thoughts better in that way than in any
other. "*L'appétit vient en mangeant*," the French
saying has it. "*L'esprit vient en causant ;*" that is,
if one can find the right persons to talk with.

The subject which has specially interested Number
Five and myself, of late, was suggested to me in the
following way.

Some two years ago I received a letter from a
clergyman who bears by inheritance one of the most
distinguished names which has done honor to the
American "Orthodox" pulpit. This letter requested
of me "a contribution to a proposed work which was
to present in their own language the views of 'many
men of many minds' on the subject of future punishment. It was in my mind to let the public hear not
only from professional theologians, but from other
professions, as from jurists on the alleged but disputed
value of the hangman's whip overhanging the witness-
box, and from physicians on the working of beliefs
about the future life in the minds of the dangerously
sick. And I could not help thinking what a good
thing it would be to draw out [the present writer]
upon his favorite borderland between the spiritual
and the material." The communication came to me,
as the writer reminds me in a recent letter, at a
"painfully inopportune time," and though it was
courteously answered, was not made the subject of a
special reply.

This request confers upon me a certain right to express my opinion on this weighty subject without fear
and without reproach even from those who might be

ready to take offence at one of the laity for meddling
with pulpit questions. It shows also that this is not a
dead issue in our community, as some of the younger
generation seem to think. There are some, there may
be many, who would like to hear what impressions
one has received on the subject referred to, after a
long life in which he has heard and read a great deal
about the matter. There is a certain gravity in the
position of one who is, in the order of nature, very
near the undiscovered country. A man who has
passed his eighth decade feels as if he were already in
the antechamber of the apartments which he may be
called to occupy in the house of many mansions. His
convictions regarding the future of our race are likely
to be serious, and his expressions not lightly uttered.
The question my correspondent suggests is a tremendous one. No other interest compares for one moment with that belonging to it. It is not only ourselves that it concerns, but all whom we love or ever
have loved, all our human brotherhood, as well as our
whole idea of the Being who made us and the relation
in which He stands to his creatures. In attempting
to answer my correspondent's question, I shall no
doubt repeat many things I have said before in different forms, on different occasions. This is no more
than every clergyman does habitually, and it would be
hard if I could not have the same license which the
professional preacher enjoys so fully.

Number Five and I have occasionally talked on religious questions, and discovered many points of agree-
ment in our views. Both of us grew up under the old
" Orthodox " or Calvinistic system of belief. Both of
us accepted it in our early years as a part of our education. Our experience is a common one. William

Cullen Bryant says of himself, " The Calvinistic system of divinity I adopted of course, as I heard nothing else taught from the pulpit, and supposed it to be the accepted belief of the religious world." But it was not the " five points " which remained in the young poet's memory and shaped his higher life. It was the influence of his mother that left its permanent impression after the questions and answers of the Assembly's Catechism had faded out, or remained in memory only as fossil survivors of an extinct or fast-disappearing theological formation. The important point for him, as for so many other children of Puritan descent, was not his father's creed, but his mother's character, precepts, and example. " She was a person," he says, " of excellent practical sense, of a quick and sensitive moral judgment, and had no patience with any form of deceit or duplicity. Her prompt condemnation of injustice, even in those instances in which it is tolerated by the world, made a strong impression upon me in early life; and if, in the discussion of public questions, I have in my riper age endeavored to keep in view the great rule of right without much regard to persons, it has been owing in a great degree to the force of her example, which taught me never to countenance a wrong because others did."

I have quoted this passage because it was an experience not wholly unlike my own, and in certain respects like that of Number Five. To grow up in a narrow creed and to grow out of it is a tremendous trial of one's nature. There is always a bond of fellowship between those who have been through such an ordeal.

The experiences we have had in common naturally

lead us to talk over the theological questions which at
this time are constantly presenting themselves to the
public, not only in the books and papers expressly devoted to that class of subjects, but in many of the
newspapers and popular periodicals, from the week-
lies to the quarterlies. The pulpit used to lay down
the law to the pews ; at the present time, it is of more
consequence what the pews think than what the minister does, for the obvious reason that the pews can
change their minister, and often do, whereas the minister cannot change the pews, or can do so only to a
very limited extent. The preacher's garment is cut
according to the pattern of that of the hearers, for the
most part. Thirty years ago, when I was writing on
theological subjects, I came in for a very pretty share
of abuse, such as it was the fashion of that day, at
least in certain quarters, to bestow upon those who
were outside of the high-walled enclosures in which
many persons, not naturally unamiable or exclusive,
found themselves imprisoned. Since that time what
changes have taken place! Who will believe that a
well-behaved and reputable citizen could have been
denounced as a " moral parricide," because he attacked
some of the doctrines in which he was supposed to
have been brought up ? A single thought should have
prevented the masked theologian who abused his in-
cognito from using such libellous language.

Much, and in many families most, of the religious
teaching of children is committed to the mother. The
experience of William Cullen Bryant, which I have
related in his own words, is that of many New England children. Now, the sternest dogmas that ever
came from a soul cramped or palsied by an obsolete
creed become wonderfully softened in passing between

the lips of a mother. The cruel doctrine at which all
but case-hardened "professionals" shudder comes out,
as she teaches and illustrates it, as unlike its original
as the milk which a peasant mother gives her babe is
unlike the coarse food which furnishes her nourishment. The virus of a cursing creed is rendered comparatively harmless by the time it reaches the young
sinner in the nursery. Its effects fall as far short of
what might have been expected from its virulence as
the pearly vaccine vesicle falls short of the terrors of
the confluent small - pox. Controversialists should
therefore be careful (for their own sakes, for they
hurt nobody so much as themselves) how they use
such terms as " parricide" as characterizing those who
do not agree in all points with the fathers whom or
whose memory they honor and venerate. They might
with as much propriety call them matricides, if they
did not agree with the milder teachings of their mothers. I can imagine Jonathan Edwards in the nursery
with his three-year-old child upon his knee. The
child looks up to his face and says to him, —

" Papa, nurse tells me that you say God hates me
worse than He hates one of those horrid ugly snakes
that crawl all round. Does God hate me so?"

" Alas! my child, it is but too true. So long as
you are out of Christ you are as a viper, and worse
than a viper, in his sight."

By and by, Mrs. Edwards, one of the loveliest of
women and sweetest of mothers, comes into the nursery. The child is crying.

" What is the matter, my darling?"

"Papa has been telling me that God hates me
worse than a snake."

Poor, gentle, poetical, sensitive, spiritual, almost

celestial Mrs. Jonathan Edwards! On the one hand
the terrible sentence conceived, written down, given to
the press, by the child's father; on the other side the
trusting child looking up at her, and all the mother
pleading in her heart against the frightful dogma of
her revered husband. Do you suppose she left that
poison to rankle in the tender soul of her darling?
Would it have been moral parricide for a son of the
great divine to have repudiated the doctrine which
degraded his blameless infancy to the condition and
below the condition of the reptile? *Was* it parricide
in the second or third degree when his descendant
struck out that venomous sentence from the page in
which it stood as a monument to what depth Christian
heathenism could sink under the teaching of the great
master of logic and spiritual inhumanity? It is too
late to be angry about the abuse a well-meaning
writer received thirty years ago. The whole atmosphere has changed since then. It is mere childish-
ness to expect men to believe as their fathers did;
that is, if they have any minds of their own. The
world is a whole generation older and wiser than
when the father was of his son's age.

So far as I have observed persons nearing the end
of life, the Roman Catholics understand the business
of dying better than Protestants. They have an expert by them, armed with spiritual specifics, in which
they both, patient and priestly ministrant, place im-
plicit trust. Confession, the Eucharist, Extreme Unc-
tion, — these all inspire a confidence which without
this symbolism is too apt to be wanting in over-sensi-
tive natures. They have been peopled in earlier years
with ghastly spectres of avenging fiends, moving in a
sleepless world of devouring flames and smothering

exhalations; where nothing lives but the sinner, the fiends, and the reptiles who help to make life an unending torture. It is no wonder that these images sometimes return to the enfeebled intelligence. To exorcise them, the old Church of Christendom has her mystic formulæ, of which no rationalistic prescription can take the place. If Cowper had been a good Roman Catholic, instead of having his conscience handled by a Protestant like John Newton, he would not have died despairing, looking upon himself as a castaway. I have seen a good many Roman Catholics on their dying beds, and it always appeared to me that they accepted the inevitable with a composure which showed that their belief, whether or not the best to live by, was a better one to die by than most of the harder creeds which have replaced it.

In the more intelligent circles of American society one may question anything and everything, if he will only do it civilly. We may talk about eschatology, — the science of last things, — or, if you will, the natural history of the undiscovered country, without offence before anybody except young children and very old women of both sexes. In our New England the great Andover discussion and the heretical missionary question have benumbed all sensibility on this subject as entirely, as completely, as the new local anæsthetic, cocaine, deadens the sensibility of the part to which it is applied, so that the eye may have its mote or beam plucked out without feeling it, — as the novels of Zola and Maupassant have hardened the delicate nerve-centres of the women who have fed their imaginations on the food they have furnished.

The generally professed belief of the Protestant

world as embodied in their published creeds is that the great mass of mankind are destined to an eternity of suffering. That this eternity is to be one of bodily pain — of "torment" — is the literal teaching of Scripture, which has been literally interpreted by the theologians, the poets, and the artists of many long ages which followed the acceptance of the recorded legends of the church as infallible. The doctrine has always been recognized, as it is now, as a very terrible one. It has found a support in the story of the fall of man, and the view taken of the relation of man to his Maker since that event. The hatred of God to mankind in virtue of their "first disobedience" and inherited depravity is at the bottom of it. The extent to which that idea was carried is well shown in the expressions I have borrowed from Jonathan Edwards. According to his teaching, — and he was a reasoner who knew what he was talking about, what was involved in the premises of the faith he accepted, — man inherits the curse of God as his principal birthright.

What shall we say to the doctrine of the fall of man as the ground of inflicting endless misery on the human race? A man to be *punished* for what he could not help! He was expected to be called to account for Adam's sin. It is singular to notice that the reasoning of the wolf with the lamb should be transferred to the dealings of the Creator with his creatures. "You stirred the brook up and made my drinking-place muddy." "But, please your wolfship, I couldn't do that, for I stirred the water far down the stream, — below your drinking-place." "Well, anyhow, your father troubled it a year or two ago, and that is the same thing." So the wolf falls upon the lamb and makes a meal of him. That is wolf logic, — and theological reasoning.

How shall we characterize the doctrine of endless torture as the destiny of most of those who have lived, and are living, on this planet? I prefer to let another writer speak of it. Mr. John Morley uses the following words: "The horrors of what is perhaps the most frightful idea that has ever corroded human character, — the idea of eternal punishment." Sismondi, the great historian, heard a sermon on eternal punishment, and vowed never again to enter another church holding the same creed. Romanism he considered a religion of mercy and peace by the side of what the English call the Reformation. — I mention these protests because I happen to find them among my notes, but it would be easy to accumulate examples of the same kind. When Cowper, at about the end of the last century, said satirically of the minister he was attacking,

"He never mentioned hell to ears polite, "

he was giving unconscious evidence that the sense of the barbarism of the idea was finding its way into the pulpit. When Burns, in the midst of the sulphurous orthodoxy of Scotland, dared to say,

" The fear o' hell 's a hangman's whip
To haud the wretch in order, "

he was only appealing to the common sense and common humanity of his fellow-countrymen.

All the reasoning in the world, all the proof-texts in old manuscripts, cannot reconcile this supposition of a world of sleepless and endless torment with the declaration that " God is love."

Where did this " frightful idea " come from? We

are surprised, as we grow older, to find that the legendary hell of the church is nothing more nor less
than the Tartarus of the old heathen world.   It has
every mark of coming from the cruel heart of a
barbarous despot.   Some malignant and vindictive
Sheik, some brutal Mezentius, must have sat for many
pictures of the Divinity.   It was not enough to kill
his captive enemy, after torturing him as much as
ingenuity could contrive to do it.   He escaped at last
by death, but his conqueror could not give him up so
easily, and so his vengeance followed him into the
unseen and unknown world.   How the doctrine got
in among the legends of the church we are no more
bound to show than we are to account for the interca-
lation of the " three witnesses " text, or the false in-
sertion, or false omission, whichever it may be, of the
last twelve verses of the Gospel of St Mark.   We
do not hang our grandmothers now, as our ancestors
did theirs, on the strength of the positive command,
" Thou shalt not suffer a witch to live."

The simple truth is that civilization has outgrown
witchcraft, and is outgrowing the Christian Tartarus.
The pulpit no longer troubles itself about witches and
their evil doings.   All the legends in the world could
not arrest the decay of that superstition and all the
edicts that grew out of it.   All the stories that can be
found in old manuscripts will never prevent the going
out of the fires of the legendary Inferno.   It is not
much talked about nowadays to ears polite or impolite.
Humanity is shocked and repelled by it.   The heart
of woman is in unconquerable rebellion against it.
The more humane sects tear it from their " Bodies of
Divinity " as if it were the flaming shirt of Nessus.
A few doctrines with which it was bound up have

dropped or are dropping away from it : the primal curse ; consequential damages to give infinite extension to every transgression of the law of God ; inverting the natural order of relative obligations ; stretching the smallest of finite offenses to the proportions of the infinite ; making the babe in arms the responsible being, and not the parent who gave it birth and determined its conditions of existence.

After a doctrine like " the hangman's whip " has served its purpose, — if it ever had any useful purpose, — after a doctrine like that of witchcraft has hanged old women enough, civilization contrives to get rid of it. When we say that civilization crowds out the old superstitious legends, we recognize two chief causes. The first is the naked individual protest ; the voice of the inspiration which giveth man understanding. This shows itself conspicuously in the modern poets. Burns in Scotland, Bryant, Longfellow, Whittier, in America, preached a new gospel to the successors of men like Thomas Boston and Jonathan Edwards. In due season, the growth of knowledge, chiefly under the form of that part of knowledge called science, so changes the views of the universe that many of its long-unchallenged legends become no more than nursery tales. The text-books of astronomy and geology work their way in between the questions and answers of the time-honored catechisms. The doctrine of evolution, so far as it is accepted, changes the whole relations of man to the creative power. It substitutes infinite hope in the place of infinite despair for the vast majority of mankind. Instead of a shipwreck, from which a few cabin passengers and others are to be saved in the long-boat, it gives mankind a vessel built to endure the tempests, and at last to reach a

port where at the worst the passengers can find rest,
and where they may hope for a home better than any
which they ever had in their old country. It is all
very well to say that men and women had their choice
whether they would reach the safe harbor or not.

> " Go to it grandam, child ;
> Give grandam kingdom, and it grandam will
> Give it a plum, a cherry and a fig."

We know what the child will take. So which course
we shall take depends very much on the way the choice
is presented to us, and on what the chooser is by nature. What he is by nature is not determined by
himself, but by his parentage. "They know not what
they do." In one sense this is true of every human
being. The agent does not know, never can know,
what makes him that which he is. What we most
want to ask of our Maker is an unfolding of the divine
purpose in putting human beings into conditions in
which such numbers of them would be sure to go
wrong. We want an advocate of helpless humanity
whose task it shall be, in the words of Milton,

> " To justify the ways of God to man."

We have heard Milton's argument, but for the reali-
zation of his vision of the time

> "When Hell itself shall pass away,
> And leave her dolorous mansions to the peering day, "

our suffering race must wait in patience.

The greater part of the discourse the reader has had
before him was delivered over the teacups one Sunday
afternoon. The Mistress looked rather grave, as if
doubtful whether she ought not to signify her disap-
probation of what seemed to her dangerous doctrine.

However, as she knew that I was a good church-goer and was on the best terms with her minister, she said nothing to show that she had taken the alarm. Number Five listened approvingly. We had talked the question over well, and were perfectly agreed on the main point. How could it be otherwise? Do you suppose that any intellectual, spiritual woman, with a heart under her bodice, can for a moment seriously believe that the greater number of the high-minded men, the noble and lovely women, the ingenuous and affectionate children, whom she knows and honors or loves, are to be handed over to the experts in a great torture-chamber, in company with the vilest creatures that have once worn human shape?

" If there is such a world as used to be talked about from the pulpit, you may depend upon it, " she said to me once, " there will soon be organized a Humane Society in heaven, and a mission established among ' the spirits in prison.' "

Number Five is a regular church-goer, as I am. I do not believe either of us would darken the doors of a church if we were likely to hear any of the "old-fashioned " sermons, such as I used to listen to in former years from a noted clergyman, whose specialty was the doctrine of eternal punishment. But you may go to the churches of almost any of our Protestant denominations, and hear sermons by which you can profit, because the ministers are generally good men, whose moral and spiritual natures are above the average, and who know that the harsh preaching of two or three generations ago would offend and alienate a large part of their audience. So neither Number Five nor I are hypocrites in attending church or " going to meeting." I am afraid it does not make a great deal

of difference to either of us what may be the established creed of the worshipping assembly.   That is a
matter of great interest, perhaps of great importance,
to them, but of much less, comparatively, to us.   Companionship in worship, and sitting quiet for an hour
while a trained speaker, presumably somewhat better
than we are, stirs up our spiritual nature, — these are
reasons enough to Number Five, as to me, for regular
attendance on divine worship.

Number Seven is of a different way of thinking and
feeling.   He insists upon it that the churches keep in
their confessions of faith statements which they do not
believe, and that it is notorious that they are afraid to
meddle with them.   The Anglo-American church has
dropped the Athanasian Creed from its service ; the
English mother church is afraid to.   There are plenty
of Universalists, Number Seven says, in the Episcopa-
lian and other Protestant churches, but they do not
avow their belief in any frank and candid fashion.
The churches know very well, he maintains, that the
fear of everlasting punishment more than any or all
other motives is the source of their power and the
support of their organizations.   Not only are the fears
of mankind the whip to scourge and the bridle to re-
strain them, but they are the basis of an almost incal-
culable material interest.   " Talk about giving up the
doctrine of endless punishment by fire ! " exclaimed
Number Seven ; " there is more capital embarked in
the subterranean fire-chambers than in all the iron-
furnaces on the face of the earth.   To think what an
army of clerical beggars would be turned loose on the
world, if once those raging flames were allowed to go
out or to calm down !   Who can wonder that the old
conservatives draw back startled and almost fright-

ened at the thought that there may be a possible escape
for some victims whom the Devil was thought to have
secured? How many more generations will pass before Milton's alarming prophecy will find itself realized in the belief of civilized mankind?"

Remember that Number Seven is called a "crank"
by many persons, and take his remarks for just what
they are worth, and no more.

Out of the preceding conversation must have origin-
ated the following poem, which was found in the common receptacle of these versified contributions: —

TARTARUS.

While in my simple gospel creed
That "God is Love" so plain I read,
Shall dreams of heathen birth affright
My pathway through the coming night?
Ah, Lord of life, though spectres pale
Fill with their threats the shadowy vale,
With Thee my faltering steps to aid,
How can I dare to be afraid?

Shall mouldering page or fading scroll
Outface the charter of the soul?
Shall priesthood's palsied arm protect
The wrong our human hearts reject,
And smite the lips whose shuddering cry
Proclaims a cruel creed a lie?
The wizard's rope we disallow
Was justice once, — is murder now!

Is there a world of blank despair,
And dwells the Omnipresent there?
Does He behold with smile serene
The shows of that unending scene,
Where sleepless, hopeless anguish lies,
And, ever dying, never dies?

Say, does He hear the sufferer's groan,
And is that child of wrath his own?

O mortal, wavering in thy trust,
Lift thy pale forehead from the dust!
The mists that cloud thy darkened eyes
Fade ere they reach the o'erarching skies!
When the blind heralds of despair
Would bid thee doubt a Father's care,
Look up from earth, and read above
On heaven's blue tablet, GOD IS LOVE!

XI.

The tea is sweetened.

WE have been going on very pleasantly of late, each of us pretty well occupied with his or her special business. The Counsellor has been pleading in a great case, and several of The Teacups were in the court-room. I thought, but I will not be certain, that some of his arguments were addressed to Number Five rather than to the jury, — the more eloquent passages especially.

Our young Doctor seems to me to be gradually getting known in the neighborhood and beyond it. A member of one of the more influential families, whose regular physician has gone to Europe, has sent for him to come and see her, and as the patient is a nervous lady, who has nothing in particular the matter with her, he is probably in for a good many visits and a long bill by and by. He has even had a call at a distance of some miles from home, — at least he has had to hire a conveyance frequently of late, for he has not yet set up his own horse and chaise. We do not like to ask him about who his patient may be, but he or she is probably a person of some consequence, as he is absent several hours on these out-of-town visits. He may get a good practice before his bald spot makes its appearance, for I have looked for it many times without as yet seeing a sign of it. I am sure he must feel encouraged, for he has been very bright

and cheerful of late ; and if he sometimes looks at our
new handmaid as if he wished she were Delilah, I do
not think he is breaking his heart about her absence.
Perhaps he finds consolation in the company of the
two Annexes, or one of them, — but which, I cannot
make out.   He is in consultation occasionally with
Number Five, too, but whether professionally or not I
have no means of knowing.   I cannot for the life of
me see what Number Five wants of a doctor for herself, so perhaps it is another difficult case in which
her womanly sagacity is called upon to help him.

In the mean time she and the Tutor continue their
readings.   In fact, it seems as if these readings were
growing more frequent, and lasted longer than they
did at first.   There is a little arbor in the grounds
connected with our place of meeting, and sometimes
they have gone there for their readings.   Some of
The Teacups have listened outside once in a while,
for the Tutor reads well, and his clear voice must be
heard in the more emphatic passages, whether one is
expressly listening or not.   But besides the reading
there is now and then some talking, and persons talking in an arbor do not always remember that lattice-
work, no matter how closely the vines cover it, is not
impenetrable to the sound of the human voice.   There
was a listener one day, — it was not one of The Teacups, I am happy to say, — who heard and reported
some fragments of a conversation which reached his
ear.   Nothing but the profound intimacy which exists
between myself and the individual reader whose eyes
are on this page would induce me to reveal what I
was told of this conversation.   The first words seem
to have been in reply to some question.

" Why, my dear friend, how can you think of such

a thing ? Do you know — I am — old enough to be
your — [I think she must have been on the point of
saying *mother*, but that was more than any woman
could be expected to say] — old enough to be your —
aunt ?"

"To be sure you are," answered the Tutor, "and
what of it ? I have two aunts, both younger than I
am. Your *years* may be more than mine, but your
life is fuller of youthful vitality than mine is. I
never feel so young as when I have been with you. I
don't believe in settling affinities by the almanac.
You know what I have told you more than once ; you
have n't ' bared the ice-cold dagger's edge ' upon me
yet ; may I not cherish the " . . .

What a pity that the listener did not hear the rest
of the sentence and the reply to it, if there was one !
The readings went on the same as before, but I
thought that Number Five was rather more silent and
more pensive than she had been.

I was much pleased when the American Annex
came to me one day and told me that she and the
English Annex were meditating an expedition, in
which they wanted the other Teacups to join. About
a dozen miles from us is an educational institution
of the higher grade, where a large number of young
ladies are trained in literature, art, and science, very
much as their brothers are trained in the colleges.
Our two young ladies have already been through
courses of this kind in different schools, and are now
busy with those more advanced studies which are ventured upon by only a limited number of " graduates."
They have heard a good deal about this institution,
but have never visited it.

Every year, as the successive classes finish their course, there is a grand reunion of the former students, with an "exhibition," as it is called, in which the graduates of the year have an opportunity of showing their proficiency in the various branches taught. On that occasion prizes are awarded for excellence in different departments. It would be hard to find a more interesting ceremony. These girls, now recognized as young ladies, are going forth as missionaries of civilization among our busy people. They are many of them to be teachers, and those who have seen what opportunities they have to learn will understand their fitness for that exalted office. Many are to be the wives and mothers of the generation next coming upon the stage. Young and beautiful, — "youth is always beautiful," said old Samuel Rogers, — their countenances radiant with developed intelligence, their complexions, their figures, their movements, all showing that they have had plenty of outdoor as well as indoor exercise, and have lived well in all respects, one would like to read on the wall of the hall where they are assembled, —

Siste, viator !
Si uxorem requiris, circumspice !

This proposed expedition was a great event in our comparatively quiet circle. The Mistress, who was interested in the school, undertook to be the matron of the party. The young Doctor, who knew the roads better than any of us, was to be our pilot. He arranged it so that he should have the two Annexes under his more immediate charge. We were all on the lookout to see which of the two was to be the favored one, for it was pretty well settled among The Teacups that a wife he must have, whether the bald spot came or not; he was getting into business, and he could not achieve a complete success as a bachelor.

Number Five and the Tutor seemed to come together as a matter of course. I confess that I could not help regretting that our pretty Delilah was not to be one of the party. She always looked so young, so fresh, — she would have enjoyed the excursion so much, that if she had been still with us I would have told the Mistress that she must put on her best dress; and if she had n't one nice enough, I would give her one myself. I thought, too, that our young Doctor would have liked to have her with us; but he appeared to be getting along very well with the Annexes, one of whom it seems likely that he will annex to himself and his fortunes, if she fancies him, which is not improbable.

The organizing of this expedition was naturally a cause of great excitement among The Teacups. The party had to be arranged in such a way as to suit all concerned, which was a delicate matter. It was finally managed in this way: The Mistress was to go with a bodyguard, consisting of myself, the Professor, and Number Seven, who was good company, with all his oddities. The young Doctor was to take the two Annexes in a wagon, and the Tutor was to drive Number Five in a good old-fashioned chaise drawn by a well-conducted family horse. As for the Musician, he had gone over early, by special invitation, to take a part in certain musical exercises which were to have a place in the exhibition. This arrangement appeared to be in every respect satisfactory. The Doctor was in high spirits, apparently delighted, and devoting himself with great gallantry to his two fair companions. The only question which intruded itself was, whether he

might not have preferred the company of one to that
of two. But both looked very attractive in their best
dresses : the English Annex, the rosier and heartier
of the two ; the American girl, more delicate in features, more mobile and excitable, but suggesting the
thought that she would tire out before the other.
Which of these did he most favor ? It was hard to
say. He seemed to look most at the English girl,
and yet he talked more with the American girl. In
short, he behaved particularly well, and neither of the
young ladies could complain that she was not attended
to. As to the Tutor and Number Five, their going
together caused no special comment. Their intimacy
was accepted as an established fact, and nothing but
the difference in their ages prevented the conclusion
that it was love, and not mere friendship, which
brought them together. There was, no doubt, a strong
feeling among many people that Number Five's affections were a kind of Gibraltar or Ehrenbreitstein, —
say rather a high table-land in the region of perpetual,
unmelting snow. It was hard for these people to believe that any man of mortal mould could find a foot-
hold in that impregnable fortress, — could climb to
that height and find the flower of love among its
glaciers. The Tutor and Number Five were both
quiet, thoughtful : he, evidently captivated ; she, —
what was the meaning of her manner to him ? Say
that she seemed *fond* of him, as she might be were he
her nephew, — one for whom she had a special liking.
If she had a warmer feeling than this, she could
hardly know how to manage it ; for she was so used
to having love made to her without returning it that
she would naturally be awkward in dealing with the
new experience.

The Doctor dróve a lively five-year-old horse, and took the lead. The Tutor followed with a quiet, steady-going nag ; if he had driven the five-year-old, I would not have answered for the necks of the pair in the chaise, for he was too much taken up with the subject they were talking of, to be very careful about his driving. The Mistress and her escort brought up the rear, — I holding the reins, the Professor at my side, and Number Seven sitting with the Mistress.

We arrived at the institution a little later than we had expected to, and the students were flocking into the hall, where the Commencement exercises were to take place, and the medal-scholars were to receive the tokens of their excellence in the various departments. From our seats we could see the greater part of the assembly, — not quite all, however of the pupils. A pleasing sight it was to look upon, this array of young ladies dressed in white, with their class badges, and with the ribbon of the shade of blue affected by the scholars of the institution. If Solomon in all his glory was not to be compared to a lily, a whole bed of lilies could not be compared to this garden-bed of youthful womanhood.

The performances were very much the same as most of us have seen at the academies and collegiate schools. Some of the graduating class read their "compositions," one of which was a poem, — an echo of the prevailing American echoes, of course, but prettily worded and intelligently read. Then there was a song sung by a choir of the pupils, led by their instructor, who was assisted by the Musician whom we count among The Teacups. There was something in one of the voices that reminded me of one I had heard before. Where could it have been ? I am

sure I cannot remember. There are some good voices
in our village choir, but none so pure and bird-like as
this. A sudden thought came into my head, but I
kept it to myself. I heard a tremulous catching of
the breath, something like a sob, close by me. It was
the Mistress, — she was crying. What was she crying for? It was impressive, certainly, to listen to
these young voices, many of them blending for the
last time, — for the scholars were soon to be scattered
all over the country, and some of them beyond its
boundaries, — but why the Mistress was so carried
away, I did not know. She must be more impressible
than most of us; yet I thought Number Five also
looked as if she were having a struggle with herself
to keep down some rebellious signs of emotion.

The exercises went on very pleasingly until they
came to the awarding of the gold medal of the year
and the valedictory, which was to be delivered by the
young lady to whom it was to be presented. The
name was called; it was one not unfamiliar to our
ears, and the bearer of it — the Delilah of our tea-
table, Avis as she was known in the school and elsewhere — rose in her place and came forward, so that
for the first time on that day, we looked upon her. It
was a sensation for The Teacups. Our modest, quiet
waiting-girl was the best scholar of her year. We
had talked French before her, and we learned that
she was the best French scholar the teacher had ever
had in the school. We had never thought of her except as a pleasing and well-trained handmaiden, and
here she was an accomplished young lady.

Avis went through her part very naturally and gracefully, and when it was finished, and she stood before
us with the medal glittering on her breast, we did not

know whether to smile or to cry, — some of us did one, and some the other.—We all had an opportunity to see her and congratulate her before we left the institution. The mystery of her six weeks' serving at our table was easily solved. She had been studying too hard and too long, and required some change of scene and occupation. She had a fancy for trying to see if she could support herself as so many young women are obliged to, and found a place with us, — the Mistress only knowing her secret.

"She is to be our young Doctor's wife!" the Mistress whispered to me, and did some more crying, — not for grief, certainly.

Whether our young Doctor's long visits to a neighboring town had anything to do with the fact that Avis was at that institution, whether she was the patient he visited or not, may be left in doubt. At all events, he had always driven off in the direction which would carry him to the place where she was at school.

I have attended a large number of celebrations, commencements, banquets, soirées, and so forth, and done my best to help on a good many of them. In fact, I have become rather too well known in connection with "occasions," and it has cost me no little trouble. I believe there is no kind of occurrence for which I have not been requested to contribute something in prose or verse. It is sometimes very hard to say no to the requests. If one is in the right mood when he or she writes an occasional poem, it seems as if nothing could have been easier. "Why, that piece run off jest like ile. I don't bullieve," the unlettered applicant says to himself, — "I don't bullieve it took him ten minutes to write them verses." The good people have no suspicion of how much a single line, a single expression, may cost its author. The wits used to say that Rogers, — the poet once before referred to, old Samuel Rogers, author of the Pleasures of Memory and giver of famous breakfasts, — was accustomed to have straw laid before the house whenever he had just given birth to a couplet. It is not quite so bad as that with most of us who are called upon to furnish a poem, a song, a hymn, an ode for some grand meeting, but it is safe to say that many a trifling performance has had more good honest work put into it than the minister's sermon of that week had cost him. If a vessel glides off the ways smoothly and easily at her launching, it does not mean that no great pains have been taken to secure the result. Because a poem is an "occasional" one, it does not follow that it has not taken as much time and skill as if it had been written without immediate, accidental, temporary motive. Pindar's great odes were occasional poems, just as much as our Commencement and Phi Beta Kappa poems are, and yet they have come down among the most precious bequests of antiquity to modern times.

The mystery of the young Doctor's long visits to the neighboring town was satisfactorily explained by what we saw and heard of his relations with our charming "Delilah," — for Delilah we could hardly help calling her. Our little handmaid, the Cinderella of the teacups, now the princess, or, what was better, the pride of the school to which she had belonged, fit for any position to which she might be called, was to be the wife of our young Doctor. It would not have been the right thing to proclaim the fact while she was a pupil, but now that she had finished her course of instruction there was no need of making a secret of the engagement.

So we have got our romance, our love-story out of our Teacups, as I hoped and expected that we should, but not exactly in the quarter where it might have been looked for.

What did our two Annexes say to this unexpected turn of events? They were good-hearted girls as ever lived, but they were human, like the rest of us, and women, like some of the rest of us. They behaved perfectly. They congratulated the Doctor, and hoped he would bring the young lady to the tea-table where she had played her part so becomingly. It is safe to say that each of the Annexes would have liked to be asked the lover's last question by the very nice young man who had been a pleasant companion at the table and elsewhere to each of them. That same question is the highest compliment a man can pay a woman, and a woman does not mind having a dozen or more such compliments to string on the rosary of her remembrances. Whether either of them was glad, on the whole, that he had not offered himself to the other in preference to herself would be a mean, shabby question, and I think altogether too well of you who are reading this paper to suppose that you would entertain the idea of asking it.

It was a very pleasant occasion when the Doctor brought Avis over to sit with us at the table where she used to stand and wait upon us. We wondered how we could for a moment have questioned that she was one to be waited upon, and not made for the humble office which nevertheless she performed so cheerfully and so well.

Commencements and other Celebrations, American and English.

The social habits of our people have undergone an immense change within the past half century, largely in consequence of the vast development of the means of intercourse between different neighborhoods.

Commencements, college gatherings of all kinds, church assemblages, school anniversaries, town centennials, — all possible occasions for getting crowds together are made the most of. " 'T is sixty years since, " — and a good many years over, — the time to which my memory extends. The great days of the year were, Election, — General Election on Wednesday, and Artillery Election on the Monday following, at which time lilacs were in bloom and 'lection buns were in order; Fourth of July, when strawberries were just going out; and Commencement, a grand time of feasting, fiddling, dancing, jollity, not to mention drunkenness and fighting, on the classic green of Cambridge. This was the season of melons and peaches. That is the way our boyhood chronicles events. It was odd that the literary festival should be turned into a Donnybrook fair, but so it was when I was a boy, and the tents and the shows and the crowds on the Common were to the promiscuous many the essential parts of the great occasion. They had been so for generations, and it was only gradually that the Cambridge Saturnalia were replaced by the decencies and solemnities of the present sober anniversary.

Nowadays our celebrations smack of the Sunday-school more than of the dancing-hall. The aroma of the punch-bowl has given way to the milder flavor of lemonade and the cooling virtues of ice-cream. A

strawberry festival is about as far as the dissipation of
our social gatherings ventures. There was much that
was objectionable in those swearing, drinking, fighting
times, but they had a certain excitement for us boys
of the years when the century was in its teens, which
comes back to us not without its fascinations. The
days of total abstinence are a great improvement over
those of unlicensed license, but there was a picturesque
element about the rowdyism of our old Commencement days, which had a charm for the eye of boyhood.
My dear old friend, — book-friend, I mean, — whom I
always called Daddy Gilpin (as I find Fitzgerald called
Wordsworth, Daddy Wordsworth), — my old friend
Gilpin, I say, considered the donkey more picturesque
in a landscape than the horse. So a village *fête* as
depicted by Teniers is more picturesque than a teetotal
picnic or a Sabbath - school strawberry festival. Let
us be thankful that the vicious picturesque is only a
remembrance, and the virtuous commonplace a reality
of to-day.

What put all this into my head is something which
the English Annex has been showing me. Most of
my readers are somewhat acquainted with our own
church and village celebrations. They know how they
are organized ; the women always being the chief
motors, and the machinery very much the same in one
case as in another. Perhaps they would like to hear
how such things are managed in England ; and that
is just what they may learn from the pamphlet which
was shown me by the English Annex, and of which I
will give them a brief account.

Some of us remember the Rev. Mr. Haweis, his
lectures and his violin, which interested and amused

us here in Boston a few years ago.   Now Mr. Haweis,
assisted by his intelligent and spirited wife, has charge
of the parish of St. James, Westmoreland Street,
Marylebone, London.   On entering upon the twenty-
fifth year of his incumbency in Marylebone, and the
twenty-eighth of his ministry in the diocese of London,
it was thought a good idea to have an " Evening Con-
versazione and Fête."   We can imagine just how such
a meeting would be organized in one of our towns.
Ministers, deacons, perhaps a member of Congress,
possibly a Senator, and even, conceivably, his Excel-
lency the Governor, and a long list of ladies lend their
names to give lustre to the occasion.   It is all very
pleasant, unpretending, unceremonious, cheerful, well
ordered, commendable, but not imposing.

Now look at our Marylebone parish celebration, and
hold your breath while the procession of great names
passes before you.   You learn at the outset that it is
held UNDER ROYAL PATRONAGE, and read the names
of two royal highnesses, one highness, a prince, and a
princess.   Then comes a list before which if you do
not turn pale, you must certainly be in the habit of
rouging : three earls, seven lords, three bishops, two
generals (one of them Lord Wolseley), one admiral,
four baronets, nine knights, a crowd of right honorable and honorable ladies (many of them peeresses),
and a mob of other personages, among whom I find
Mr. Howells, Bret Harte, and myself.

Perhaps we are disposed to smile at seeing so much
made of titles ; but after what we have learned of Lord
Timothy Dexter and the high-sounding names appropriated by many of our own compatriots, who have
no more claim to them than we plain Misters and
Misseses, we may feel to them something as our late

friend Mr. Appleton felt to the real green turtle soup
set before him, when he said that it was almost as
good as mock.

The entertainment on this occasion was of the most
varied character. The programme makes the following announcement: —

Friday, 4 July, 18—.

At 8 P. M. the Doors will Open.
Mr. Haweis will receive his Friends.
The Royal Handbell Ringers will Ring.
The Fish-pond will be Fished.
The Stalls will be Visited.
The Phonograph will Utter.

Refreshments will be called for, and they will come, — Tea,
Coffee, and Cooling Drinks. Spirits will not be called for, —
from the Vasty Deep or anywhere else, — nor would they come
if they were.

At 9.30 Mrs. Haweis will join the assembly.

I am particularly delighted with this last feature in
the preliminary announcement. It is a proof of the
high regard in which the estimable and gifted lady
who shares her husband's labors is held by the people
of their congregation, and the friends who share in
their feelings. It is such a master stroke of policy,
too, to keep back the principal attraction until the
guests must have grown eager for her appearance. I
can well imagine how great a saving it must have
been to the good lady's nerves, which were probably
pretty well tried already by the fatigues and responsibilities of the busy evening. I have a right to say
this, for I myself had the honor of attending a meeting at Mr. Haweis's house, where I was a principal
guest, as I suppose, from the fact of the great number
of persons who were presented to me. The minister

must be very popular, for the meeting was a regular jam, — not quite so tremendous as that greater one, where but for the aid of Mr. Smalley, who kept open a breathing-space round us, my companion and myself thought we should have been asphyxiated.

The company was interested, as some of my readers may be, to know what were the attractions offered to the visitors besides that of meeting the courteous entertainers and their distinguished guests. I cannot give these at length, for each part of the show is introduced in the programme with apt quotations and pleasantries, which enlivened the catalogue. There were eleven stalls, " conducted on the coöperative principle of division of profits and interest; they retain the profits, and you take a good deal of interest, we hope, in their success."

Stall No. 1. Edisoniana, or the Phonograph. Alluded to by the Roman Poet as *Vox, et præterea nihil.*

Stall No. 2. Money-changing.

Stall No. 3. Programmes and General Enquiries.

Stall No. 4. Roses.
A rose by any other name, etc. Get one. You can't expect to smell one without buying it, but you may buy one without smelling it.

Stall No. 5. Lasenby Liberty Stall.

(I cannot explain this. Probably articles from Liberty's famous establishment.)

Stall No. 6. Historical Costumes and Ceramics.

Stall No. 7. The Fish-pond.

Stall No. 8. Varieties.

Stall No. 9. Bookstall.
(Books) " highly recommended for insomnia ; friends we never speak to, and always cut if we want to know them well."

Stall No. 10. Icelandic.

> "Mrs. Magnusson, who is devoted to the North Pole and all its works, will thaw your sympathies, enlighten your minds," etc., etc.

Stall No. 11. Call Office.

> All you buy may be left at the stalls, ticketed. A duplicate ticket will be handed to you on leaving. Present your duplicate at the Call Office.

At 9.45, First Concert.

At 10.45, An Address of Welcome by Rev. H. R. Haweis.

At 11 P. M., Bird-warbling Interlude by Miss Mabel Stephenson, U. S. A.

At 11.20, Second Concert.

NOTICE !

Three Great Pictures.

LORD TENNYSON	G. F. Watts, R. A.
JOHN STUART MILL	G. F. Watts, R. A.
JOSEPH GARIBALDI	Sig. Rondi.

NOTICE !

A Famous Violin.

A world-famed Stradivarius Violin, for which Mr. Hill, of Bond Street, gave £1000, etc., etc.

REFRESHMENTS.

Tickets for Tea, Coffee, Sandwiches, Iced Drinks, or Ices, Sixpence each, etc., etc.

I hope my American reader is pleased and interested by this glimpse of the way in which they do these things in London.

There is something very pleasant about all this, but what specially strikes me is a curious flavor of city provincialism. There are little centres in the heart of great cities, just as there are small fresh-water ponds in great islands with the salt sea roaring all round them, and bays and creeks penetrating them

as briny as the ocean itself. Irving has given a charming picture of such a *quasi*-provincial centre in one of
his papers in the Sketch-Book, — the one with the
title " Little Britain." London is a nation of itself,
and contains provinces, districts, foreign communities,
villages, parishes, — innumerable lesser centres, with
their own distinguishing characteristics, habits, pursuits, languages, social laws, as much isolated from
each other as if " mountains interposed " made the
separation between them. One of these lesser centres
is that over which my friend Mr. Haweis presides as
spiritual director. Chelsea has been made famous as
the home of many authors and artists, — above all,
as the residence of Carlyle during the greater part of
his life. Its population, like that of most respectable
suburbs, must belong mainly to the kind of citizens
which resembles in many ways the better class, — as
we sometimes dare to call it, — of one of our thriving
New England towns. How many John Gilpins there
must be in this population, — citizens of " famous
London town," but living with the simplicity of the
inhabitants of our inland villages! In the mighty
metropolis where the wealth of the world displays itself they practise their snug economies, enjoy their
simple pleasures, and look upon ice-cream as a luxury,
just as if they were living on the banks of the Connecticut or the Housatonic, in regions where the summer locusts of the great cities have not yet settled on
the verdure of the native inhabitants. It is delightful to realize the fact that while the West End of
London is flaunting its splendors and the East End
in struggling with its miseries, these great middle-
class communities are living as comfortable, unpretending lives as if they were in one of our thriving

townships in the huckleberry districts. Human beings are wonderfully alike when they are placed in similar conditions.

We were sitting together in a very quiet way over our teacups. The young Doctor, who was in the best of spirits, had been laughing and chatting with the two Annexes. The Tutor, who always sits next to Number Five of late, had been conversing with her in rather low tones. The rest of us had been soberly sipping our tea, and when the Doctor and the Annexes stopped talking there was one of those dead silences which are sometimes so hard to break in upon, and so awkward while they last. All at once Number Seven exploded in a loud laugh, which startled everybody at the table.

What is it that sets you laughing so? said I.

"I was thinking," Number Seven replied, "of what you said the other day of poetry being only the ashes of emotion. I believe that some people are disposed to dispute the proposition. I have been putting your doctrine to the test. In doing it I made some rhymes, — the first and only ones I ever made. I will suppose a case of very exciting emotion, and see whether it would probably take the form of poetry or prose. You are suddenly informed that your house is on fire, and have to scramble out of it, without stopping to tie your neckcloth neatly or to put a flower in your buttonhole. Do you think a poet turning out in his night-dress, and looking on while the flames were swallowing his home and all its contents, would express himself in this style?

My house is on fire!
Bring me my lyre!
Like the flames that rise heavenward my song shall aspire!

He would n't do any such thing, and you know he
would n't.   He would yell Fire! Fire! with all his
might.   Not much rhyming for him just yet!   Wait
until the fire is put out, and he has had time to look
at the charred timbers and the ashes of his home, and
in the course of a week he may possibly spin a few
rhymes about it.   Or suppose he was making an offer
of his hand and heart, do you think he would declaim
a versified proposal to his Amanda, or perhaps write
an impromptu on the back of his hat while he knelt
before her ?

> My beloved, to you
> I will always be true.
> Oh, pray make me happy, my love, do ! do ! do !

What would Amanda think of a suitor who courted
her with a rhyming dictionary in his pocket to help
him make love ?"

You are right, said I, — there 's nothing in the
world like rhymes to cool off a man's passion.   You
look at a blacksmith working on a bit of iron or steel.
Bright enough it looked while it was on the hearth,
in the midst of the sea-coal, the great bellows blowing
away, and the rod or the horse-shoe as red or as white
as the burning coals.   How it fizzes as it goes into
the trough of water, and how suddenly all the glow
is gone !   It looks black and cold enough now.   Just
so with your passionate incandescence.   It is all well
while it burns and scintillates in your emotional centres, without articulate and connected expression ; but
the minute you plunge it into the rhyme-trough it
cools down, and becomes as dead and dull as the cold
horse-shoe.   It is true that if you lay it cold on the
anvil and hammer away on it for a while it warms up
somewhat.   Just so with the rhyming fellow, — he

pounds away on his verses and they warm up a little.
But don't let him think that this afterglow of composition is the same thing as the original passion. *That*
found expression in a few *oh, oh's, àι àι's, eheu,
eheu's, hélas, hélas's,* and when the passion had burned
itself out you got the rhymed verses, which, as I have
said, are its ashes.

I thanked Number Seven for his poetical illustra-
tion of my thesis. There is great good to be got out
of a squinting brain, if one only knows how to profit
by it. We see only one side of the moon, you know,
but a fellow with a squinting brain seems now and
then to get a peep at the other side. I speak metaphorically. He takes new and startling views of
things we have always looked at in one particular
aspect. There is a rule invariably to be observed
with one of this class of intelligences : *Never contradict a man with a squinting brain.* I say a *man,*
because I do not think that squinting brains are
nearly so common in women as they are in men. The
" eccentrics " are, I think, for the most part of the
male sex.

That leads me to say that persons with a strong
instinctive tendency to contradiction are apt to become unprofitable companions. Our thoughts are
plants that never flourish in inhospitable soils or chill-
ing atmospheres. They are all started under glass,
so to speak; that is, sheltered and fostered in our
own warm and sunny consciousness. They must
expect some rough treatment when we lift the sash
from the frame and let the outside elements in upon
them. They can bear the rain and the breezes, and
be all the better for them ; but perpetual contradiction
is a pelting hailstorm, which spoils their growth and
tends to kill them out altogether.

Now stop and consider a moment. Are not almost
all brains a little wanting in bilateral symmetry? Do
you not find in persons whom you love, whom you
esteem, and even admire, some marks of obliquity in
mental vision?   Are there not some subjects in looking at which it seems to you impossible that they
should ever see straight?   Are there not moods in
which it seems to you that they are disposed to see all
things out of plumb and in false relations with each
other?   If you answer these questions in the affirma-
tive, then you will be glad of a hint as to the method
of dealing with your friends who have a touch of cerebral strabismus, or are liable to occasional paroxysms
of perversity. Let them have their head. Get them
talking on subjects that interest them. As a rule,
nothing is more likely to serve this purpose than letting them talk about themselves; if authors, about
their writings; if artists, about their pictures or statues; and generally on whatever they have most pride
in and think most of their own relations with.

Perhaps you will not at first sight agree with me in
thinking that slight mental obliquity is as common as
I suppose.   An analogy may have some influence on
your belief in this matter.   Will you take the trouble
to ask your tailor how many persons have their two
shoulders of the same height?   I think he will tell
you that the majority of his customers show a distinct
difference of height on the two sides. Will you ask
a portrait-painter how many of those who sit to him
have both sides of their faces exactly alike? I believe he will tell you that one side is always a little
better than the other. What will your hatter say
about the two sides of the head? Do you see equally
well with both eyes, and hear equally well with both

ears ? Few persons past middle age will pretend that
they do. Why should the two halves of a brain not
show a natural difference, leading to confusion of
thought, and very possibly to that instinct of contradiction of which I was speaking? A great deal of
time is lost in profitless conversation, and a good
deal of ill temper frequently caused, by not considering these organic and practically insuperable conditions. In dealing with them, acquiescence is the best
of palliations and silence the sovereign specific.

I have been the reporter, as you have seen, of my
own conversation and that of the other Teacups. I
have told some of the circumstances of their personal
history, and interested, as I hope, here and there a
reader in the fate of different members of our company. Here are our pretty Delilah and our Doctor
provided for. We may take it for granted that it will
not be very long that the young couple will have to
wait; for, as I have told you all, the Doctor is certainly getting into' business, and bids fair to have a
thriving practice before he saddles his nose with an
eyeglass and begins to think of a pair of spectacles.
So that part of our little domestic drama is over, and
we can only wish the pair that is to be all manner
of blessings consistent with a reasonable amount of
health in the community on whose ailings must
depend their prosperity.

All our thoughts are now concentrated on the relation existing betwen Number Five and the Tutor.
That there is some profound instinctive impulse which
is drawing them closer together no one who watches
them can for a moment doubt. There are two principles of attraction which bring different natures to-

gether: that in which the two natures closely resemble each other, and that in which one is complementary of the other. In the first case, they coalesce, as do two drops of water or of mercury, and become intimately blended as soon as they touch; in the other, they rush together as an acid and an alkali unite, — predestined from eternity to find all they most needed in each other. What is the condition of things in the growing intimacy of Number Five and the Tutor? He is many years her junior, as we know. Both of them look that fact squarely in the face. The presumption is against the union of two persons under these circumstances. Presumptions are strong obstacles against any result we wish to attain, but half our work in life is to overcome them. A great many results look in the distance like six-foot walls, and when we get nearer prove to be only five-foot hurdles, to be leaped over or knocked down. Twenty years from now she may be a vigorous and active old woman, and he a middle-aged, half-worn-out invalid, like so many overworked scholars. Everything depends on the number of drops of the elixir vitæ which Nature mingled in the nourishment she administered to the embryo before it tasted its mother's milk. Think of Cleopatra, the bewitching old mischief-maker; think of Ninon de L'Enclos, whose own son fell desperately in love with her, not knowing the relation in which she stood to him; think of Dr. Johnson's friend, Mrs. Thrale, afterward Mrs. Piozzi, who at the age of eighty was full enough of life to be making love ardently and persistently to Conway, the handsome young actor. I can readily believe that Number Five will outlive the Tutor, even if he is fortunate enough to succeed in storming that Ehrenbreitstein, — say

rather in winning his way into the fortress through
gates that open to him of their own accord. If he
fails in his siege, I do really believe he will die early ;
not of a broken heart, exactly, but of a heart starved,
with the food it was craving close to it, but unattain-
able. I have, therefore, a deep interest in knowing
how Number Five and the Tutor are getting along together. Is there any danger of one or the other growing tired of the intimacy, and becoming willing to get
rid of it, like a garment which has shrunk and grown
too tight ? Is it likely that some other attraction may
come in to disturb the existing relation ? The problem is to my mind not only interesting, but exceptionally curious. You remember the story of Cymon and
Iphigenia as Dryden tells it. The poor youth has the
capacity of loving, but it lies hidden in his undevel-
oped nature. All at once he comes upon the sleeping
beauty, and is awakened by her charms to a hitherto
unfelt consciousness. With the advent of the new
passion all his dormant faculties start into life, and
the seeming simpleton becomes the bright and intelligent lover. The case of Number Five is as different
from that of Cymon as it could well be. All her
faculties are wide awake, but one emotional side
of her nature has never been called into active exercise. Why has she never been in love with any one
of her suitors ? Because she *liked* too many of them.
Do you happen to remember a poem printed among
these papers, entitled " I Like You and I Love You " ?
No one of the poems which have been placed in the
urn, — that is, in the silver sugar-bowl, — has had any
name attached to it ; but you could guess pretty nearly
who was the author of some of them, certainly of the
one just referred to. Number Five was attracted to

the Tutor from the first time he spoke to her. She dreamed about him that night, and nothing idealizes and renders fascinating one in whom we have already an interest like dreaming of him or of her. Many a calm suitor has been made passionate by a dream; many a passionate lover has been made wild and half beside himself by a dream; and now and then an infatuated but hapless lover, waking from a dream of bliss to a cold reality of wretchedness, has helped himself to eternity before he was summoned to the table.

Since Number Five had dreamed about the Tutor, he had been more in her waking thoughts than she was willing to acknowledge. These thoughts were vague, it is true, — emotions, perhaps, rather than worded trains of ideas; but she was conscious of a pleasing excitement as his name or his image floated across her consciousness; she sometimes sighed as she looked over the last passage they had read from the same book, and sometimes when they were together they were silent too long, — too long! What were they thinking of?

And so it was all as plain sailing for Number Five and the young Tutor as it had been for Delilah and the young Doctor, was it? Do you think so? Then you do not understand Number Five. Many a woman has as many atmospheric rings about her as the planet Saturn. *Three* are easily to be recognized. First, there is the wide ring of attraction which draws into itself all that once cross its outer border. These revolve about her without ever coming any nearer. Next is the inner ring of attraction. Those who come within its irresistible influence are drawn so close that it seems as if they must become one with her sooner or later. But within this ring is another, — an atmos-

pheric girdle, one of repulsion, which love, no matter
how enterprising, no matter how prevailing or how insinuating, has never passed, and, if we judge of what
is to be by what has been, never will. Perhaps Nature loved Number Five so well that she grudged her
to any mortal man, and gave her this inner girdle of
repulsion to guard her from all who would know her
too nearly and love her too well. Sometimes two vessels at sea keep each other company for a long distance, it may be during a whole voyage. Very pleasant it is to each to have a companion to exchange
signals with from time to time ; to come near enough,
when the winds are light, to hold converse in ordinary
tones from deck to deck; to know that, in case of
need, there is help at hand. It is good for them to be
near each other, but not good to be too near. Woe is
to them if they touch! The wreck of one or both is
likely to be the consequence. And so two well-
equipped and heavily freighted natures may be the
best of companions to each other, and yet must never
attempt to come into closer union. Is this the
condition of affairs between Number Five and the
Tutor? I hope not, for I want them to be joined together in that dearest of intimacies, which, if founded
in true affinity, is the nearest approach to happiness to
be looked for in our mortal experience. We must
wait. The Teacups will meet once more before the
circle is broken, and we may, perhaps, find the solu-
tion of the question we have raised.

In the mean time, our young Doctor is playing
truant oftener than ever. He has brought Avis, — if
we must call her so, and not Delilah, — several times
to take tea with us. It means something, in these
days, to graduate from one of our first-class academies

or collegiate schools. I shall never forget my first visit to one of these institutions. How much its pupils know, I said, which I was never taught, and have never learned! I was fairly frightened to see what a teaching apparatus was provided for them. I should think the first thing to be done with most of the husbands they are likely to get would be to put them through a course of instruction. The young wives must find their lords wofully ignorant, in a large proportion of cases. When the wife has educated the husband to such a point that she can invite him to work out a problem in the higher mathematics or to perform a difficult chemical analysis with her as his collaborator, as less instructed dames ask their husbands to play a game of checkers or backgammon, they can have delightful and instructive evenings together. I hope our young Doctor will take kindly to his wife's (that is to be) teachings.

When the following verses were taken out of the urn, the Mistress asked me to hand the manuscript to the young Doctor to read. I noticed that he did not keep his eyes very closely fixed on the paper. It seemed as if he could have recited the lines without referring to the manuscript at all.

AT THE TURN OF THE ROAD.

The glory has passed from the goldenrod's plume,
The purple-hued asters still linger in bloom :
The birch is bright yellow, the sumachs are red,
The maples like torches aflame overhead.

But what if the joy of the summer is past,
And winter's wild herald is blowing his blast ?
For me dull November is sweeter than May,
For my love is its sunshine, — she meets me to-day !

Will she come ? Will the ring-dove return to her nest ?
Will the needle swing back from the east or the west ?
At the stroke of the hour she will be at her gate ;
A friend may prove laggard, — love never comes late.

Do I see her afar in the distance ? Not yet.
Too early ! Too early ! She could not forget !
When I cross the old bridge where the brook overflowed,
She will flash full in sight at the turn of the road.

I pass the low wall where the ivy entwines ;
I tread the brown pathway that leads through the pines ;
I haste by the boulder that lies in the field,
Where her promise at parting was lovingly sealed.

Will she come by the hillside or round through the wood ?
Will she wear her brown dress or her mantle and hood ?
The minute draws near, — but her watch may go wrong ;
My heart *will* be asking, What keeps her so long ?

Why doubt for a moment ? More shame if I do !
Why question ? Why tremble ? Are angels more true ?
She would come to the lover who calls her his own
Though she trod in the track of a whirling cyclone !

— I crossed the old bridge ere the minute had passed.
I looked : lo ! my Love stood before me at last.
Her eyes, how they sparkled, her cheeks, how they glowed,
As we met, face to face, at the turn of the road !

XII

THERE was a great tinkling of teaspoons the other evening, when I took my seat at the table, where all The Teacups were gathered before my entrance. The whole company arose, and the Mistress, speaking for them, expressed the usual sentiment appropriate to such occasions. "Many happy returns" is the customary formula. No matter if the object of this kind wish is a centenarian, it is quite safe to assume that he is ready and very willing to accept as many more years as the disposing powers may see fit to allow him.

The meaning of it all was that this was my birthday. My friends, near and distant, had seen fit to remember it, and to let me know in various pleasant ways that they had not forgotten it. The tables were adorned with flowers. Gifts of pretty and pleasing objects were displayed on a side table. A great green wreath, which must have cost the parent oak a large fraction of its foliage, was an object of special admiration. Baskets of flowers which had half unpeopled greenhouses, large bouquets of roses, fragrant bunches of pinks, and many beautiful blossoms I am not botanist enough to name had been coming in upon me all day long. Many of these offerings were brought by the givers in person; many came with notes as fragrant with good wishes as the flowers they accompanied with their natural perfumes.

How old was I, The Dictator, once known by another equally audacious title, — I, the recipient of all these favors and honors? I had cleared the eight-barred gate, which few come in sight of, and fewer, far fewer, go over, a year before. I was a trespasser on the domain belonging to another generation. The children of my coevals were fast getting gray and bald, and *their* children beginning to look upon the world as belonging to them, and not to their sires and grandsires. After that leap over the tall barrier, it looks like a kind of impropriety to keep on as if one were still of a reasonable age. Sometimes it seems to me almost of the nature of a misdemeanor to be wandering about in the preserve which the fleshless game-keeper guards so jealously. But, on the other hand, I remember that men of science have maintained that the natural life of man is nearer fivescore than three-score years and ten. I always think of a familiar experience which I bring from the French *cafés*, well known to me in my early manhood. One of the illustrated papers of my Parisian days tells it pleasantly enough.

A guest of the establishment is sitting at his little table. He has just had his coffee, and the waiter is serving him with his *petit verre*. Most of my readers know very well what a *petit verre* is, but there may be here and there a virtuous abstainer from alcoholic fluids, living among the bayberries and the sweet ferns, who is not aware that the words, as commonly used, signify a small glass — a very small glass — of spirit, commonly brandy, taken as a *chasse-café*, or coffee-chaser. [This drinking of brandy, " neat," I may remark by the way, is not quite so bad as it looks. Whiskey or rum taken unmixed from a *tum-*

bler is a knock-down blow to temperance, but the little
thimbleful of brandy, or Chartreuse, or Maraschino, is
only, as it were, tweaking the nose of teetotalism.]
Well, — to go back behind our brackets, — the guest
is calling to the waiter, "*Garçon! et le bain de
pieds!*" Waiter! and the foot-bath! — The little
glass stands in a small tin saucer or shallow dish, and
the custom is to more than fill the glass, so that some
extra brandy runs over into this tin saucer or cup-
plate, to the manifest gain of the consumer.

Life is a *petit verre* of a very peculiar kind of
spirit. At seventy years it used to be said that the
little glass was full. We should be more apt to put
it at eighty in our day, while Gladstone and Tennyson
and our own Whittier are breathing, moving, thinking, writing, speaking, in the green preserve belonging to their children and grandchildren, and Bancroft
is keeping watch of the gamekeeper in the distance.
But, returning resolutely to the *petit verre*, I am willing to concede that all after fourscore is the *bain de
pieds*, — the slopping over, so to speak, of the full
measure of life. I remember that one who was very
near and dear to me, and who lived to a great age, so
that the ten-barred gate of the century did not look
very far off, would sometimes apologize in a very
sweet, natural way for lingering so long to be a care
and perhaps a burden to her children, themselves getting well into years. It is not hard to understand the
feeling, never less called for than it was in the case of
that beloved nonagenarian. I have known few persons, young or old, more sincerely and justly regretted
than the gentle lady whose memory comes up before
me as I write.

Oh, if we could all go out of flower as gracefully,

as pleasingly, as we come into blossom! I always think of the morning-glory as the loveliest example of a graceful yielding to the inevitable. It is beautiful before its twisted corolla opens; it is comely as it folds its petals inward, when its brief hours of perfection are over. Women find it easier than men to grow old in a becoming way. A very old lady who has kept something, it may be a great deal, of her youthful feelings, who is daintily cared for, who is grateful for the attentions bestowed upon her, and enters into the spirit of the young lives that surround her, is as precious to those who love her as a gem in an antique setting, the fashion of which has long gone by, but which leaves the jewel the color and brightness which are its inalienable qualities. With old men it is too often different. They do not belong so much indoors as women do. They have no pretty little manual occupations. The old lady knits or stitches so long as her eyes and fingers will let her. The old man smokes his pipe, but does not know what to do with his fingers, unless he plays upon some instrument, or has a mechanical turn which finds business for them.

But the old writer, I said to The Teacups, as I say to you, my readers, labors under one special difficulty, which I am thinking of and exemplifying at this moment. He is constantly tending to reflect upon and discourse about his own particular stage of life. He feels that he must apologize for his intrusion upon the time and thoughts of a generation which he naturally supposes must be tired of him, if they ever had any considerable regard for him. Now, if the world of readers hates anything it sees in print, it is apology. If what one has to say is worth saying, he need not

beg pardon for saying it. If it is not worth saying —
I will not finish the sentence. But it is so hard to
resist the temptation, notwithstanding that the terrible line beginning " Superfluous lags the veteran "
is always repeating itself in his dull ear !

What kind of audience or reading parish is a man
who secured his constituency in middle life, or before
that period, to expect when he has reached the age of
threescore and twenty? His coevals have dropped
away by scores and tens, and he sees only a few units
scattered about here and there, like the few heads
above the water after a ship has gone to pieces.
Does he write and publish for those of his own time
of life ? He need not print a large edition. Does he
hope to secure a hearing from those who have come
into the reading world since his coevals ? They have
found fresher fields and greener pastures. Their
interests are in the out-door, active world. Some of
them are circumnavigating the planet while he is
hitching his rocking-chair about his hearth-rug. Some
are gazing upon the pyramids while he is staring at
his andirons. Some are settling the tariff and fixing
the laws of suffrage and taxation while he is dozing
over the weather bulletin, and going to sleep over the
obituaries in his morning or evening paper.

Nature is wiser than we give her credit for being ;
never wiser than in her dealings with the old. She
has no idea of mortifying them by sudden and wholly
unexpected failure of the chief servants of consciousness. The sight, for instance, begins to lose something of its perfection long before its deficiency calls
the owner's special attention to it. Very probably,
the first hint we have of the change is that a friend
makes the pleasing remark that we are " playing the

trombone," as he calls it ; that is, moving a book we are holding backward and forward, to get the right focal distance. Or it may be we find fault with the lamp or the gas-burner for not giving so much light as it used to. At last, somewhere between forty and fifty, we begin to dangle a jaunty pair of eye-glasses, half plaything and half necessity. In due time a pair of sober, business-like spectacles bestrides the nose. Old age leaps upon it as his saddle, and rides triumphant, unchallenged, until the darkness comes which no glasses can penetrate. Nature is pitiless in carrying out the universal sentence, but very pitiful in her mode of dealing with the condemned on his way to the final scene. The man who is to be hanged always has a good breakfast provided for him.

Do not think that the old look upon themselves as the helpless, hopeless, forlorn creatures which they seem to young people. Do these young folks suppose that all vanity dies out of the natures of old men and old women ? A dentist of olden time told me that a good-looking young man once said to him, " Keep that incisor presentable, if you can, till I am fifty, and then I sha'n't care how I look." I venture to say that that gentleman was as particular about his personal appearance and as proud of his good looks at fifty, and many years after fifty, as he was in the twenties, when he made that speech to the dentist.

My dear friends around the teacups, and at that wider board where I am now entertaining, or trying to entertain, my company, is it not as plain to you as it is to me that I had better leave such tasks as that which I am just finishing to those who live in a more interesting period of life than one which, in the order of nature, is next door to decrepitude ? Ought I not to regret having undertaken to report the doings and sayings of the members of the circle which you have known as The Teacups?

Dear, faithful reader, whose patient eyes have followed my reports through these long months, you and I are about parting company. Perhaps you are one of those who have known me under another name, in those far-off days separated from these by the red sea of the great national conflict. When you first heard the tinkle of the teaspoons, as the table was being made ready for its guests, you trembled for me, in the kindness of your hearts. I do not wonder that you did, — I trembled for myself. But I remembered the story of Sir Cloudesley Shovel, who was seen all of a tremor just as he was going into action. "How is this?" said a brother officer to him. "Surely you are not afraid?" "No," he answered, "but my flesh trembles at the thought of the dangers into which my intrepid spirit will carry me."

I knew the risk of undertaking to carry through a series of connected papers. And yet I thought it was better to run that risk, more manly, more sensible, than to give way to the fears which made my flesh tremble as did Sir Cloudesley Shovel's. For myself the labor has been a distraction, and one which came at a time when it was needed. Sometimes, as in one of those poems recently published, — the reader will easily guess which, — the youthful spirit has come over me with such a rush that it made me feel just as I did when I wrote the history of the "One-hoss Shay" thirty years ago. To repeat one of my comparisons, it was as if an early fruit had ripened on a graft upon an old, steady-going tree, to the astonishment of all its later-maturing products. I should hardly dare to

say so much as this if I had not heard a similar opinion expressed by others.

Once committed to my undertaking, there was no
turning back. It is true that I had said I might stop
at any moment, but after one or two numbers it
seemed as if there were an informal pledge to carry
the series on, as in former cases, until I had completed
my dozen instalments.

Writers and speakers have their idiosyncrasies,
their habits, their tricks, if you had rather call them
so, as to their ways of writing and speaking. There
is a very old and familiar story, accompanied by a
feeble jest, which most of my readers may probably
enough have met with in Joe Miller or elsewhere. It
is that of a lawyer who could never make an argument without having a piece of thread to work upon
with his fingers while he was pleading. Some one
stole it from him one day, and he could not get on at
all with his speech, — he had lost the thread of his
discourse, as the story had it. Now this is what I
myself once saw. It was at a meeting where certain
grave matters were debated in an assembly of professional men. A speaker, whom I never heard before
or since, got up and made a long and forcible argument. I do not think he was a lawyer, but he spoke
as if he had been trained to talk to juries. He held
a long string in one hand, which he drew through the
other hand incessantly, as he spoke, just as a shoemaker performs the motion of waxing his thread. He
appeared to be dependent on this motion. The physiological significance of the fact I suppose to be that
the flow of what we call the nervous current from the
thinking centre to the organs of speech was rendered

freer and easier by the establishment of a simulta-
neous collateral nervous current to the set of muscles
concerned in the action I have described.

I do not use a string to help me write or speak, but
I must have its equivalent. I must have my paper
and pen or pencil before me to set my thoughts flow-
ing in such form that they can be written continu-
ously. There have been lawyers who could think out
their whole argument in connected order without a
single note. There are authors, — and I think there
are many, — who can compose and finish off a poem
or a story without writing a word of it until, when
the proper time comes, they copy what they carry in
their heads. I have been told that Sir Edwin Arnold
thought out his beautiful "Light of Asia" in this
way.

I find the great charm of writing consists in its
surprises. When one is in the receptive attitude of
mind, the thoughts which are sprung upon him, the
images which flash through his consciousness, are a
delight and an excitement. I am impatient of every
hindrance in setting down my thoughts, — of a pen
that will not write, of ink that will not flow, of paper
that will not receive the ink. And here let me pay
the tribute which I owe to one of the humblest but
most serviceable of my assistants, especially in poetical composition. Nothing seems more prosaic than
the stylographic pen. It deprives the handwriting of
its beauty, and to some extent of its individual character. The brutal communism of the letters it forms
covers the page it fills with the most uniformly uninteresting characters. But, abuse it as much as you
choose, there is nothing like it for the poet, for the
imaginative writer. Many a fine flow of thought has

been checked, perhaps arrested, by the ill behavior of a goose-quill. Many an idea has escaped while the author was dipping his pen in the inkstand. But with the stylographic pen, in the hands of one who knows how to care for it and how to use it, unbroken rhythms and harmonious cadences are the natural products of the unimpeded flow of the fluid which is the vehicle of the author's thoughts and fancies. So much for my debt of gratitude to the humble stylographic pen. It does not furnish the proper medium for the correspondence of intimates, who wish to see as much of their friends' personality as their handwriting can hold, — still less for the impassioned interchange of sentiments between lovers; but in writing for the press its use is open to no objection. Its movement over the paper is like the flight of a swallow, while the quill pen and the steel pen and the gold pen are all taking short, laborious journeys, and stopping to drink every few minutes.

A chief pleasure which the author of novels and stories experiences is that of becoming acquainted with the characters he draws. It is perfectly true that his characters must, in the nature of things, have more or less of himself in their composition. If I should seek an exemplification of this in the person of any of my Teacups, I should find it most readily in the one whom I have called Number Seven, — the one with the squinting brain. I think that not only I, the writer, but many of my readers, recognize in our own mental constitution an occasional obliquity of perception, not always detected at the time, but plain enough when looked back upon. What extravagant fancies you and I have seriously entertained at one time or another! What superstitious notions have got into our heads and taken possession of its empty chambers, — or, in the language of science, seized on the groups of nerve-cells in some of the idle cerebral convolutions!

The writer, I say, becomes acquainted with his characters as he goes on. They are at first mere embryos, outlines of distinct personalities. By and by, if they have any organic cohesion, they begin to assert themselves. They can say and do such and such things; such and such other things they cannot and must not say or do. The story-writer's and play-writer's danger is that they will get their characters mixed, and make A say what B ought to have said. The stronger his imaginative faculty, the less liable will the writer be to this fault; but not even Shakespeare's power of throwing himself into his characters prevents many of his different personages from talking philosophy in the same strain and in a style common to them all.

You will often observe that authors fall in love with the imaginary persons they describe, and that they bestow affectionate epithets upon them which it may happen the reader does not consider in any way called for. This is a pleasure to which they have a right. Every author of a story is surrounded by a little family of ideal children, as dear to him, it may be, as are flesh-and-blood children to their parents. You may forget all about the circle of Teacups to which I have introduced you, — on the supposition that you have followed me with some degree of interest; but do you suppose that Number Five does not continue as a presence with me, and that my pretty Delilah has left me forever because she is going to be married? No, my dear friend, our circle will break apart, and

its different members will soon be to you as if they
had never been. But do you think that I can forget
them? Do you suppose that I shall cease to follow
the love (or the loves; which do you think is the true
word, the singular or the plural?) of Number Five
and the young Tutor who is so constantly found in her
company? Do you suppose that I do not continue my
relations with the "cracked Teacup," — the poor old
fellow with whom I have so much in common, whose
counterpart, perhaps, you may find in your own complex personality?

I take from the top shelf of the hospital department
of my library — the section devoted to literary cripples,
imbeciles, failures, foolish rhymesters, and silly eccentrics — one of the least conspicuous and most hopelessly feeble of the weak-minded population of that
intellectual almshouse. I open it and look through its
pages. It is a story. I have looked into it once before, — on its first reception as a gift from the author.
I try to recall some of the names I see there: they
mean nothing to me, but I venture to say the author
cherishes them all, and cries over them as he did when
he was writing their history. I put the book back
among its dusty companions, and, sitting down in my
reflective rocking-chair, think how others must forget,
and how I shall remember, the company that gathered
about this table.

Shall I ever meet any one of them again, in these
pages or in any other? Will the cracked Teacup hold
together, or will he go to pieces, and find himself in
that retreat where the owner of the terrible clock
which drove him crazy is walking under the shelter of
the high walls? Has the young Doctor's crown yet
received the seal which is Nature's warrant of wisdom

and proof of professional competency? And Number Five and her young friend the Tutor, — have they kept on in their dangerous intimacy? Did they get through the *tutto tremante* passage, reading from the same old large edition of Dante which the Tutor recommended as the best, and in reading from which their heads were necessarily brought perilously near to each other?

It would be very pleasant if I could, consistently with the present state of affairs, bring these two young people together. I say *two* young people, for the one who counts most years seems to me to be really the younger of the pair. That Number Five foresaw from the first that any tenderer feeling than that of friendship would intrude itself between them I do not believe. As for the Tutor, he soon found where he was drifting. It was his first experience in matters concerning the heart, and absorbed his whole nature as a thing of course. Did he tell her he loved her? Perhaps he did, fifty times; perhaps he never had the courage to say so outright. But sometimes they looked each other straight in the eyes, and strange messages seemed to pass from one consciousness to the other. Will the Tutor ask Number Five to be his wife; and if he does, will she yield to the dictates of nature, and lower the flag of that fortress so long thought impregnable? Will he go on writing such poems to her as " The Rose and the Fern " or " I Like You and I Love You, " and be content with the pursuit of that which he never can attain? That is all very well on the " Grecian Urn " of Keats, — beautiful, but not love such as mortals demand. Still, that may be all, for aught that we have yet seen.

" Fair youth, beneath the trees, thou canst not leave
    Thy song, nor ever can those trees be bare ;
      Bold lover, never, never, canst thou kiss,
  Though winning near the goal, — yet do not grieve ;
    She cannot fade, though thou hast not thy bliss,
      Forever wilt thou love, and she be fair !

" More happy love ! more happy, happy love !
    Forever warm, and still to be enjoyed,
      Forever panting and forever young ! "

And so, good-bye, young people, whom we part with
here. Shadows you have been and are to my readers ;
very real you have been and are to me, — as real as
the memories of many friends whom I shall see no
more.

As I am not in the habit of indulging in late sup-
pers, the reader need not think that I shall spread
another board and invite him to listen to the conversations which take place around it. If, from time to
time, he finds a slight refection awaiting him on the
sideboard, I hope he may welcome it as pleasantly as
he has accepted what I have offered him from the
board now just being cleared.

It is a good rule for the actor who manages the
popular street drama of Punch not to let the audience
or spectators see his legs. It is very hard for the
writer of papers like these, which are now coming to
their conclusion, to keep his personality from showing
itself too conspicuously through the thin disguises of
his various characters. As the show is now over, as
the curtain has fallen, I appear before it in my proper
person, to address a few words to the friends who have
assisted, as the French say, by their presence, and as

we use the word, by the kind way in which they have received my attempts at their entertainment.

This series of papers is the fourth of its kind which I have offered to my readers. I may be allowed to look back upon the succession of serial articles which was commenced more than thirty years ago, in 1857. "The Autocrat of the Breakfast-Table" was the first of the series. It was begun without the least idea what was to be its course and its outcome. Its characters shaped themselves gradually as the manuscript grew under my hand. I jotted down on the sheet of blotting paper before me the thoughts and fancies which came into my head. A very odd-looking object was this page of memoranda. Many of the hints were worked up into formal shape, many were rejected. Sometimes I recorded a story, a jest, or a pun for consideration, and made use of it or let it alone as my second thought decided. I remember a curious coincidence, which, if I have ever told in print, — I am not sure whether I have or not, — I will tell over again. I mention it, not for the pun, which I rejected as not very edifying and perhaps not new, though I did not recollect having seen it.

Mulier, Latin for woman; why apply that name to one of the gentle but occasionally obstinate sex? The answer was that a woman is (sometimes) more mulish than a mule. Please observe that I did not like the poor pun very well, and thought it rather rude and inelegant. So I left it on the blotter, where it was standing when one of the next numbers of " Punch " came out and contained that very same pun, which must have been hit upon by some English contributor at just about the same time I fell upon it on this side of the Atlantic. This fact may be added to the chapter of coincidences which belongs to the first number of this series of papers.

The "Autocrat" had the attraction of novelty, which of course was wanting in the succeeding papers of similar character. The criticisms upon the successive numbers as they came out were various, but generally encouraging. Some were more than encouraging; very high-colored in their phrases of commendation. When the papers were brought together in a volume their success was beyond my expectations. Up to the present time the "Autocrat" has maintained its position. An immortality of a whole generation is more than most writers are entitled to expect. I venture to think, from the letters I receive from the children and grandchildren of my first set of readers, that for some little time longer, at least, it will continue to be read, and even to be a favorite with some of its readers. *Non omnis moriar* is a pleasant thought to one who has loved his poor little planet, and will, I trust, retain kindly recollections of it through whatever wilderness of worlds he may be called to wander in his future pilgrimages. I say "poor little planet." Ever since I had a ten cent look at the transit of Venus, a few years ago, through the telescope in the Mall, the earth has been wholly different to me from what it used to be. I knew from books what a speck it is in the universe, but nothing ever brought the fact home like the sight of the sister planet sailing across the sun's disk, about large enough for a buckshot, not large enough for a full-sized bullet. Yes, I love the little globule where I have spent more than fourscore years, and I like to think that some of my thoughts and some of my emotions may live themselves over again when I am sleeping. I cannot thank all the

kind readers of the "Autocrat" who are constantly
sending me their acknowledgments. If they see this
printed page, let them be assured that a writer is always rendered happier by being told that he has made
a fellow-being wiser or better, or even contributed to
his harmless entertainment. This a correspondent
may take for granted, even if his letter of grateful
recognition receives no reply. It becomes more and
more difficult for me to keep up with my correspondents, and I must soon give it up as impossible.

"The Professor at the Breakfast Table" followed
immediately on the heels of the "Autocrat." The
Professor was the *alter ego* of the first personage. In
the earlier series he had played a secondary part, and
in this second series no great effort was made to create
a character wholly unlike the first. The Professor
was more outspoken, however, on religious subjects,
and brought down a good deal of hard language on
himself and the author to whom he owed his existence.
I suppose he may have used some irritating expressions, unconsciously, but not unconscientiously, I am
sure. There is nothing harder to forgive than the
sting of an epigram. Some of the old doctors, I fear,
never pardoned me for saying that if a ship, loaded
with an assorted cargo of the drugs which used to be
considered the natural food of sick people, went to the
bottom of the sea, it would be "all the better for mankind and all the worse for the fishes." If I had not
put that snapper on the end of my whip-lash, I might
have got off without the ill temper which my antithe-
sis provoked. Thirty years set that all right, and the
same thirty years have so changed the theological atmosphere that such abusive words as "heretic" and
"infidel," applied to persons who differ from the old

standards of faith, are chiefly interesting as a test of
breeding, being seldom used by any people above the
social half-caste line. I am speaking of Protestants;
how it may be among Roman Catholics I do not know,
but I suspect that with them also it is a good deal a
matter of breeding. There were not wanting some
who liked the Professor better than the Autocrat. I
confess that I prefer my champagne in its first burst
of gaseous enthusiasm; but if my guest likes it better
after it has stood awhile, I am pleased to accommodate
him. The first of my series came from my mind
almost with an explosion, like the champagne cork;
it startled me a little to see what I had written, and
to hear what people said about it. After that first
explosion the flow was more sober, and I looked upon
the product of my wine-press more coolly. *Continua-
tions* almost always sag a little. I will not say that
of my own second effort, but if others said it, I should
not be disposed to wonder at or to dispute them.

"The Poet at the Breakfast Table" came some
years later. This series of papers was not so much a
continuation as a resurrection. It was a doubly hazardous attempt, made without any extravagant expectations, and was received as well as I had any right
to anticipate. It differed from the other two series in
containing a poem of considerable length, published in
successive portions. This poem holds a good deal of
self-communing, and gave me the opportunity of expressing some thoughts and feelings not to be found
elsewhere in my writings. I had occasion to read the
whole volume, not long since, in preparation for a new
edition, and was rather more pleased with it than I had
expected to be. An old author is constantly rediscov-
ing himself in the more or less fossilized productions

of his earlier years. It is a long time since I have read the "Autocrat," but I take it up now and then and read in it for a few minutes, not always without some degree of edification.

These three series of papers, "Autocrat," "Professor," "Poet," are all studies of life from somewhat different points of view. They are largely made up of sober reflections, and appeared to me to require some lively human interest to save them from wearisome didactic dulness. What could be more natural than that love should find its way among the young people who helped to make up the circle gathered around the table? Nothing is older than the story of young love. Nothing is newer than that same old story. A bit of gilding here and there has a wonderful effect in enlivening a landscape or an apartment. Napoleon consoled the Parisians in their year of defeat by gilding the dome of the Invalides. Boston has glorified her State House and herself at the expense of a few sheets of gold leaf laid on the dome, which shines like a sun in the eyes of her citizens, and like a star in those of the approaching traveller. I think the gilding of a love-story helped all three of these earlier papers. The same need I felt in the series of papers just closed. The slight incident of Delilah's appearance and disappearance served my purpose to some extent. But what should I do with Number Five? The reader must follow out her career for himself. For myself, I think that she and the Tutor have both utterly forgotten the difference of their years in the fascination of intimate intercourse. I do not believe that a nature so large, so rich in affection, as Number Five's is going to fall defeated of its best inheritance of life, like a vine which finds no support

for its tendrils to twine around, and so creeps along
the ground from which nature meant that love should
lift it. I feel as if I ought to follow these two personages of my sermonizing story until they come together
or separate, to fade, to wither, — perhaps to die, at
last, of something like what the doctors call *heart-fail-
ure*, but which might more truly be called *heart-star-
vation*. When I say *die*, I do not mean necessarily
the death that goes into the obituary column. It may
come to that, in one or both ; but I think that, if they
are never united, Number Five will outlive the Tutor,
who will fall into melancholy ways, and pine and
waste, while she lives along, feeling all the time that
she has cheated herself of happiness. I hope that is
not going to be their fortune, or misfortune. *Vieille
fille fait jeune mariée.* What a youthful bride Number Five would be, if she could only make up her
mind to matrimony ! In the mean time she must be
left with her lambs all around her. May heaven
temper the winds to them, for they have been shorn
very close, every one of them, of their golden fleece
of aspirations and anticipations.

I must avail myself of this opportunity to say a few
words to my distant friends who take interest enough
in my writings, early or recent, to wish to enter into
communication with me by letter, or to keep up a
communication already begun. I have given notice in
print that the letters, books, and manuscripts which I
receive by mail are so numerous that if I undertook
to read and answer them all I should have little time
for anything else. I have for some years depended
on the assistance of a secretary, but our joint efforts
have proved unable, of late, to keep down the accumu-
lations which come in with every mail. So many of

the letters I receive are of a pleasant character that it
is hard to let them go unacknowledged.   The extreme
friendliness which pervades many of them gives them
a value which I rate very highly.   When large numbers of strangers insist on claiming one as a friend, on
the strength of what he has written, it tends to make
him think of himself somewhat indulgently.   It is the
most natural thing in the world to want to give expression to the feeling the loving messages from far-
off unknown friends must excite.   Many a day has
had its best working hours broken into, spoiled for all
literary work, by the labor of answering correspondents whose good opinion it is gratifying to have
called forth, but who were unconsciously laying a new
burden on shoulders already aching.   I know too well
that what I say will not reach the eyes of many who
might possibly take a hint from it.   Still I must
keep repeating it before breaking off suddenly and
leaving whole piles of letters unanswered.   I have
been very heavily handicapped for many years.   It is
partly my own fault.   From what my correspondents
tell me, I must infer that I have established a dangerous reputation for willingness to answer all sorts of
letters.   They come with such insinuating humility,
— they cannot bear to intrude upon my time, they
know that I have a great many calls upon it, — and
incontinently proceed to lay their additional weight on
the load which is breaking my back.

The hypocrisy of kind-hearted people is one of the
most painful exhibitions of human weakness.   It has
occurred to me that it might be profitable to reproduce some of my unwritten answers to correspondents.
If those which were actually written and sent were
to be printed in parallel columns with those mentally

formed but not written out responses and comments, the reader would get some idea of the internal conflicts an honest and not unamiable person has to go through, when he finds himself driven to the wall by a correspondence which is draining his vocabulary to find expressions that sound as agreeably, and signify as little, as the phrases used by a diplomatist in closing an official communication.

No. 1. Want my autograph, do you? And don't know how to spell my name! An *a* for an *e* in my middle name. Leave out the *l* in my last name. Do you know how people hate to have their names misspelled? What do you suppose are the sentiments entertained by the Thompsons with a *p* towards those who address them in writing as Thomson?

No. 2. Think the lines you mention are by far the best I ever wrote, hey? Well, I did n't write those lines. What is more, I think they are as detestable a string of rhymes as I could wish my worst enemy had written. A very pleasant frame of mind I am in for writing a letter, after reading yours!

No. 3. I am glad to hear that my namesake, whom I never saw and never expect to see, has cut another tooth; but why write four pages on the strength of that domestic occurrence?

No. 4. You wish to correct an error in my Broomstick poem, do you? You give me to understand that Wilmington is not in Essex County, but in Middlesex. Very well; but are they separated by *running water?* Because if they are not, what could hinder a witch from crossing the line that separates Wilmington from Andover, I should like to know? I never meant to imply that the witches made no excursions beyond the district which was more especially their seat of operations.

As I come towards the end of this task which I had set myself, I wish, of course, that I could have performed it more to my own satisfaction and that of my readers. This is a feeling which almost every one must have at the conclusion of any work he has undertaken. A common and very simple reason for this disappointment is that most of us overrate our capacity. We expect more of ourselves than we have any right to, in virtue of our endowments. The figurative descriptions of the last Grand Assize must no more be taken literally than the golden crowns, which we do not expect or want to wear on our heads, or the golden harps, which we do not want or expect to hold in our hands. Is it not too true that many religious sectaries think of the last tribunal complacently, as the scene in which they are to have the satisfaction of saying to the believers of a creed different from their own, "I told you so"? Are not others oppressed with the thought of the great returns which will be expected of them as the product of their great gifts, the very limited amount of which they do not suspect, and will be very glad to learn, even at the expense of their self-love, when they are called to their account? If the ways of the Supreme Being are ever really to be "justified to men," to use Milton's expression, every human being may expect an exhaustive explanation of himself. No man is capable of being his own counsel, and I cannot help hoping that the ablest of the archangels will be retained for the defence of the worst of sinners. He himself is unconscious of the agencies which made him what he is. Self-determining he may be, if you will, but who determines the self which is the proximate source of the determination? Why was the A self like his good uncle in bodily aspect and mental and moral qualities, and the B self like the bad uncle in look and character? Has not a man a right to ask this question in the here or in the hereafter, — in this world or in any world in which he may find himself? If the Allwise wishes to satisfy his reasonable and reasoning creatures, it will not be by a display of elemental convulsions, but by the still small voice, which treats with him as a dependent entitled to know the meaning of his existence, and if there was anything wrong in his adjustment to the moral and spiritual conditions of the world around him to have full allowance made for it. No melodramatic display of warring elements, such as the white-robed Second Adventist imagines, can meet the need of the human heart. The thunders and lightnings of Sinai terrified and impressed the more timid souls of the idolatrous and rebellious caravan which the great leader was conducting, but a far nobler manifestation of divinity was that when "the Lord spake unto Moses face to face, as a man speaketh unto his friend."

I find the burden and restrictions of rhyme more and more troublesome as I grow older. There are times when it seems natural enough to employ that form of expression, but it is only occasionally; and the use of it as the vehicle of the commonplace is so prevalent that one is not much tempted to select it as the medium for his thoughts and emotions. The art of rhyming has almost become a part of a high-school education, and its practice is far from being an evidence of intellectual distinction. Mediocrity is as much forbidden to the poet in our days as it was in those of Horace, and the immense majority of the verses written are stamped with hopeless mediocrity.

When one of the ancient poets found he was trying to grind out verses which came unwillingly, he said he was writing

INVITÂ MINERVÂ.

Vex not the Muse with idle prayers, —
  She will not hear thy call ;
She steals upon thee unawares,
  Or seeks thee not at all.

Soft as the moonbeams when they sought
  Endymion's fragrant bower,
She parts the whispering leaves of thought
  To show her full-blown flower.

For thee her wooing hour has passed,
  The singing birds have flown,
And winter comes with icy blast
  To chill thy buds unblown.

Yet, though the woods no longer thrill
  As once their arches rung,
Sweet echoes hover round thee still
  Of songs thy summer sung.

Live in thy past ; await no more
  The rush of heaven-sent wings ;
Earth still has music left in store
  While Memory sighs and sings.

I hope my special Minerva may not always be unwilling, but she must not be called upon as she has been in times past.   Now that the teacups have left the table, an occasional evening call is all that my readers must look for.   Thanking them for their kind companionship, and hoping that I may yet meet them in the now and thens of the future, I bid them goodbye for the immediate present.

INDEX.